AND SIN
NO MORE

RIMA D. APPLE AND JANET GOLDEN, EDITORS

The Selling of Contraception
The Dalkon Shield Case, Sexuality, and Women's Autonomy
Nicole J. Grant

AND SIN
NO MORE

◆ ◆ ◆

SOCIAL POLICY AND
UNWED MOTHERS
IN CLEVELAND,
1855–1990

MARIAN J. MORTON

OHIO STATE UNIVERSITY PRESS
COLUMBUS

Morton, Marian J., 1937–
    And sin no more : social policy and unwed mothers in Cleveland,
1855–1990 / Marian J. Morton.
        p.   cm.
    Includes bibliographical references and index.
    ISBN 0–8142–0602–6. — ISBN 0–8142–0603–4 (pbk.)
    1. Unmarried mothers—Services for—Ohio—Cleveland—History.
2. Social policy—Ohio—Cleveland—History.   I. Title.
HV700.5.M66   1993
362.83′928′0977132—dc20   92–39087
                                                              CIP

Text and jacket design by Hunter Graphics.
Type set in Sabon by G & S Typesetters, Austin, TX.
Printed by Thomson-Shore, Dexter, MI.

The paper in this book meets the guidelines for permanence and
durability of the Committee on Production Guidelines for Book
Longevity of the Council on Library Resources. ∞

9   8   7   6   5   4   3   2   1

With love and gratitude to my own children, Margaret, Elizabeth, John, and Sarah, who taught me much about motherhood

◆ CONTENTS ◆

Contents

◆ TABLES ◆

◆ Editors' Foreword ◆

Marian Morton's study illuminates the historical roots of an emotionally charged contemporary social issue: single motherhood. By tracing the care of unwed mothers in Cleveland and exploring how the changing dynamics of social welfare, religion, and race affected private and public choices, this research enables us to better understand today's responses to single parenthood.

As demographers chart the rise of single parenthood in the late twentieth century, politicians vigorously debate appropriate methods for discouraging out-of-wedlock births. Appropriately dubbed "bridefare," these are modifications of the Aid to Dependent Children (AFDC) programs and are designed to encourage marriage and to punish single mothers. Pilot programs in Wisconsin and New Jersey aim to reward AFDC recipients who marry and include financial disincentives for additional out-of-wedlock births. The success of "bridefare" will be judged, at least in part, on whether the programs reduce or delay subsequent pregnancies and on whether they increase the number of two-parent families. These and other programs proposed throughout the country demonstrate a political agenda informed by discussions of particular definitions of "family values."

Clearly, the single mother today, as in the nineteenth century, evokes a cultural response deeply rooted in our notions of morality, economics, sexuality, health care, and family. In analyzing the experiences of reformers providing maternity services, and in probing the ways race and religion shaped institutions serving what were once termed "unwed mothers," Morton has given us a vital history of an enduring social condition.

Rima D. Apple
Janet Golden

◆ Acknowledgments ◆

What's a nice girl like me doing in a place like this?

As have thousands of unwed mothers, I asked myself that question innumerable times in the last several years as I found myself living with—but thankfully not in—maternity homes and hospitals. Like most of those mothers' stories, mine began innocently enough. I had a simple desire to spend a summer looking out of the windows of the Western Reserve Historical Society library at its lovely formal gardens. This desire, and the fortuitous discovery in that library that respectable Victorian women had sought the reclamation of their fallen sisters, led me down my own primrose path. A book that started out to be about private homes for unwed mothers came to include public institutions, which I now believe may have been more important. So it was that half a dozen years later I found myself in a dark, cluttered basement hallway of Cleveland Metropolitan General Hospital en route to an interview with a very knowledgeable woman on whose office wall hung her degree in sex education. I had come a long way from those formal gardens.

Along that way I acquired many debts. I would like to here thank some of those who helped me.

For time off, thanks to the National Endowment for the Humanities for a summer research grant and a research fellowship, and to John Carroll University for a Grauel Faculty Fellowship and a summer research grant.

For a research and travel grant, thanks to the Association of American Colleges.

For help with research on the Cleveland Infirmary/City Hospital/Metropolitan General Hospital/MetroHealth Services, thanks to archivists Dianne O'Malia and Martin Hauserman; Victor Hersch, manager of computer systems for MetroHealth Services; and Lynn Zaremba, administrative director of the Maternity and Infant Care Project.

For help with research on the Florence Crittenton Home, thanks to Ed McCabe, director of the Florence Crittenton Services, and David Klassen of the Social Welfare History Archives Center at the University of Minnesota.

For help with research on St. Ann's Infant and Maternity Asylum, thanks to Chris Krosel of the Cleveland Catholic Diocesan Archives and Sr. Cheryl Keehner of the Archives of the Sisters of Charity of St. Augustine in Richfield, Ohio.

For help with research on the Salvation Army Booth Memorial Hospital and Mary B. Talbert Home, thanks to Susan Williams of the Salvation Army Archives and Research Center in New York City; Monica Hagland and Joanne Provident of Booth Memorial Hospital; and Commissioner Edward Carey, former director of Booth.

For *The Encyclopedia of Cleveland History*, thanks to David D. Van Tassel and John J. Grabowski.

For technical assistance, thanks to Jean Belin and Bill Barker of John Carroll University.

For reading, thanks to David D. Van Tassel (again), Lois Scharf, Earl Landau, Tom Fullmer, and especially Mike McTighe and Brenda Wirkus.

For listening, thanks to the Cleveland Social Welfare History and Spaghetti Society and Women Historians of Greater Cleveland.

Finally, for warm encouragement, thanks to Charlotte Dihoff of the Ohio State University Press, and for enthusiastic support and shrewd editing, thanks to Janet Golden.

◆ INTRODUCTION ◆

*A HOMELESS OUTCAST falls with her Babe on the Hospital
steps. . . . A Pathetic story of a Fallen Woman turned on the streets
with her Baby in her arms. Worn out and ill and homeless, the
despised [Salvation] Army takes her in.*
Salvation Army Rescue Home, Annual Report

This 1893 vignette is the very stuff of Victorian melodrama. Its heroine,
the unwed mother, is penniless and homeless until sheltered by the Salvation Army, which would save her soul and send her forth to sin no
more. The devastating depression of 1893 ruined thousands of Americans, and the destitution of this unwed mother, although certainly piti-
able, was not unusual. Her "fallen-ness" and the "baby in her arms"
distinguished this woman from other dependent people, making her a
sinner, an outcast, turned out by the public hospital and welcome only at
the Salvation Army home for fallen women.

The plight of this "homeless outcast" symbolizes American social
policy toward unwed motherhood from the mid-nineteenth century until
today. Unwed mothers have shared some experiences of others dependent
on public or private aid, and this book underscores several familiar
themes of social policy history—most obviously, the growing public responsibility for the maintenance and health care of dependent people.
The book's first and last chapters, on Cleveland's public facility for the
indigent, illustrate the importance of this theme. Also familiar are the
shifting strategies for relieving dependence from residential institutions
to relief checks, the change from volunteer to professional care providers,
the persistence of racial segregation, and the enduring identification of
dependence with delinquency, institutionalized in the all-purpose poorhouse sheltering the poor, the ill, and the criminal.

Nevertheless, the sexual delinquency of unwed mothers, defined as
sin by the powerful rhetoric of organized religion, has distinguished them
from other dependents. Pregnancy out-of-wedlock affronts deeply held
beliefs that a woman should remain within her home, subordinate to a
male breadwinner, and that female sexuality should remain within marriage. Receiving secular sanction in custom and law, this social construc-

1

tion of womanhood undergirds the American social welfare system, differentiating not only between policies regarding men and women but between policies for married and unmarried women.[1] Government has intended to provide unmarried mothers with the least possible support: the least residential care, the least relief, and the fewest medical services. As a result, the private sector has played an unusually significant role, reflected in the four chapters on private maternity homes. These institutions have remained "women's work," created and sustained by churches or church-related organizations and committed to the nineteenth-century strategies of the spiritual reclamation of fallen women.

The story of social policy and unwed motherhood reinforces and dramatizes much of what we already know about the interactions between gender and the allocation of public and private aid to dependent people. First, dependence is clearly linked to gender in a society that provides women with the fewest opportunities for self-support and the greatest responsibilities for child rearing. Second, gendered definitions of appropriate sexual conduct have an impact on public relief. Women with husbands sometimes receive preferential treatment; mothers without husbands often receive uncertain and minimal public benefits. Third, gender shapes the practices of private institutions for unwed mothers, guaranteeing that these practices would be women's work. Fourth, gender explains the relative powerlessness of both unwed mothers and middle-class caretakers, reflected in the very minimal private and public support they receive.[2]

In 1989 the federal government spent an estimated $21.5 billion on welfare programs for families of teenage mothers, most of them unmarried.[3] This enormous expense is compounded by the astronomical social cost of unfinished educations, unemployment, and the persistent poverty of female-headed families.[4] Proposed solutions to the problems of pregnancy out-of-wedlock from the political left and center have included more sex education for teenagers, more readily accessible abortions, and more adequate income maintenance programs.

These proposals have encountered vigorous political opposition during the last decade. The political right has proposed its own solutions. Conservative analyst Charles Murray has suggested that unwed mothers be placed in public poorhouses rather than on income maintenance programs. Murray believes that "a good correctional 'half-way house' might serve as an incentive for an unwed mother, if she has no money, to accept abortion or to give her child to the state."[5]

The religious right has generated renewed enthusiasm for maternity homes, the private sector's historic solution to unwed motherhood. After declining during the 1960s and 1970s, the number of such homes in this country rose from 99 to 140 during the 1980s. The new homes are modeled on those of the last century: "A rambling Victorian house . . . with lace curtains at the windows and religious samplers on the wall." Most are sponsored by churches or anti-abortion advocates such as the Reverend Jerry Falwell, the National Right to Life Committee, and the Christian Action Council. The facilities can shelter only about sixty-two hundred women, an admittedly tiny fraction of those who become pregnant out-of-wedlock each year.[6]

Public poorhouses and private maternity homes were nineteenth-century strategies that became less able to solve the problems of unwed mothers and unwed motherhood. They certainly are not able to do so in the vastly different late twentieth century. Intelligent policy for the future must be informed by the past, not captive to it. Therefore, it is to the study of past institutions and policies that this book turns.

HISTORIANS AND UNWED MOTHERS

Historians have written much about hospitals, prisons, orphanages, reformatories, insane asylums, and poorhouses, but, until recently, little about the institutions that sheltered unwed mothers. The lack of interest may be due to the fact that unwed mothers constituted a very small proportion of the country's institutionalized population. A national census taken in 1923, when institutional care was still widely used, revealed that of the 204,888 dependent, neglected, and delinquent children in institutions, only 2,389—.011 percent—were sheltered in homes for unmarried mothers and babies. (These numbers include both women and children.)[7]

Unwed mothers inspire less interest than comparable populations for other reasons. They are less sympathetic than orphans and less exciting than prostitutes.[8] Moreover, they defy easy identification; it is much easier for a woman to conceal her marital status than her pregnancy. The Cleveland Infirmary distributed outdoor relief to mothers described as "widows" and "grass widows," allegedly deserted by spouses. Members of neither group were married at the time, but whether they ever had been was not clear. Cleveland's public hospital even today simply notes whether a woman is "married" or "not married," which can mean separated, divorced, or widowed. The City of Cleveland, on the other hand, records as illegitimate the children of women who keep their maiden names because those names are different from their husbands' names.

Consequently, illegitimate childbirth is hard to quantify. Although social workers and city officials counted illegitimate births and unwed mothers, and although those numbers will be treated here as evidence, the data are far from precise. Prior to the hospitalization of most child-births and the end of midwife deliveries in the 1930s, registration of birth, although required in most states, was not always done. In 1915 the U.S. Children's Bureau found that only a few states and cities could provide accurate figures on births. On the strength of these, the bureau estimated that 1.8 percent of all births were illegitimate—"probably a gross underestimate," according to historian Susan Tiffin.[9] The chief of the Cleveland Division of Health commented in 1925: "For many years, at least as far back as 1891, birth registration has been a favorite subject for annual lamentations by health officials. . . . Some years it was estimated as low as 75 percent." Therefore, although Cleveland annually recorded illegitimate births, the numbers should be regarded with caution. As Daniel Scott Smith has noted (not entirely correctly): "The most easily counted events in American history tend to be those belonging to people who 'counted' at the time; these are not the people most likely to conceive children out of wedlock."[10]

Standard histories of the public welfare system discuss unwed mothers only briefly, mostly as recipients of federal public assistance, especially Aid to Families of Dependent Children. Such peripheral attention sometimes overlooks the gender-based capriciousness and inequities of the welfare state, which have been discussed by feminist historians and appear here in unusually vivid ways.[11]

Historians of women have paid closer attention to private agencies and institutions, in which women have been prominently involved as agents as well as recipients of relief. However, only the largest of the private agencies for unwed mothers, the National Florence Crittenton Mission, has received extensive scholarly attention, and the focus has been on the Mission as it began to secularize, downplaying its long-standing evangelical thrust. Other research has also focused on Protestant maternity homes, all of them for a white clientele. In general, these historians have underestimated the tenacity of the woman-centered traditions of private benevolence described here, arguing that those traditions either died or became co-opted into male traditions during the 1930s.[12]

This book paints both a broader and a more specific picture. It is broader because it describes practices from the mid-nineteenth to the late twentieth centuries, and because it describes both Protestant and Catholic institutions as well as those that sheltered both black and white women.

At the same time, it is a case study of institutions in one specific city, Cleveland. Like charity, and sometimes *as* charity, social welfare began at home. From the colonial period until the mid-1930s and the New

Deal, local government and local private agencies cared for those who could not care for themselves. For this reason, much social welfare history is local history.[13] Policy statements may be made by national boards in New York City, or national conferences of social workers in Chicago, or the federal Congress in Washington, D.C., but policies are implemented—and just as often *not* implemented—at the local level in homes and hospitals in Cleveland and other cities across the country.

MATERNITY HOMES AND HOSPITALS IN CLEVELAND

Cleveland's economic and demographic development has been typical of midwestern cities. Originally part of colonial Connecticut's Western Reserve, Cleveland was founded by Connecticut land developers in 1796, and the city's elite retained a New England and staunchly Protestant flavor for several decades. In the first quarter of the nineteenth century, Cleveland and cities such as Pittsburgh, Detroit, and Buffalo constituted the urban frontier of the lower Great Lakes. Although Cleveland remained a tiny struggling hamlet (population barely more than one thousand in 1830), its location at the mouth of the Cuyahoga River on Lake Erie made it perfectly situated to take advantage of the national transportation revolution. In 1825 Cleveland became the northern terminus of the Ohio Canal and an important link between the cities of the East and the farmlands of the Northwest. By the 1830s and 1840s it was a prospering commercial village. Cleveland's population had increased to forty-four thousand by 1860 as immigrants from Germany and Ireland and from nearby country towns were attracted by early factories and transported by early railroads.[14]

The Civil War encouraged the growth of Cleveland industry, especially oil refining and iron manufacture, and in the last three decades of the century the city became a center for the production of iron and steel products and ships. By the early twentieth century, it had added the manufacture of automobiles and automotive parts to its industrial base. Cleveland's population continued to grow rapidly. In 1870, it was the fifteenth largest city in the country; by 1910, with a population of 560,663, it was the nation's "Sixth City." A third of its population was foreign-born, increasing numbers of them from southeastern Europe. Beginning in the 1910s, these Italian, Polish, and Russian newcomers were joined by blacks, part of the great migration from the American South. Cleveland's black population tripled between 1910 and 1920.[15]

The host of social and economic problems attendant upon rapid industrialization and urbanization inspired Progressive reformers across the country and also inspired Cleveland's energetic Progressive mayor, Tom L. Johnson. During Johnson's administration, 1901–1909, journalist Lincoln Steffens called Cleveland "the best governed city" in the country. The first three decades of this century were probably the city's glory years: its great fortunes were made or increased, its great public buildings were erected according to a design by city planner Daniel Burnham, and its great cultural institutions were founded.

In 1930, Cleveland's population of 900,429 ranked it behind New York, Chicago, Philadelphia, Detroit, and Los Angeles. But in April of that year one-seventh of the city's work force was unemployed, and by January 1931, 100,000 Clevelanders were out of work.[16] Federal relief funds and New Deal public works projects, including the country's first public housing units, rescued Cleveland, but the Depression ended the city's growth. Although defense industries sustained its economy during World War II, Cleveland began to lose population to its surrounding suburbs. The loss was slow at first, then, during the 1950s and 1960s, the middle-class and working-class white population rushed to flee the second migration of southern blacks who had arrived during and after the war.

The shift of industry and commerce to the suburbs and the postwar deindustrialization of the national economy brought a crippling loss of jobs and tax monies. Neighborhoods and services deteriorated, and in July 1966, a race riot devastated the Hough inner-city area, causing four deaths and millions of dollars worth of property damage. Despite the election in 1967 of a black mayor, Carl B. Stokes, another outburst of racial violence occurred in July 1968. The city's economy began the gradual transition to a service base, which did not provide adequate jobs or income for the city's steadily declining population. Cleveland's poverty rate, already well above the national average, continued to climb through the 1980s. Historians Carol Poh Miller and Robert Wheeler have concluded that "Cleveland not only shared America's urban crisis, it epitomized it."[17]

Cleveland has one notable geographical and historical peculiarity. The Cuyahoga River divides the city into east and west sides, which originally were separate political entities, Cleveland and Ohio City respectively, until their merger in 1854. Clevelanders still joke about the alleged cultural differences between the two sides of town. But nobody jokes about the fact that the East Side is predominantly black and the West Side predominantly white, and that consequently, Cleveland is reputedly the most racially segregated city in the country. This residential segregation has had serious political and economic consequences, such as the forced busing of schoolchildren. Segregation also means that black

TABLE I.1
CLEVELAND MATERNITY HOMES AND HOSPITALS, 1855–1990

Cleveland Infirmary, 1855
   Cleveland City Hospital, 1889
   Cleveland Metropolitan General Hospital, 1958
   Cleveland MetroHealth Services, 1989

The Retreat, 1869–1936

St. Ann's Infant and Maternity Asylum, 1873
   St. Ann's Loretta Hall, 1918
   DePaul Infant and Maternity Home, 1951
   DePaul Family Services, 1973

Salvation Army Rescue Home, 1892
   Booth Memorial Hospital and Home, 1923–87
   Mary B. Talbert Home, 1925–60
   Booth-Talbert Clinic, 1960–76
   Booth Home, 1987

Florence Crittenton Home, 1912
   Florence Crittenton Services, 1970

Maternity Hospital, 1917
   MacDonald House of University Hospitals, 1936

Cleveland Federation for Charity and Philanthropy, 1913
   Cleveland Welfare Federation, 1917
   Cleveland Federation for Community Planning, 1971

women living on the East Side have to travel four miles across the city for health care at the public hospital on the West Side, which may partially account for the city's very high black infant mortality rates.[18] Although the use of the public facility by nonwhite, medically indigent women is not unique, the four-mile trip may be.

The Cleveland facilities that cared for unwed mothers have often changed their names. (See Table I.1.) When the city took over the small township poorhouse in 1855, it became the Cleveland Infirmary. In 1909, when the institution moved to the outskirts of the city, it became Farm Colony, then Cooley Farm. The medical department of the poorhouse in 1889 became an independent institution, City Hospital. In 1958 it was renamed Cleveland Metropolitan General Hospital, and in 1989 the complex of health facilities became Cleveland MetroHealth Services.

Cleveland's first private maternity home, the Retreat, was opened by the Woman's Christian Association (later the Young Women's Christian Association). The Catholic facility for unwed mothers began as St. Ann's Infant and Maternity Asylum or Home, but in 1918 the separate facility for unmarried women became St. Ann's Loretta Hall. In 1951 it was renamed DePaul Infant and Maternity Home, and from 1973 to 1983 it was called DePaul Family Services, indicating its shift to outpatient programs.

The Salvation Army Rescue Home became Booth Memorial Hospital and Home in the 1920s and then simply Booth Memorial Hospital, although the hospital housed both married and unmarried women. Booth Memorial Hospital was purchased by Cleveland Metropolitan General Hospital in 1987, but the Army maintained the city's last residential program for unwed mothers at the Booth site. In 1925 the Army opened Mary B. Talbert Home for black women, which in 1960 was replaced by Booth-Talbert Clinic. The clinic closed in 1976.

In 1912 the National Florence Crittenton Mission opened a home in Cleveland, and when in 1970 the Cleveland Florence Crittenton Home changed its clientele to delinquent, nonpregnant adolescents, it changed its name to Florence Crittenton Services.

The most significant private hospital to provide medical care for unwed mothers was Maternity Hospital, which in 1936 was renamed MacDonald House of University Hospitals. The last agency that needs to be identified here was founded in 1913 as the Cleveland Federation for Charity and Philanthropy, whose goal was to systematize the policies and practices of the city's myriad private agencies. After a 1917 merger with the Cleveland Welfare Council, the organization became the Welfare Federation, and in 1971, the Federation for Community Planning. It will be referred to here as the Federation.

SOURCES

Few institutions record, and fewer are willing to share, accounts of daily life within their walls: the dull, dreary routines or the out-of-the-ordinary and untoward incidents that might illuminate or enliven the historian's account. Like most histories of institutions, therefore, this one focuses on their public faces, revealed through their public documents. Most are clearly self-serving. Many were intended to raise money or justify its expenditure. For example, in 1857 the superintendent of the Infirmary blamed its escalating costs on the early onset of winter and the expenses of transporting idle transients out of town. Many documents emphasized successes: in 1905, the Salvation Army boasted that 90 percent of the 2,482 inmates received since the Rescue's founding had "proved satisfactory." Many accounts were partial: a Federation study of private maternity homes probably undercounted their infant or maternal mortality because the homes transferred their seriously ill clients to hospitals.[19] In the 1920s and 1930s, feeling pressure from the Federation and from professional social workers, homes' public records occasionally adopted the language of social work, stressing the expertise of their own staff, for example. The jargon of psychoanalytic theory appears in homes' reports of the 1950s and 1960s. The language is deceptive, however; homes talked far more about new services than they provided them.

Nevertheless, some revealing records survive. The registers of the Cleveland Infirmary provide glimpses of life inside walls that housed not only pregnant women but men and women with syphilis, frozen feet, or "sore eyes," who were insane, intemperate, or just down on their luck. Births and deaths are also a matter of public record, and public reports contain helpful although sometimes puzzling information. In 1905 the Cleveland Public Health Department reported an astonishingly high mortality rate for the foundlings and illegitimate infants at St. Ann's: 145 deaths, compared with 3 at the Jewish Orphan Asylum, the city's largest orphanage with a population of more than five hundred. The statistics are probably evidence of an outbreak of infectious disease, not poor medical care provided by St. Ann's.[20]

Other records contain hints about life within the institutions. The minutes of the board of managers of the Florence Crittenton Home during the 1910s painstakingly detail squabbles with local grocers over past-due bills; the 1968 board of trustees minutes record a break-in at the home even as the board discussed the dangers of the neighborhood. The archives of the Cleveland Catholic Diocese contain a stern letter to the sister superior of St. Ann's Hospital from the bishop of Cleveland because she challenged his appointment of a doctor to the hospital staff.[21]

Because the Federation acted as a watchdog for Cleveland's voluntary agencies, its records sometimes contain unflattering comments. A frank letter from a Federation official to Maud Morlock at the U.S. Children's Bureau describes the matron at one of the homes as "the worst yet."[22] The Federation, dedicated to research and professionalism, also collected invaluable data, including the most thorough study of the city's maternity facilities, the 1936 Bolt Report, which will be referred to often.[23]

The sources also dictate that this history of social policy is less often about the choices of female clients—unwed mothers—than about the decisions of female policymakers.[24] We know a good deal about the women who wrote and signed the surviving reports, letters, and minutes of meetings. We know, for example, that the meetings of the Retreat and Florence Crittenton boards opened with a prayer (sometimes we even know what the Florence Crittenton board had for lunch). We know these women's names and sometimes their addresses and occupations. Almost all of them were white, but they did not constitute a homogeneous group. The founders of the Retreat belonged to Cleveland's social elite; the founders of the Florence Crittenton Home did not. The Catholic nuns and the Salvation Army officers belonged to different churches and probably came from different ethnic and socioeconomic backgrounds as well. In general, however, most of these women can be described as middle-class by virtue of their financial resources, which allowed them to pursue religious vocations, professional training, or volunteer benevolence.

We know almost nothing about the unmarried women who bore children unaided and unnoticed by public and private agencies. Their fates have been unrecorded and remain inaccessible to the historian. This study, consequently, deals only with those unwed mothers whose recorded dependency on public and private welfare agencies has made them visible. They were generally, although not exclusively, working-class. The clientele of the public hospitals were indigent, or they would have been somewhere else. Throughout the Depression, the inmates of maternity homes sometimes were factory workers and waitresses, but most were domestic servants, as were unwed mothers in other cities. (See Table I.2.)[25] Even after World War II, when the maternity home clientele became middle-class, unmarried women remained anonymous, because it was the homes' policy never to record a client's real name in order to hide her shame.[26] There are no case records available, and in the surviving case studies, the women have only pseudonyms. Like most social welfare clients, these women were almost always literally and figuratively inarticulate.

For the most part, we see and try to understand the unmarried women through the eyes of their middle-class benefactors, whose perspectives were sometimes distorted. For example, the early twentieth-century description of women pregnant out-of-wedlock as "feeble-minded," although derived in part from the contemporary vocabulary of intelligence testing, came in larger part from the class and ethnic differences that often made the tests incomprehensible to those being tested: "feebleminded" often meant someone who could not read English. In the same way, racial stereotypes shaped white women's interpretation of black unwed motherhood, reflected even in the thinking of the respected

TABLE I.2
CONFERENCE ON ILLEGITIMACY SURVEY
OF UNWED MOTHERS, 1914

Occupation at time of fall
14 no occupation (at home)
37 domestic
 2 telephone girls
 4 dressmakers
15 factory girls
 9 waitresses
 4 clerks

Earnings at time of fall
Average $8.88 per week
Maximum $12.50 per week
Minimum $6.00 per week

Religion
46 Catholic
48 Protestant
 1 Jewish
 1 Russian Catholic

Causes of Downfall
19 misplaced confidence
10 mental and moral weakness
 2 bad company
 2 bad home influence
 1 lack of protection
 1 propinquity following separation from husband
 1 propinquity and lack of protection

Source: Conference on Illegitimacy, May 25, 1914, FCP MS 3788, container 21, folder 516, WRHS.

experts at the U.S. Children's Bureau: "Illegitimacy among Negroes . . . must be studied . . . in relation to . . . social and economic conditions," specifically "laxness of marriage relations."[27]

Middle-class distortions were compounded by the deliberate deceptions of working-class clients. Certainly they lied, telling matrons or social workers that they were domestic servants because "barmaid" or "occasional prostitute" would not have gained them the shelter and medical care they needed.

We do find a few authentic voices. In interviews done for her master's thesis in social work, Mabel Mattingly carefully recorded some women's responses. Most mothers told her that they had become pregnant after repeated sexual intercourse with a long-time sexual partner, whom they had "liked . . . at least at the time." The women also recounted some unpleasant memories of maternity homes, such as the smells of the laundry and the burden of caring for numerous babies: "One girl ran away from the institution because she couldn't bear the thought of doing the same job, in the same way, and at the same time each day." Another, however, recalled that "she had found her salvation" in her work at the home. Mattingly also includes an eloquent letter written by an unwed mother to her social worker: "I shall never forget all you did for the baby and me. I can just say that it was what a real mother would do for a daughter of her own whom she loved very dearly." The Salvation Army Rescue occasionally published appreciative letters like this one: "I thought I would write you a letter this evening to let you know how I am getting along. I am striving hard to be good. . . . Adjutant, I know Jesus will help me to conquer my tongue. I do want to get the victory over it. . . . Do pray for me, Adjutant." The Florence Crittenton Home scrapbooks contain fond notes from former residents, as well as proud birth and wedding announcements; some women regularly returned to the home for its June fund-raiser. The DePaul Home papers include a few monthly newsletters written at the home in the early 1970s. In them, girls spoke affectionately of each other and of the staff, but with great pathos about giving up their infants for adoption: "Make the most of the little time you have left here. Appreciate your baby while you still have her. . . . The hardest time you will have is when you must . . . give them your baby. I know it was the hardest thing I ever did in my whole life. . . . Please pray for me and my baby. I need God's help so much now."[28]

Because the unwed mothers too seldom speak for themselves, I have included as much descriptive and anecdotal material about them as possible in order to capture their individuality, if not their voices, and to allow them to become actors in this story.[29] Here is a woman whose actions say more about her than did the exasperated social worker who wrote the account: "This woman of good American stock, a woman of 25 years of age now, is of normal intelligence and healthy. Under proper influences, her behavior is socially acceptable. She has been pregnant five times, had two miscarriages, and placed her three children up for adoption. All confinements had been in Cleveland maternity homes. The social agencies had known her. . . . [S]he had married the father of her first child, but he had not provided a home, and he was not the father of the other two children. The father of one child was colored, and the father of the other Jewish. While one social agency was attempting to follow her up on two separate cases reported, she was being confined in a maternity home for the second time under a different name. The case work agency never did catch up with her. At Probate Court two separate cases on her children were being investigated when it was discovered she was one and the same mother going by different names." [30]

WOMEN AND SOCIAL POLICY

Two of the most important leaders in this work were male, William Booth and Charles Crittenton, founders of the largest chains of homes for unwed mothers. Generous gifts from male philanthropists and financial aid and moral direction from Catholic bishops supported maternity homes decade after decade. But within homes and hospitals in Cleveland and elsewhere, women—founders, boards of managers, volunteers, matrons, nuns, nurses, and social workers—admitted and dismissed inmates, established rules and routines, cared for children and mothers, and managed the day-to-day operations that made institutional life livable or at least bearable.

Like other social policymakers, these women simultaneously "preach[ed] compassion and stress[ed] deterrence." [31] Genuine compassion prompted the establishment and shaped the administration of the scores of institutions for unmarried mothers. Women provided temporary and sometimes long-term housing and necessary medical attention for mothers and infants. They were well aware of the other, grim options: public humiliation, infanticide, illegal and dangerous abortion, prostitution, homelessness, and almost certain destitution for the mother, and for the infant, perhaps abandonment, the disgrace of bastardy, poverty, or even infanticide.

Deterrence was also a primary goal. The prescribed regimen of the homes—long confinements, religious instruction, domestic chores, rigid rules—was undeniably restrictive. At least until very recently, workers at facilities for unwed mothers would have freely admitted that they were trying to control their clients' behavior and prevent additional illegitimate pregnancies.

Although it was an obvious attempt at social control, the work of these middle-class women, while perhaps intellectually or spiritually empowering for them as individuals, did not empower them as a group. Like much women's work, theirs was private and domestic, done inside the walls of institutions, unpaid or ill-paid. Even within the closed universe of the homes, there were failures. In 1872 the Retreat board noted sadly: "Some [women] have returned to their former lives of sin, tis true, and that is the experience of every such institution [as ours]." In 1915 the

13

TABLE I.3
INFORMATION ON UNMARRIED MOTHERS REPORTED
HAVING TWO OR MORE CHILDREN, 1936

					Places of Confinement		
Case	Age	Color	Religion	Occupation	First	Second	Third
1	16	W	Protestant	Student	Booth	Crittenton	—
2	16	N	Protestant	At home	City	Talbert	—
3	17	W	Catholic	At home	Retreat	St. Ann's	—
4	18	N	Protestant	At home	Talbert	Talbert	—
5	19	W	Catholic	Waitress	Mansfield	St. Ann's	—
6	19	W	Catholic	Factory	St. Alexis	St. Ann's	—
7	19	W	Catholic	Waitress	Own home	Own home	—
8	19	W	Protestant	At home	Retreat	Booth	—
9	20	W	Protestant	Unemployed	Retreat	Booth	—
10	20	W	Catholic	Domestic	Miscarried	Booth	—
11	20	N	Protestant	At home	Talbert	City	—
12	20	W	Protestant	Factory	Booth	Own home	Booth
13	21	W	Protestant	At home	Hospital	Own home	—
14	21	W	Catholic	Domestic	St. Ann's	Crittenton	—
15	21	W	Protestant	Waitress	Toledo	Booth	—
16	21	W	Catholic	Domestic	Retreat	Booth	—
17	22	W	Protestant	Domestic	Crittenton	Booth	—
18	22	W	Protestant	At home	St. Ann's	Own home	—
19	22	W	Catholic	Domestic	Own home	St. Ann's	—
20	22	W	Catholic	Waitress	Abortion	Unknown	—
21	23	W	Protestant	Salesgirl	Unknown	St. Luke's	—
22	23	W	Protestant	Waitress	Abortion	Booth	—
23	24	W	Protestant	Waitress	Booth	Unknown	Crittenton
24	24	W	Catholic	Unemployed	St. Ann's	Own home	—
25	25	W	Catholic	Domestic	St. Ann's	Booth	—
26	25	W	Catholic	Stenographer	St. Ann's	Own home	—
27	26	W	Protestant	At home	Unknown	Booth	—
28	26	W	Catholic	Domestic	St. Ann's	St. Ann's	—
29	26	W	Catholic	Unknown	Lorain	City	—
30	27	W	Catholic	Factory	St. Ann's	Booth	—

Source: Committee on Unmarried Mothers, Oct. 19, 1936, FCP MS 3788, container 33, folder 829, WRHS.

Florence Crittenton matron puzzled over what to do with "a young woman with a second illegitimate baby who shows no disposition to work or even to be of any service in the household . . . and is back with her original bad companions and seems altogether indifferent." [32] The Federation in 1936 discovered women who had multiple illegitimate pregnancies. (See Table I.3.) Many of these second- and sometimes third-time offenders had earlier been confined to maternity homes where they had obviously refused to be reformed.[33]

Women workers certainly did not have power over men, who continued to make the important financial and policy decisions for every institution examined in this book. The Cleveland Infirmary was run by a male superintendent who took his orders and funds from the men in the city council or the mayor's office. The Retreat, perhaps the most autonomous of all the institutions, was even so financially dependent on male philanthropists. The Florence Crittenton Home's female board of managers had to beg for grocery money from the male board of trustees, just as the Sisters of Charity had to beg the bishop of Cleveland for subsidies and do the bidding of doctors whom the bishop appointed. At City Hospital male doctors headed the obstetrical staff and male politicians allocated crucial funding. In the Cleveland Federation the social workers were mostly women; the Federation's director, however, was male, and the Federation controlled much of the homes' funding. The most prominent women in this story were the social work professionals at the U.S. Children's Bureau, a federal agency with a small budget and only investigative powers, under the direction of the male-headed Department of Commerce and Labor.

The unwed mothers themselves may have occasionally frustrated their middle-class benefactors, but they too were clearly less powerful than men. Too many sources describe the women as seduced and abandoned by deceitful men to dismiss the characterization as a middle-class distortion or working-class deception. This description appears first in late-nineteenth-century promotional materials for the maternity homes that abound with tales of "romance, ruin, and rescue," and it surfaces again and again. At the 1917 National Conference on Social Work, a trained caseworker for the Cleveland Humane Society described "Martha" to the audience: "[She was] of American parentage, neatly and modestly dressed, and altogether pleasing in appearance. She was unmarried and the mother of a perfectly normal baby two months of age. . . . [S]he had left her home in a small town in Virginia . . . [and] had first been employed at housework in Cleveland, but just previous to her confinement worked as a marker in a laundry. She told us that she had the father of her baby arrested, but for some reason she could not explain, nothing came of it. He disappeared after giving her fifty dollars. She described him as a sturdy American, four years her senior, and a carpenter by trade." Half a century later, a social worker for Cleveland's Children Services, the descendant of the Humane Society, discovered that the "majority of the clients confided in the father first, telling him of the pregnancy," and that they continued to "hold out hope for marriage" as long as possible, coming to the agency for help only after the men refused to marry them.[34]

This is not to deny the scattered evidence of a more entrenched illegitimacy found, for example, in the Federation Bolt Report. Occasional case studies describe unwed mothers who were illegitimate themselves or who had sisters who bore children out-of-wedlock. An example would be one "American girl, 19 years old," who bore two illegitimate children, the first of which was taken from her and died in an institution. Angry and resentful because her family had not institutionalized her sister's illegitimate child, the young woman refused to care for her second child until a social worker talked with her and the police charged her with neglect.[35]

Like most women's history, this study is less about power than about degrees of powerlessness. The American social welfare system not only distinguishes between the undeserving and deserving poor but rewards those with power and punishes those with none. Public and private social policy and practice have often penalized most heavily those women who have obviously violated sexual norms and provided least not only for them but for their caretakers.

Powerlessness is not the whole story. Both groups of women were able to use the system to their advantage. Middle-class women, church members, nuns, Salvation Army lassies, volunteers, and social workers kept alive a religious mission in a secular age, maintained nineteenth-century institutions into the twentieth, and at the very least kept themselves employed. Similarly, unwed mothers succeeded in getting outdoor relief from the city, mothers' pensions from the state, and ADC/AFDC, despite all efforts to make it impossible. Women weren't enticed or coerced into maternity homes and hospitals, but they used private and public facilities as temporary way stations or medical facilities for themselves and their children. Even dependent, unwed mothers were resourceful enough to care for themselves and their children.

In and Out of the Social Welfare Mainstream

The development of national social welfare policies and practices from the mid-nineteenth to the late twentieth century will provide a rough chronology for this study. Each of the Cleveland institutions receives a separate chapter, but each also operated within the larger context and in conjunction with national organizations: the National Conference on Charities and Corrections and its later manifestations, the National

Conference on Social Work and the National Conference on Social Welfare; the Young Women's Christian Association; the National Florence Crittenton Mission; the Salvation Army; and the Conference of Catholic Charities. Each chapter focuses on the local institution that best illustrates the ways in which care for unwed mothers conformed to and deviated from mainstream social welfare policy as it was applied to other dependent groups.

Chapter 1 describes the Cleveland Infirmary or poorhouse, built in the mid-nineteenth century when the only public responsibility for dependence was borne by the local government, in accordance with custom and statute inherited from seventeenth-century poor law. Like government itself, that responsibility at first was minimal: to provide enough outdoor relief to stave off starvation. However, a commercializing economy and a surge of European immigrants to American cities multiplied the number of destitute people during the first third of the century, prompting Americans to search for a better remedy for dependence. That remedy was institutionalization, shelter within a public facility for the absolutely destitute where material sustenance could be combined with moral improvement that would prevent further reliance on local taxpayers.

The Cleveland Infirmary was one of scores of public institutions founded throughout the country during this period. The Infirmary housed growing numbers of the city's destitute and homeless, including some unwed mothers. Because Americans made little distinction between dependence and delinquency, women pregnant out-of-wedlock initially received the same treatment as did male inmates. By the last decades of the century, as welfare reformers argued for an end to the undifferentiated poorhouse, mothers, most of them unmarried, were removed from the Infirmary and it became a home for elderly men. Subsequently, there have been in general no public funds to shelter unwed mothers.

Denied long-term care at public facilities like the Infirmary, Cleveland's unwed mothers became the special responsibility of private sectarian refuges and maternity homes such as the Retreat, the subject of chapter 2. Throughout the nineteenth century, churches were significant welfare providers, especially in the nation's cities, where rapid industrialization created vast economic opportunity and great poverty in the post–Civil War decades. The century's powerful religious impulses, fanned by waves of revivalism and sectarian rivalries, culminated in the last third of the century in the proliferation of evangelical social welfare institutions. Their mission was to rescue destitute co-religionists and proselytize everyone else. Of particular concern were dependent children, whose religious conversion would ensure the future of the faith, and "fallen women," with whose sexual exploitation middle-class evangelical women could empathize. Institutions that sheltered women became women's work.

The Retreat typified this female evangelical benevolence. Founded and administered by middle- and upper-class members of the Woman's Christian Association (and financed by their fathers and husbands), the Retreat sought to rescue its clientele—at first prostitutes and then unmarried mothers—through conversion to Christ within the cloistered walls of the home. Unlike the care of children, which began to move out of sectarian institutions and to receive significant public funding, the care of unwed mothers remained the province of women and private, church-related organizations. Although the Retreat closed in 1936, the other Cleveland maternity homes remained privately funded, committed through the 1980s to their original goal of spiritual reclamation through long institutionalization.

Chapter 3 focuses on the professionalization of social work as it gathered steam in the 1910s. The growth of professionalization is illustrated by the changing relationship between the Cleveland Florence Crittenton Home and the Cleveland Federation. Professional social work emerged from the same social and economic disorder of the early twentieth century that spawned Progressive reformism. The graduates of the first social work schools did in fact hope to reform existing social welfare practices by remedying the haphazard delivery of relief and services by sectarian private agencies such as the Retreat and the corruption of local welfare systems such as Cleveland's. These early social workers were mostly women, and child-saving became a paramount interest of theirs as well as of Progressive reformers in general.

The Cleveland Crittenton Home opened in 1912, almost simultaneously with the founding of the Federation, which sought to professionalize the staffs and practices of social agencies. Initially the pious volunteers and matrons of the maternity homes and the new Federation-endorsed professional caseworkers agreed on strategies and goals. In the late 1930s and early 1940s, differences emerged, stemming from the rescue work tradition of the maternity homes and the child-saving orientation of professional workers. The Crittenton Home nevertheless evaded Federation pressures through much of the post–World War II period and retained historic practices at odds with social work standards. When the goal of the Crittenton Home and the goals of professional social workers diverged too widely in the late 1960s, the Federation ended the home's life as a shelter for unwed mothers.

Chapter 4 describes a simultaneous version of the professionalization of social policy, the medicalization of childbirth, best exemplified by the institutional development of St. Ann's Infant and Maternity Asylum. Since the colonial period, home had been the birth setting preferred by both women and doctors. Hospitals, like poorhouses, initially were places for poor people without homes, and early lying-in hospitals sheltered mostly poor and unmarried mothers. Hospital childbirth, therefore, was correctly identified with sexual immorality and even more correctly with disease, especially puerperal fever. In the first decades of this century, doctors became convinced of the professional and medical advantages of hospital care, and hospital administrators became convinced that private patients must pay the rising costs of that care. When middle-class women became convinced that hospitals and doctors were both safe and respectable, childbirth moved from home to hospital. In 1930 the majority of Cleveland women giving birth did so in hospitals.

St. Ann's was founded as a charitable shelter for destitute unwed mothers, one of scores of Catholic social welfare institutions including hospitals, orphanages, and schools administered by thousands of Catholic nuns. During the 1910s and 1920s, St. Ann's spawned a separate maternity hospital where middle-class married women could receive the best of medical care from professionally trained doctors and nurses. For unwed mothers, housed after 1918 in a separate facility, childbirth remained an occasion for spiritual reclamation under the direction of nuns, not a medical event under the direction of doctors. The postwar psychiatric interpretation of unwed motherhood as symptomatic of personality disorder merely added the patina of medical expertise to what remained essentially a moral and religious rather than a medical assessment of pregnancy out-of-wedlock.

Chapter 5 is the story of the Salvation Army Rescue and especially Mary B. Talbert Home for black women. Mary B. Talbert illustrates the ways in which twentieth-century white social policymakers tried to solve the problems created by a black clientele. In the late nineteenth century, social welfare institutions for blacks were separate and unequal, reflecting contemporary racist ideas and practices. In response the black community, especially black clubwomen, struggled to serve their people by building their own institutions. However, the great migrations of blacks to northern cities during the first and second world wars taxed to the limit the abilities of the private sector, black and white, to provide adequate care. Although segregationist policies were retained by private social welfare agencies even through the second postwar period, these policies were mitigated by the diminished importance of institutional care for most dependent populations.

Initiated by the Cleveland Council of Colored Women, the Mary B. Talbert Home was administered by the Salvation Army, a church receptive to the spiritual needs of black Americans but susceptible also to the racist ideas and practices of the white social work establishment. Segregation at Mary B. Talbert was standard social welfare practice. Moreover, white assumptions about black women's sexual mores outweighed traditional assumptions about the desirability of institutional care for unwed mothers, guaranteeing that the segregated home would never adequately serve black women. In 1960 the Federation closed Mary B. Talbert, and it was replaced by outpatient services for women pregnant out-of-wedlock. The closing thus marked the effective end to the institutionalization that had been the private sector's historic solution to unwed motherhood.

By the 1960s, Cleveland's public hospital, the subject of chapter 6, had become the city's largest single provider of health care to unwed mothers, many of them black. The story of this hospital best illustrates the ways in which responsibilities for relief and health care have shifted from the private to the public sectors during the twentieth century. Public hospitals and local governments were the primary providers of financial and medical aid to the urban destitute, but private hospitals and private relief agencies also played important welfare roles during the first decades of the century. During the Great Depression, however, private agencies and institutions could not handle the sustained economic emergency. The New Deal then (briefly) provided relief, and public hospitals supplied increased medical services to more people. During the 1960s, expanded funds for relief and health care—AFDC and Medicaid—provided more but never adequate public aid for the dependent.

Cleveland's city hospital began as the city poorhouse, and it retained much of its almshouse flavor because it was forced to care for the indigent at the least possible expense to taxpayers. Among the indigent were unwed mothers. During the 1930s, when private maternity homes and hospitals began to abandon charitable patients, this public facility delivered greater numbers of illegitimate children, especially to black women. By the early 1960s it became the largest home for unwed mothers, just as its parent Infirmary had been in the mid-nineteenth century. Here at the public hospital where patients were not only poor and nonwhite but sexually delinquent, they received again the ungenerous and politically vulnerable care of the old poorhouse.

POORHOUSE BEGINNINGS: THE CLEVELAND INFIRMARY, 1855–1910

Name	Age	Nativity	Cause of Present Indigence
[illegible]	19	Ireland	Seduction

This notation in the Cleveland Infirmary's 1856 register[1] tells us that this anonymous woman's indigence resulted from her "seduction" and illicit pregnancy and that she lived among other homeless dependents in the Cleveland poorhouse. Although not intended as a shelter for unwed mothers, the Infirmary nevertheless became the city's first institution for women pregnant out-of-wedlock, for whom it provided some medical attention and a temporary reprieve from poverty. During the 1880s the Infirmary became a less hospitable refuge for women, particularly those with children, and by 1910 the all-purpose poorhouse had become a showpiece of Progressive institutional reform and a home for elderly men.

The mid-nineteenth-century poorhouse sheltered all dependents, regardless of the cause of their indigence: illness, insanity, transience, old age, bad luck, or seduction. The sexual immorality of unwed mothers soon provided justification for their early eviction from this shelter and an end to substantial public aid.

POOR RELIEF AND POORHOUSES

The American poorhouse developed in response to the changing dimensions and perceptions of poverty. The institution ambitiously sought to reform both the traditional poor relief system and the poor themselves.

The English colonists had brought with them seventeenth-century poor laws that assumed that if a family could not take care of its members, the local government would.[2] Government was responsible only for its own residents, and town fathers and overseers of the poor refused entry or warned away "strangers"—men, women, and children who might become public charges, especially unwed mothers.[3]

Although commonly called outdoor relief, public assistance took several forms. The indigent who had homes received food, clothing, or fuel distributed by public officials. An able-bodied adult might be auctioned off to the lowest bidder, typically a private householder for whom the pauper would work. A woman might be bound out as a servant, but her children might be placed elsewhere.[4] All indigent parents, and especially women, were suspect, and state and local governments often took custody of children whose parents asked for public assistance. An 1811 Ohio law, for example, provided for the relief of abandoned women by permitting the court to bind out their children as apprentices.[5]

During the first quarter of the nineteenth century, economic and demographic changes multiplied the number of people dependent on public aid. The commercialization of the economy encouraged migration from family farms and country villages to growing cities, where there were jobs in stores, the trades, and early factories. The fortunes of urban workers became linked to the prosperity of their employers and the national economy, and frequent recessions and depressions such as those that followed the War of 1812 or the land speculations of 1837 had immediate impact on vulnerable working people.

To worsen matters, the ranks of American paupers were swelled by new immigrants, particularly from Ireland and Germany after the 1830s. These too gathered in the growing cities, contributing to urban rioting and labor unrest. The poor relief system, designed for small, homogenous communities where public officials knew residents and where dependent people might actually find refuge with friends or even family at public expense, no longer worked.

The solution to this new dependence, more widespread and seemingly more disruptive than in earlier decades, was a single public facility that would house all homeless dependents: the poorhouse. Boston had built a poorhouse in 1662, Philadelphia in 1732, and New York in 1736. By the nineteenth century, poorhouses were "among the most important . . . residential institutions," touching more lives during this period than any institutions except jails.[6] Poorhouses were only one of a host of new nineteenth-century caretaker institutions, including jails, orphanages, and insane asylums, whose purpose was to promote social stability by confining dependent and delinquent persons.[7]

Like these institutions, the poorhouse reflected changing ideas about the cures and causes of poverty and delinquency. On the one hand, poorhouses represented humanitarian attempts to eliminate some of the callousness of outdoor relief. Auctioning off the poor allowed employers to brutalize and exploit their dependent charges and smacked too much of slavery, distasteful to northerners. In addition, the custom of shipping out nonresident paupers was particularly hard on their children, who might be shuttled from one township to another. On the other hand, although the poorhouse was meant to be a "refuge for the helpless," it was also to be "a deterrent to the able-bodied."[8] Americans had come to believe that in the land of opportunity, the destitution of able-bodied adults must be the result of individual failings, and that outdoor relief simply fostered pauperism by allowing recipients to remain in their own homes, free to pursue the vices and bad habits that had made them poor in the first place.

The poorhouse, therefore, would serve several purposes. Within its walls officials could control and improve inmates' behavior. Vices would be forbidden, and virtues, especially industry, would be encouraged. The absence of amenities and the rigorous discipline would discourage dependence upon the taxpayers, thereby saving money in the long run. Because illness was a primary cause of dependence, poorhouses were also hospitals where doctors and medical students provided free health care in return for clinical experience. And at the very least, poorhouses would keep the growing numbers of poor out of sight behind high fences or brick walls.

DEPENDENCE AND UNWED MOTHERHOOD

Unmarried mothers and their children appeared on the poorhouse registers of many cities. Their admission into poorhouses tacitly acknowledged the close connections between female dependence and marital status.

All women had limited economic opportunities. In the agricultural economy of colonial America, most wealth derived from the ownership of land, and colonial proprietors, joint stock companies, and town fathers had granted land almost exclusively to men. Women most often acquired property through inheritance from fathers or husbands. Most women married because a wife's labor was as essential to a husband's success as his was to hers, but because common law assumed that a woman's legal identity was subsumed in her husband's, a married woman usually had to relinquish her property to her spouse. Her livelihood became bound up with his good luck and good will.

Urbanization and the development of a market economy in the nineteenth century created opportunities for some free women who followed their traditional domestic chores into the factory, the store, or the school. Most income-earning women, however, even in urban settings, were domestic servants. Moreover, the changing economy disrupted families and communities as husbands lost jobs or pursued them across the country and into cities, and even married women and their children lost the economic security of a spouse or extended family.

It is not surprising that women appear to have been the majority of those dependent on public assistance at mid-century.[9] Some were married women whose husbands were disabled or absent. Most probably were husbandless, and certainly many were never-married mothers. Women who had children but no male breadwinners—widows, deserted wives, and unwed mothers—were at great risk of becoming dependent upon public support.

Pregnancy out-of-wedlock was interpreted as both sin and public expense. The prescriptive literature, secular and religious, emphasized the sinfulness of extramarital sex and pregnancy, the deviation from the primary purpose of sexual activity, procreation within the family. But public behavior recognized the practical implications of illegitimate birth. In the colonial period, an unmarried pregnant woman was required to identify her sexual partner, often while she was in labor, so that he could be punished and, more important, required to support her illegitimate child. If paternity was not established or the father could not support the child, the mother became financially responsible. An unmarried indentured servant, for example, was compelled to serve her master longer to compensate for the time lost during her pregnancy and for the child's expenses. In early nineteenth-century Philadelphia, an unwed mother who had given birth in the poorhouse could not receive outdoor relief until she had identified her child's father so that authorities could force him to pay for her lying-in expenses and for child support.[10] Unmarried mothers with financial resources, on the other hand, won the legal right to custody of their children, and "governments . . . gradually lost interest in prosecuting sexual sinners so long as the children of sin were financially cared for."[11]

The Cleveland Infirmary, 1855–1880

Four of the thirty-three women admitted to the Cleveland Infirmary in the first quarter of 1856 were pregnant and probably unmarried.[12] These

24

women received the same treatment as male inmates in this early, undifferentiated facility.

Although the city's commercial success created wealth for many, Cleveland's working people were often impoverished. Lake Erie and the newly built Erie and Ohio canals provided seasonal work for Cleveland men. Equally sporadic were the construction trades, even for skilled craftsmen. "Winter has truly been called 'the enemy of the poor' . . . as the accumulations of warmer and brighter days are steadily and rapidly decreasing . . . while the ring of the trowel is still, and the stroke of the hammer or axe is unheard," commented Infirmary superintendent Madison Miller in his 1857 annual report.[13] National depressions affected Cleveland's economy. In the wake of the depression of 1873, the directors of the Infirmary explained that heavy demands were being made upon the institution by "the almost total cessation of work in all manufactories and other establishments which were the means of giving a livelihood to the laboring classes."[14]

Many of the poor were recent arrivals from northwestern Europe or nearby Ohio villages, and many lacked both money and skills for urban living. In 1854 the Infirmary director reported, "Whole families of emigrants from foreign countries, having wholly exhausted their limited means to reach a land of liberty and home for the oppressed, or fleeced of their hard earnings by sharks and cut-throats of the Eastern cities and while they were expecting in a few days more to reach a home on the prairies of the West, were dropped in our streets, with the assurance that their tickets would carry them no further."[15] The city provided many of these transients with temporary shelter and train or canal tickets out of town.

Illness also caused destitution. Endemic malaria slowed the city's early settlement, cholera struck in 1832 and 1849, and smallpox scares hit in 1838 and 1845. The city's rapid growth caused overcrowding and exacerbated bad sanitation in poorer neighborhoods. Infirmary officials thus noted typical causes of indigence at the time of inmates' admissions: "sore leg," "debility," "consumption," "fever," "sickness," "sickness and misfortune," "sickness and age," "insane," or "idiotic."[16] Ill health and the hazards of working-class life compelled many people to use the poorhouse as a temporary residence to tide them over hard times or a medical emergency, or until they found permanent housing.

Therefore, although the population of Cleveland multiplied two and a half times between 1850 and 1860,[17] the numbers of the city's poor multiplied even more rapidly. The Ohio state legislature in 1816 had authorized township or county poorhouses to replace the earlier system of contracting out the poor or providing them with outdoor relief.[18] In 1827 the township of Cleveland opened the city's first poorhouse, located on the future site of the Erie Street Cemetery. The small building housed "twenty-five inmates of both sexes and all ages, some infirm, a few insane or feeble-minded," and was enlarged in 1837 to accommodate those impoverished by that year's depression.[19] In 1855 the city built an imposing brick structure and named it the Infirmary, suggesting its medical function. The Infirmary's population grew from 40 inmates in 1855 to 240 just five years later.[20]

In 1864 a reporter for the *Cleveland Leader* who accompanied the city council on its annual tour of the Infirmary described it this way: "Our infirmary is at once an asylum for the aged and infirm, a hospital, and a house of corrections. . . . In the basement . . . are confined the dangerously and violently insane. . . . Above there are the separate rooms for the little boys. . . . [Above them are] the old men, old women, and little girls."[21] The fourth floor housed the city workhouse.

Despite their occasional expressions of sympathy, Infirmary officials shared the prevalent negative attitudes about the poor. These are revealed in the Infirmary registers, which often attributed poverty to "bad management," "dissipation," or "bad habits." Particularly noticeable are the frequent references to "intemperance" or "delirium tremens" that reflect not only the results of heavy drinking but popular temperance sentiments, which blamed a vast array of social ills, including destitution and dependence, on alcohol.[22] An 1856 Infirmary report noted suspiciously that each applicant must be investigated thoroughly so that "no sum however small be expended upon an unworthy object." In addition, "great care should be taken at the outset not to make the place so attractive as to invite the indolent to enjoy the luxuries which the charity of a liberal people has provided."[23]

Within the Infirmary, women and men were housed separately but were subject to the same strict regimen: "The bell is rung at half past four o'clock in the summer, and half past five o'clock in the winter. . . . No ardent spirits or tobacco will be allowed the inmates, except in special cases ordered by the physician."[24] In reality, both male and female inmates probably were disorderly and disobedient. Superintendent Miller bemoaned the difficulties of his job: "To enforce obedience to the rules of the house—to compel those to obey law who have spent their whole lives following their own inclinations regardless of all law—to compel the unclean to be clean, and the quarrelsome and turbulent to be gentle and quiet—the indolent to become industrious and the profane to cease their profanity."[25]

Although work was divided along gender lines, the Infirmary bylaws provided that all "inmates shall work as far as their health and condition permit, faithfully and diligently for the benefit of the Infirmary."[26] The Infirmary maintained a farm so that inmates could produce their own food, and there were sporadic attempts at manufacturing, especially of clothing for the inmates. Men worked outside, and the women were responsible for much of the cleaning, sewing, and cooking.

Religious conversion was also considered a crucial means of control and an effective cure for dependence of both men and women. The third-floor hall was used as a chapel for occasional visits by ministers. Charged with neglect of the "spiritual needs of the poor," the Infirmary director conceded that only the Catholic priests were regular visitors and that he would "welcome sincere laborers belonging to any or all of the Christian denominations." In the meantime, he would strive "to improve and elevate the morals of the unfortunate."[27] Missionaries from various women's organizations, such as the local Woman's Christian Association and the Woman's Christian Temperance Union, sought to teach female inmates virtue and convert them to evangelical Protestantism.

Neither men nor women got adequate medical care. The city physician was supposed to visit the institution "at least once each day and oftener if necessary," but an 1858 newspaper account claimed that although the Infirmary was "a very excellent and pleasant farm[,] at present there is no physician in attendance." Since the job paid little or nothing, it is not surprising that it was vacant. One heroic doctor served the entire Infirmary population from 1878 until 1891, when a medical staff was appointed.[28] Inmates of the Infirmary or the workhouse, very possibly pregnant or newly delivered women, did the nursing.

The physical plant itself was simply not conducive to good medical practices. Dr. J. H. Marshall, acting health officer and city physician, on his first visit in 1864 found the Infirmary cramped and uncomfortable: "There were only two or three bedsteads for patients, no shades or blinds, and the stove and furniture was dilapidated to a woeful degree."[29] In 1887 the *Cleveland Medical Gazette* charged that the wards of the Infirmary were so crowded that patients were lodged in bathrooms and some "poor sufferers" offered to sleep on the floor if only they could be admitted.[30] The close relationship between the relief of poverty and the relief of illness stigmatized both, ensuring bad medical care for the poor and moralistic care for the ill.

The women who gave birth in this setting were probably not only dependent but unmarried. The evidence about their marital status is admittedly indirect but conclusive. The Infirmary registers, extant only through 1882, are so severely water-damaged that the first names and sometimes surnames of inmates and often their discharge dates are missing. The registers do identify women whose cause of indigence was pregnancy. After 1857 the registers do not use the term "seduction" but describe as "near confinement" women such as the nineteen-year-old German girl, "three weeks in the city," who entered alone in 1856, or the twenty-six-year-old Irish woman with two children but no husband in tow.[31]

During the late 1860s and 1870s another record-keeper substituted "enceinte" for "near confinement" or "pregnant." Significantly, these designations are not pejoratives like "dissipation" or "bad habits," commonly used to describe other inmates, and may reflect the same tolerance evidenced in the changing laws regarding custodial rights of unwed mothers with financial resources. It must have been almost impossible, in any case, for Infirmary officials to determine which pregnant women had never married and which were simply deserted, so it may have seemed easier not to try. The practical difference was minimal; the women were likely to be destitute in either case. Only in 1882 did a scrupulous record-keeper distinguish one "Mrs." from the other women.[32]

In contrast to the descriptions of women pregnant but without spouses, the registers did clearly identify prostitutes. Public officials took them in grudgingly, "especially those cases whose poverty, want, and disease is brought on by frequenting theatres, saloons, and houses of ill fame. Their allowance of food and medicine should be such as to sustain life and health, but no luxuries, or even condiments, which can stimulate vicious habits, should be allowed," the superintendent advised.[33] Prostitutes such as a sixteen-year-old "miserable diseased creature"[34] may have entered the Infirmary specifically for medical treatment. Registers also contain frequent references to syphilis: eight of the thirty-three women in the Infirmary in early 1856 were syphilitic.[35] The presence of prostitutes and syphilitics almost guaranteed that few respectable married women, no matter how destitute, would bear their children in the poorhouse, and that the women who did were in fact pregnant out-of-wedlock.

The fragmentary evidence allows some tentative comparisons between those women and the male inmates. Both were almost exclusively working-class. The men were laborers and occasionally skilled artisans. When their occupations were listed, the women were almost always described as servants.

Like the men, the women were disproportionately Irish or German. (See Table 1.1.) The records from the mid-1850s to 1882 are full of Bridgets and Marys, Kates and Maggies: Bridget Carl, 28 years old, born in Ireland and a resident in Cleveland for two years, entered the Infirmary

TABLE 1.1
REPORT OF THE INFIRMARY SUPERINTENDENT, 1856

ADMITTED from Dec. 18, 1855, to April 1, 1856

Men	47
Women	50
Boys	41
Girls	21

REMAINING on April 1, 1856

Men	37
Women	37
Boys	32
Girls	18

NATIVITY

America	48[a]	France	1
Ireland	42	Germany	59
England	4	Canada	3
Scotland	1	Isle of Man	1

[a] 19 had foreign-born parents.

Source: City of Cleveland, Annual Report, 1856 (Cleveland, 1856), 44.

February 10, 1859, but died in childbirth; her child was discharged two weeks later.[36] Unmarried Irish women were encouraged to emigrate so that they could support themselves, and the resulting low sex ratios in Cleveland and other American cities made it difficult for immigrant women to find husbands. At the same time, although customs from the old country or among the native-born working class might have sanctioned sexual activity for couples considering marriage, the lack of restraints in the new urban environment might encourage a man to desert his pregnant fiancée.[37] As late as 1880, 45 percent of Infirmary inmates were German- or Irish-born.[38] There were almost no black inmates. In 1859 a forty-four-year-old blacksmith was admitted; for cause of indigence the record-keeper noted, apparently without irony, "coloured."[39]

Like the men, the pregnant women often were transients and temporarily homeless, particularly in the 1850s and 1860s. A poignant example is the thirty-year-old English immigrant who had been in Cleveland only one day and was admitted in 1857 "about to be confined." In that same year the Infirmary admitted a young Irish woman who had arrived from Toronto only three days earlier; after a short stay she was discharged with her two children, one of whom had been born seven months before in the Cincinnati Infirmary.[40] City officials were supposed to turn away nonresident paupers, but the appearance of these women on the registers suggests that exceptions were made in the case of pregnant women.

There also were significant differences between male and female inmates. Men appear to have been generally older than women.[41] Female inmates came to the Infirmary in their childbearing or child-rearing years, their twenties and less often their early thirties: "Sarah Jackson, 21, Tailoress, American"; "——— Sterling, 26, [no occupation], Ireland"; "———, 23, [no occupation], Ireland"; "———, 30, [no occupation], Bohemia."[42]

The crucial relationship between women's dependence and their child-raising responsibilities is revealed also in the differences in the way men and women entered the Infirmary and how long they stayed. Occasionally, whole families, usually in transit, entered together. Patrick and Margaret Ryan, en route from Buffalo and after only one day in Cleveland, ended up in the Infirmary in 1859. In that same year a thirty-one-year-old Irish carpenter, his twenty-eight-year-old wife, and their five-year-old child were admitted; the parents were described as "intemperate."[43]

More typically, men entered the Infirmary alone and, by the 1870s, in far greater numbers than women. Men's stays were also shorter because men could more easily be discharged to find work outside the Infirmary when the weather changed or their health improved. In 1873, although 244 men and 102 women had been admitted, at the end of the year there were in residence 87 men and 85 women.[44] Women, on the other hand, entered the Cleveland poorhouse with child—near confinement or enceinte—or with children. ——— Murray was admitted in 1857 with her four children aged thirteen years to eighteen months, described as orphans because, in the parlance of the day, they were considered destitute without a father to support them.[45]

Without a male breadwinner, a woman might be in poverty year-round, not seasonally. Cleveland's changing economy offered women few jobs in factories, which required physical strength, or in stores, which required literacy. For that reason the Infirmary registers listed no occupations for many women. Almost the only exception to "servant" was "prostitute."

Earning a living was doubly hard because women had to care for their children. Of course, newborns often did not survive in the poorhouse. One of the few black women registered entered in 1867 enceinte and gave birth to a stillborn son. Adeline ———, a twenty-two-year-old German servant, gave birth in March 1875; she was hired as a "housewife" in June, but her infant son had died of pneumonia soon after his birth. On May 19, 1877, Mary O'Brien, daughter of Rosey O'Brien, died in the Infirmary, where she had been born eight weeks before. One page in the 1882 register recorded the deaths of three never-named infants.[46] Given the total absence of prenatal care and the poverty of the mothers, it is remarkable that any infants survived.

Further, a woman unable to support herself and an infant might be forced to leave her child at the poorhouse. The Infirmary regularly placed out or indentured children: in 1867 the superintendent boasted, "Homes for twenty-one children born or left at the Infirmary have been secured in the past year. . . . [A] great benefit has been conferred upon the children, as also a large item of expense saved to the city."[47] Several children were sent to the orphanages, which generally housed destitute rather than orphaned children.

As the superintendent acknowledged, a woman's responsibility for her child had serious economic consequences not only for herself but for the taxpayers of Cleveland. Although she most often took her child with her, a mother might stay months after her delivery until living arrangements could be made, or until she wore out her welcome. In February 1859, ——— Patten, a twenty-year-old Irish woman, was admitted although she had been in Cleveland only four days; her child was born in the Infirmary and lived there until December, and the mother stayed until January 1860. Later registers indicate that some stays lasted two to three months after confinement.[48] In the 1850s the Infirmary even organized occasional classes for children. After that, only food and shelter were provided.[49] Still, a woman in the poorhouse, because she had her children with her, was an expensive proposition.

EXIT WOMEN AND CHILDREN, 1880–1910

By the 1880s differences in the treatment of male and female dependents had become marked, and the Infirmary sheltered far more men than women. As relief costs rose, public disapproval of illegitimate pregnancy increased and the Infirmary began to specialize its functions. Women and their children became unwelcome guests, a trend encouraged by Progressive welfare reformers.

A serious business depression in 1873 and a subsequent scandal in the Infirmary first aroused concern about the costs of sheltering women. In 1878, a public official attempted unsuccessfully to reinstitute a policy of making inmates pick oakum, which would allow female inmates to earn money: "Some may shrink from the idea of exacting labor from women, but honest labor is no disgrace, and is it not more honorable for a woman to earn a living than to be supported in the degraded and degrading character of a pauper?"[50]

The grudging tolerance for public support of unmarried women gave way to the "sexual politics" of the social purity movement in the 1870s and 1880s. The movement's chief target was prostitution, but the once-clear line between prostitute and unmarried but enceinte became blurred—both represented the practice of sex outside of marriage. By the 1890s the social purity movement had gained considerable political clout.[51] Public officials accordingly feared that sheltering unwed mothers implied their approval of illicit sexual behavior. At the National Conference on Charities and Corrections meetings in 1889, the secretary of the Wisconsin Board of Charities and Reform described the common practice in his state: "To receive these women in the last stages of pregnancy, and to discharge them as soon as they are able to work." He was not complaining that the procedure was heartless. On the contrary, he argued, "the poorhouse, or the hospital, . . . thus becomes a convenience for lying-in women and an encouragement to licentiousness." Like Charles Murray a century later, the secretary wanted unwed mothers "to stay and work long enough to pay for the care and expense to which they have put the public."[52]

There also was swelling criticism of the poorhouse as a "charitable catch-all," housing under one roof "idiots, epileptics, incurables, incompetents, the aged, abandoned children, foundlings, women for confinement, and a considerable number of the insane, the blind, and the deaf and dumb." The growing number of public and private welfare administrators who gathered at the conventions of the National Conference on Charities and Corrections viewed the undifferentiated poorhouse as a careless institution that sheltered the worthy and the unworthy alike, the respectable elderly with debauched drunkards and diseased prostitutes.[53] Therefore, the Cleveland Infirmary in the 1880s began to divide its various populations into "departments" presumably requiring different treatment: the insane department; the "middle" department, which sheltered the indigent; and the hospital department. In 1889 the hospital department became a separate facility, City Hospital. By the 1890s more women gave birth at the hospital than at the Infirmary: in 1899, for example, there were twenty births at the hospital and only twelve at the Infirmary. By 1904 all births in a public facility were recorded at the hospital.[54]

Perhaps most important, women were removed from the poorhouse because their children were. Many Americans had come to believe that dependent children and adults should not be housed together. Accordingly, scores of orphanages and county children's homes were founded. Between 1850 and 1880, the number of children in almshouses dropped from seventeen thousand to eleven thousand, and the number in orphanages escalated from seventy-seven hundred to sixty thousand. From 1866 to 1899 the state of Ohio established fifty county homes (none in Cuyahoga County, where Cleveland is located).[55] An 1884 Ohio law prohibited children from staying in an almshouse unless it had separate quarters for them. The Infirmary superintendent complained that the law made it difficult to provide for "an increasing number of illegitimate children" because there was no county home for them.[56]

But the law also made it difficult for women who wanted to keep their children to stay in the Infirmary. A mother without resources now was forced to choose between shelter in the Infirmary without her child or a precarious existence on outdoor relief for them both after a short confinement in the hospital. Most dependent women chose or were forced to choose the latter.[57] The declining use of the Cleveland Infirmary can also be explained by the availability in the 1880s of two private maternity homes: St. Ann's Infant and Maternity Asylum and the Retreat. Furthermore, the Retreat, in the 1870s at least, received some public funding because the home housed destitute women who might earlier have been sheltered at the public facility.

The removal of women and children can be seen in the Infirmary's changing sex ratio and birth rate. During the 1850s the Infirmary sheltered almost equal numbers of men and women and recorded relatively large numbers of births in proportion to its population. In its first few months, from December 1855 to April 1856, the Infirmary actually admitted more women than men—fifty and forty-seven, respectively, and there were four births. In 1880, 233 males and 161 females were admitted, and 10 children were born. By 1893, the population of 938 men and 404 women yielded only 28 births.[58]

As women moved out of the poorhouse, they moved onto the outdoor relief rolls. Cleveland officials had remarked as early as the 1860s that outdoor relief recipients were often women "in the lowest state of destitution" or "widows with from five to ten small children."[59] That trend accelerated in the 1890s. In December 1883 the Infirmary sheltered 197 men and 150 women; during the year, it had given outdoor relief to 782 married persons, but also to 441 widows and 123 grass widows, a euphemism for women of undetermined marital status. In 1890 more than twice as many men as women were admitted to the Infirmary (383 and 181), but nearly twice as many single female heads of household (580 widows and 408 grass widows) received outdoor relief than did married couples (499). The city annual report lamented that "desertions of families is [sic] on the increase," but in fact husbandless women consistently received more outdoor relief, except when the severe depression of 1893 created massive unemployment for male breadwinners.[60]

CONCLUSION

In the first decade of this century, strategies for coping with dependence continued to change. Those changes further differentiated the public residential care received by men and women.

Progressive welfare reformers of this period supported greater public responsibility for the relief of poverty but in principle opposed the institutionalization of dependents. They proposed instead a variety of programs that would substitute flexible treatment of individuals, particularly children, for institutions. The best known of these programs was a system of juvenile justice that substituted probation for incarceration.[61] Progressives were proponents of outdoor relief for similar reasons: it allowed for more individualized treatment of poverty, whether by public or private agencies.

Tom L. Johnson, Cleveland's mayor from 1901 to 1909, personified the Progressive reform impulse for his contemporaries and for later historians. His energetic and flamboyant campaigning made him a popular political candidate, a four-time Democratic winner in a Republican town. He fought vigorously and unsuccessfully for publicly owned streetcars so that Clevelanders could get to work, and he improved public parks so that they would have places to play.

The Johnson administration also prided itself on its reformist efforts on behalf of the disadvantaged. The city's 1902 annual report expressed a generous willingness to assume obligation for those who could not care for themselves. Some people were simply unable to work, the report said: the crippled, the blind, and "destitute mothers, left alone with a number of small children. . . . The fact of the congestion of the poor in districts by themselves makes it difficult for private charity to reach many who are in distress and want." The city, therefore, must help: "Under present industrial and social conditions, no other method seems possible."[62]

Even as it provided outdoor relief for these unfortunates, the administration built several new welfare institutions. In nearby Hudson the city purchased a 285-acre farm for a correctional institution for boys. Ten miles east of the city on 850 acres of rolling farmland and orchards, the city built Cooley Farm, named after Cleveland's director of charities and corrections, the Reverend Harris R. Cooley. On the grounds was a new workhouse where Cooley's liberal parole program was implemented. The insane were transferred to a state institution, and the ill stayed at City Hospital on the site of the old Infirmary. The showpiece of this model welfare complex was the facility for those who were simply dependent. This handsome Spanish mission–style building with a red tile roof was informally referred to as the Old Couples' Cottage because almost all the residents were elderly.

These welfare reformers, however, provided no shelter for dependent women who were not married and in fact gave them less outdoor assistance than had previous administrations. In contrast to the 1890s, in both 1905 and 1909 women without husbands—widows or grass widows—constituted less than half of the adult relief recipients.[63] Moreover, the Johnson administration served poor men more generously than poor women. In 1903 the city spent $3.66 per capita on outdoor relief; most of that went to women and children. A stay in the Infirmary cost $133.55 per person, and most of those persons were male.[64] In 1910 447 men and 48 women lived in the Old Couples' Cottage. Like other poorhouses, the Cleveland Infirmary had become a home for old men.[65]

The poorhouse in particular and institutions for dependents in general have few defenders today. Critics maintain that such institutions were haphazardly and stingily administered, repressive of individual liberties, and careless of inmates' physical well-being. Much of the evidence from the Cleveland Infirmary bears out those criticisms. Historians like David J. Rothman have lamented that despite Progressive reforms, the "convenience" of institutions often won out over the "conscience" that urged their reform.[66]

As early as the 1880s, however, Cleveland public officials found a way to satisfy both conscience and convenience. It was more convenient, and cheaper, to distribute outdoor relief to a woman and her children from the backdoor of the Infirmary than to house them inside. Conscience could be served too if the recipient of cheap relief was a woman pregnant out-of-wedlock whose sexual delinquency had clearly caused her dependence. Moreover, while the poorhouse may seem repressive to twentieth-century male historians, it may have appeared quite otherwise to a nineteenth-century woman—without husband or resources and pregnant or with children—whose probable options were homelessness and utter destitution.

The removal of women from the poorhouse also established the pattern of care for unwed mothers that persists to this day: no public shelter and minimal public relief, which can be cut in the name of political necessity or reform. Further, private residential care remained "in the shadow of the poorhouse," in Michael B. Katz's phrase. There would be the same emphasis on work and moral improvement, and there would never be enough money.[67]

By the second decade of this century, Americans no longer saw the public poorhouse as a cure for poverty or as a place where unwed mothers could bear and care for their children. In Cleveland, four private maternity homes would attempt to provide shelter, medical care, and spiritual reclamation for unwed mothers: the Retreat, founded by the Woman's Christian Association; St. Ann's Infant and Maternity Asylum; the Salvation Army Rescue; and the Florence Crittenton Home.

◆ 2 ◆

RELIGION TO THE RESCUE: THE RETREAT, 1869–1936

She often expressed her gratitude to God that she was permitted to come to the Retreat—that here she had learned her way to Heaven. . . . Her delight was in having texts of Scriptures read . . . and in prayer by Christian friends who knelt at her bedside. Her end was perfect peace through Christ.
                                                                    Earnest Worker, July 1874

The Retreat was to be the way to Heaven for Cleveland's fallen women. Its well-to-do founders shared the contemporary view that a woman pregnant but not married had fallen from the grace of God and polite society. They also believed, however, that fallen women could be redeemed by conversion to Christ and by the cultivation of domestic skills and virtues within that most female of institutions, the home. The Retreat closed in 1936, a victim of the Great Depression, but its mission and strategies were carried on through the 1980s by the city's remaining homes for unwed mothers.

Like many late nineteenth-century social welfare institutions, particularly those that cared for children, the Retreat was a sectarian institution. Unlike sectarian child-care facilities, the Retreat and other maternity homes remained privately funded, committed to religious goals, institutionalization, and women's work.

PROTESTANT CHURCHES AND SOCIAL WELFARE INSTITUTIONS

Churches acted as social welfare agencies in nineteenth-century cities for both religious and secular reasons. Conversion was a key strategy in their efforts to save the souls and bodies of those they served.

37

The traditional belief that Christians have a responsibility to care for the less fortunate gained new energy in the nineteenth century. The religious revivals of the Second Great Awakening prompted a burst of activism and perfectionism that infused efforts to ameliorate the lot of the urban poor as well as a multitude of antebellum reforms such as temperance, utopian community-building, and abolitionism. The unwillingness or inability of local governments to provide adequately for the needy also encouraged churches and church-related organizations to assume responsibility for dependent people when cities denied or cut back on aid.[1]

Protestant welfare activities were also energized by lively competition among denominations and particularly by rivalry with the Catholic church. As German and Irish Catholics arrived in American cities by the hundreds of thousands in mid-century, long-standing animosities surfaced in the "Protestant crusades" of church-burnings, scurrilous anti-Catholic literature, and Know-Nothing political machinations. Less dramatic and more constructive were Protestant efforts to provide for the impoverished of their denominations.[2]

Although temporarily diverted from the cities to the battlefields of the Civil War, crusading Protestantism enjoyed a vigorous rebirth in the postwar years, "the great age for American Protestant missions."[3] Like the secular state, churches identified Protestant Christianity with their own ethnocentric and class-bound definition of civilization and felt a moral obligation to spread the blessings of both to the heathen. The foreign mission movement sought to evangelize the heathen of Asia and India, and the equally vigorous home mission movement tackled the heathen of southeastern Europe—Jews, Catholics, and other unbelievers—who poured into American ports and cities by the millions in the late nineteenth century.

At the heart of this evangelical Protestantism lay its emotional and intellectual commitment to the individual's conversion to Christ, which would bring release from the sin of this world and the promise of salvation in the next. In the 1880s and 1890s, the powerful preachers of this gospel included the Young Men's Christian Association, which proselytized on street corners and college campuses, and the revivalist Dwight L. Moody, who was converted by the YMCA and then began a hugely successful ministry preaching the "simple old-time Gospel of salvation through rebirth in Christ." Moody inspired the formation in 1888 of the Student Volunteer Movement of college students, the leaders of evangelical Protestantism for the next decades whose motto was "the evangelization of the world in this generation."[4]

Evangelicalism had important social welfare repercussions. For Americans who steadfastly believed that poverty resulted from an individual's lapse from grace, religious conversion remained a logical solution to dependence. Efforts to provide social services were always accompanied by efforts to proselytize. Dozens of charity groups such as the Association for Improving the Condition of the Poor in New York distributed religious tracts along with food and fuel.

Conversion was also a central strategy of caretaker institutions, including those for children, most of which were established by religious organizations. Because public institutions such as the Cleveland Infirmary had a strongly Protestant aura, Catholics founded dozens of childcare institutions before the 1880s.[5] The Cleveland Catholic Diocese opened the city's first orphanage, St. Mary's Female Asylum, in 1851, and the diocese built two more orphanages by the mid-1870s.

Cleveland Protestants kept pace. Members of the First Presbyterian Church founded the Protestant Orphan Asylum in 1852. In 1864 the first Methodist orphanage in the United States opened in nearby Berea. In 1869 the Independent Order of B'nai B'rith established the Jewish Orphan Asylum for the children of Jewish Civil War veterans. In these facilities religious services and Bible classes were as mandatory as instruction in carpentry for boys or sewing for girls. Lengthy stays, sometimes four to five years in the Catholic institutions and eight to nine years in the Jewish asylum, acknowledged both the sustained poverty of the children's parents (most "orphans" had at least one parent) and the difficulties of achieving the desired religious and moral regeneration.[6]

"Women's Work for Women"

Embarking on missions of their own, Protestant women established separate female institutions that became "women's work for women."

Nineteenth-century religion was regarded particularly as women's sphere, and church-related benevolent activities were often explicitly gender-linked. Women constituted the majority of Protestant church members, their numbers added to by each of the century's great revivals. Recognizing and reinforcing this, prescriptive literature "insisted that the 'true woman's' very nature was pious; . . . religiosity was synonymous with femininity." Easily converted herself, the evangelical Protestant woman had a responsibility to convert others. Her most acceptable ministry lay within her own home, her primary sphere, where as wife and especially as mother she might Christianize her family.[7]

Without overtly challenging this limitation, Protestant women expanded their religious domain. Growing numbers became foreign missionaries, but far more supported missionary work at home, mostly through fund-raising for female missionaries. Gathered into single-sex organizations, women sought to save and uplift heathen women abroad and at home and simultaneously enhance their own status within their churches.[8]

This women's work for women became the mission of one of the largest nondenominational organizations of women, the Woman's Christian Association (WCA). The first WCAs were founded by well-to-do Englishwomen in the mid-1850s as prayer circles. The first American WCA, the Ladies Christian Association of New York City, was established in 1858, coinciding with a series of urban revivals. "Any lady who is in a good standing of an Evangelical church may become an active member," according to the organization's constitution. By 1875 the twenty-eight Associations in the United States had this ambitious goal: "The temporal, moral, and spiritual welfare of self-supporting young women."[9] (The American WCAs united to form the Young Women's Christian Association in 1893.)

The women borrowed some strategies from the Young Men's Christian Association, whose workers preached on street corners and in jails, taught Bible classes and Sunday schools, and provided outdoor relief and temporary shelter for the homeless in "friendly inns."[10] The WCA journal, the *Earnest Worker*, describes similar activities: street preaching; visits to homes, hospitals, or poorhouses like the Cleveland Infirmary; and prayer meetings and Bible classes. Like the YMCA, the WCA organized on college campuses. The WCAs and then the YWCAs administered day nurseries, employment bureaus, and classes in cooking, sewing, nursing, and other domestic skills.

In the late nineteenth century, the WCAs specialized in building institutions for women. The first twenty-eight associations had founded thirteen homes by 1878, most of them boarding homes for working women.[11] In the decade of the Civil War alone, the percentage of women in the labor force increased from 9.7 to 13.7.[12] They worked in laundries, factories, shops, and offices, and hired themselves out as seamstresses, washerwomen, and domestic servants.

The typical woman worker was young, single, underpaid, and, from the perspective of her middle-class benefactors, sexually vulnerable. Unable to support herself, a woman might become the victim of economic and sexual exploitation by her employer, or she might turn to prostitution to earn a living. Cast adrift from family and church, loosed from the restraints of neighborhood and village, she might too eagerly yield to the temptation of premarital sex, especially if it was accompanied by the promise of marriage.

Victorians used the terms "fallen" and "ruined" to describe women who had engaged in premarital sex. Fallen meant fallen from God's grace by breaking divinely ordained rules of female chastity, but as Joan Jacobs Brumberg has explained, ruined also meant "to be less than physically perfect, to be non-virginal. . . . It also suggested . . . truncated marital and educational opportunities—a liability that would be particularly deadly to the economic and social aspirations of the Victorian middle class." [13] A ruined or fallen woman thus symbolized the fragility of all women's control over their bodies and their lives, as well as many of the ills of an urbanizing America: its growing commercialization and sexual permissiveness, the weakening of the family, the decay of small-town morality, and the decline of orthodox religion.

The WCA, therefore, sought to rescue fallen women. Rescue work began in the 1830s and 1840s, when female moral reform societies opened shelters for prostitutes, and it gained strength in the post—Civil War period from the broader-ranging social purity movement, which had made Infirmary administrators wary of providing public shelter for women pregnant out-of-wedlock and had hastened the exodus of women from the poorhouse. [14] WCA members believed—and the evidence bears them out—that women did not fare well in public poorhouses where there were male administrators and male inmates. Unfortunate women would be far better served and saved in private institutions that sheltered only other women, with religious rather than secular purposes. Unlike the poorhouses, these would be "homes," where religious influences were pervasive and where middle-class women could best serve their own ministries. Such homes institutionalized a "search for female moral authority" as women sought to promulgate their ideal of female sexual purity and moral superiority and gain a measure of control over the behavior of errant inmates within the homes and errant men outside. [15]

THE RETREAT, 1869–1912

The Cleveland Retreat, opened in 1869 by the Cleveland WCA, was the product of this female religious zeal and energy. In its first decades, the Retreat sheltered fallen but not necessarily pregnant women.

In 1868 a YMCA missionary urged the women in his Cleveland audience to do "practical work." Three weeks later an enthusiastic meeting of six hundred churchwomen at the YMCA led to the WCA's formal organization. Its motto: "Everything we do is religious." WCA leaders were members of Cleveland's social elite. Many had wealthy fathers or husbands who provided not only financial assistance and direction but social sanction for their efforts. Flora Stone Mather, for example, was the daughter of a rich industrialist and the wife of another, and herself endowed both a settlement and a college for women. Other WCA officers, such as long-time president Sarah Fitch, were single women with leisure time and financial independence. The Cleveland WCA also spawned both the local Woman's Christian Temperance Union and the long-lived Cleveland Day Nursery Association, and for several decades it supported four residential institutions for women.

Although there was no national WCA at this time, the Cleveland group's objective closely paralleled that of other WCAs: the "spiritual, moral, mental, social and physical welfare of the women in our midst," especially of "young women who [were] dependent upon their own exertions for support."[16] The Cleveland WCA justified its work in familiar terms: "In the bustle and activity of the age the women are following hard after the men. Not satisfied with their quiet country homes, many of them press their way to cities. What shall be done to care for these women? Be they never so pure, they are liable to fall into disgrace and sin, and they must be tenderly watched over and cared for. . . . They do not realize the snares and pitfalls that lie so thickly about them. They do not know that many men go about 'like roaring lions seeking whom they devour.' "[17]

Although the images of women painted here and elsewhere borrowed from Victorian popular literature, they also reflected demographic and economic realities. Women did indeed follow hard after the men during the Civil War in pursuit of jobs made available by departing soldiers or by new commercial needs. The *Cleveland Leader*, worried about "the difficulties experienced by young women in employment," suggested that "selling jewelry, books, shoes, sewing machines, and drygoods, and bookkeeping" were appropriate female jobs. Police court records reveal that some women found prostitution more lucrative.[18]

The Cleveland WCA set out to save women who had already fallen and, better yet, to prevent the fall of others. The first step was a missionary committee of volunteers and a paid Bible reader who visited private homes and charitable institutions such as the Infirmary and hospitals. But, as WCA historian and member Mrs. Howard Ingham commented: "As the early work of this committee was done, one great need stared it in the face: the need of a safe and inexpensive boarding-house for young women, whose dreary lives in the comfortless quarters to which poverty often drove them, filled tender hearts with pity."[19] Therefore, the second step toward saving women was the establishment of the Boarding Home for Working Women, which provided daily religious services and strict discipline. Railroad president Stillman Witt, whose wife, along with his daughter, Mrs. Daniel P. Eells, served on the WCA board, donated the building.[20] Boarders were expected to pay something for their rooms, but the home never became self-supporting and was always sustained by charitable contributions.

Almost simultaneously, the WCA opened the Retreat for women whose needs, although slightly different, were even more pressing: "Those who, from want, or sorrow, or deception, had lost the glory of their womanhood." Retreat founders often claimed that their work was despised, implying that like fallen women, they had become social outcasts for allegedly "encouraging vice."[21] This was not the case. Like its parent WCA, the Retreat received substantial financial gifts and moral support from well-to-do, socially prominent Clevelanders. Its first residence was donated by industrialist Joseph Perkins. Perkins provided ten thousand dollars more when the Retreat moved in 1873 to a site given by Leonard Case, whose fortune also endowed Case School of Applied Science. When the new facility opened, it was visited by Cleveland's elite and described in glowing detail by the local newspapers. Another generous supporter was Cleveland's best-known millionaire, John D. Rockefeller.[22]

Nevertheless, the Retreat was chronically in debt and always in need of donations. Consequently, its board lavished praise on the institution's male benefactors even as it portrayed other men as wicked seducers. The main danger to women, board members insisted, was men: "Stepfathers, fathers, physicians, and clergymen, . . . married men . . . libidinous lovers."[23] The 1873 annual report described one pathetic eighteen-year-old who had found refuge at the Retreat: "Banished from home by her father because one whom she had fondly and foolishly trusted had basely abused her confidence and deprived her of woman's priceless dower."[24] Retreat founders protested the double standard: "We would not excuse vice in woman more than in men, but are impelled to ask, why a man should go unscathed and be allowed to walk uncondemned and with the mein of innocence among his fellow men, aye, and among virtuous and refined women too, while his surely no more guilty companion in sin is a branded criminal?"[25] Such public utterances may have been more moderate than what was said in private, but the Retreat's energies were directed more at changing the women inside its walls than the men outside.

The Retreat was in the vanguard of the wave of rescue home—building that soon followed in Cleveland and elsewhere. The Sisters of the Good Shepherd opened their convent for wayward women in 1869 (to which Joseph Perkins also gave money), and the Sisters of Charity of St. Augustine founded St. Ann's Infant and Maternity Asylum in 1873. In 1878 the Cleveland WCTU sponsored the Open Door for homeless women, both "respectable" and "disreputable."[26] The WCA opened at least two similar institutions in other cities. The Sheltering Arms in Pittsburgh, opened in 1872, was dedicated to the "work of reform among those girls who, having strayed from the paths of virtue, manifest a desire to return"; and a White Cross home was opened in St. Louis in 1888 to aid and protect "young women who have been tempted or betrayed under promise of marriage and who desire to lead pure lives in the future, and to procure suitable homes for their children."[27] In the 1880s, the Salvation Army and Charles Crittenton initiated their chains of homes for unwed mothers.

These institutions shared the Retreat's goal: spiritual conversion and physical reclamation. The WCA *Earnest Worker* captured that mission in this poetic tribute in 1874:

> A blest Retreat in mercy lent
> Poor fallen woman to restore,
> If she but heed the Savior's voice,
> "Go sin no more, go sin no more."[28]

Christ's admonition to Mary Magdalene was often repeated by rescue workers, and "Go sin no more" became the motto of the Florence Crittenton homes. The Salvation Army Rescue's mission, although expressed more prosaically, was identical: "To provide a home for fallen girls who wish to reform; . . . to teach them habits of industry and self-help . . . to lead them to Christ for salvation."[29] The Retreat's reports scrupulously recorded conversions and spiritual awakenings. "It is believed by the Matron that many of the inmates have really become humble Christians and though rejoicing with trembling, they still hope greatly and give fervent thanks," boasted the minutes of an 1879 meeting.[30] The presence of the two Catholic homes, St. Ann's and the Convent of the Good Shepherd, probably meant that few Catholic women were forced to submit to this energetic Protestant missionizing.

Crucial to conversion was the presence of other women whose pious practices and principles provided models of female Christianity. Most important was the matron. The Pittsburgh Sheltering Arms' 1874 report claimed, "It is the aim of the Matron to teach these girls to earn an honest living and to govern all their actions upon Christian principles . . . to throw around them the beauty of Christianity."[31] At the Retreat and the Florence Crittenton Home, matrons were aided by women on the boards of managers who visited the homes, taught classes, or gave fund-raisers and parties there. In the Salvation Army and Catholic homes, the role of Christian exemplar was played by female religious, Army officers, and nuns.

The proper environment was also crucial, for woman could reclaim and be reclaimed best within her domestic sphere. Although the first Retreat was rather modest, the second building was a massive and imposing brick edifice with Italianate elements in a style popular for both public institutions and private homes of the wealthy, designed to inspire awe in passersby and generosity in philanthropists. High stone walls enclosed the home and grounds. The cloistered privacy hid the inmates' guilty secrets and preserved their families' good names. Thus sheltered from the world, the Retreat, like the private homes of middle-class Victorians, could create a "Christian atmosphere" where the institution's chief goal of spiritual reclamation could be achieved by daily prayers, Bible classes, or the embroidering of samplers with pious mottos: "Through Christ we hope"; "God is our refuge and our strength." [32]

Within this domestic and familial environment, the matron and the board could discipline inmates just as mothers discipline children. "The life at the Retreat is in every sense a home life. Our girls live together as one family, and the superintendent endeavours to be a true house mother to them all." This was not always easy, as the 1879 minutes of the Retreat board noted: "As a rule, the inmates [there were forty-six] have been law-abiding and well behaved, but in some cases discipline has been a necessity. . . . 'Eternal vigilance' is the price of good order in a family such as ours." (The term "inmate" did not suggest, at least to the Retreat managers, that the institution was a jail. Victorian women described their family members as inmates of their own homes.) The regimen also imposed discipline: the "girls are required to devote their forenoons to housework. In the afternoons they sew for their personal outfits. During four evenings each week, they study, under efficient teaching; one evening is devoted to a prayer meeting, and the remaining one to recreation." Girls who did not conform might be dismissed. [33]

The regimen nurtured woman's domestic instincts and skills. The care of infants, for example, encouraged mothers to develop their "God-given desire for maternity." [34] Although these tasks were supposed to have spiritual value, they also had practical implications for inmates and for the institution. Women were taught domestic skills at the Retreat so that they could earn a living. "The instruction which is given in housework, in sewing, and in the care of children, is in most cases, very much needed, and makes possible and probable a life of virtuous independence," claimed a Retreat annual report. [35] At the White Cross home, "All inmates are expected to share in the household duties. Only the matron is paid for work. All girls are taught plain sewing, nursing, and cooking." [36] Mothers at the Retreat, like women in other YWCA classes, were trained chiefly in domestic service, and annual reports regularly recorded the large number of women who left the Retreat to go into service. Consequently, the YWCA has been charged with being primarily a producer of domestic servants for its middle-class patrons, but such training made sense, given women's limited job options. Moreover, domestic service was considered an honest occupation, certainly more honest than prostitution, and working and living in someone else's home was better than having no home at all.[37] In addition, inmates occasionally were able to raise money for the Retreat by selling their "fancywork," and their free labor held down the home's expenses.

According to the home's annual reports, about equal numbers of women went into service as "returned to friends." Very few married. This speaks volumes about the social realities of being ruined and then abandoned. Marriage would clearly have been the first choice of home founders and inmates, but it was clearly not the choice of the men involved.

During its first twenty years, the Retreat had a varied clientele. In the tradition of the antebellum moral reform societies, the Retreat's first targets were prostitutes, for Cleveland already had flourishing red-light districts. The Retreat missionaries "visited the haunts of vice" in search of prostitutes who would be "willing to leave a house of sin," and Retreat officers claimed to have found two such women in 1875.[38] The missionaries probably found more recruits in the city workhouse and Infirmary than in brothels and saloons. Like the Protestant Orphan Asylum, the Retreat in its very earliest years received funds from the city because the home's missionaries had removed some women from the public facilities.[39] These women may have been prostitutes, but it is far more likely that they were simply destitute and therefore, by WCA standards, in danger of sexual exploitation. "It is comforting to know," commented the Missionary Committee, "that these weak and degraded women have opportunities of hearing the gospel invitation lovingly and persistently." A missionary also reported visits to women who were thus far guilty only of "low dances and . . . bad company"—working-class women whose relaxed behavior with men appeared promiscuous and dangerous by middle-class standards.[40]

Women, therefore, entered the Retreat and other rescue homes for a variety of reasons and stayed varying lengths of time. Some simply needed shelter, perhaps having been banished from their homes. Some needed long-term medical care. One young woman with tuberculosis came to the Retreat after two years of "sin and shame"; the institution could not heal her body, but at her death, "her fearful burden of sin she laid at the cross."[41] (Such death-bed conversions were, of course, triumphs for the institution.) The home also had a small paying clientele, probably young women committed by parents because they were incorrigible, pregnant, or potentially delinquent.[42] Some received temporary or transient care; others stayed for months.

Most early inmates, however, were not pregnant, as is indicated by the low ratio of births to inmates during the home's first decade. By 1879 the institution had cared for 556 women but only 260 children.[43] The Retreat did not begin to specialize in the care of unwed mothers until the 1880s. Prostitutes proved difficult to reclaim, better left to police and anti-vice squads. Indigent women might receive outdoor relief. Other institutions such as the WCTU's Training Home for Friendless Women or the Catholic Convent of the Good Shepherd cared for delinquent or pre-delinquent women who were not criminals. Women pregnant out-of-wedlock, on the other hand, were being removed from the Infirmary by unsympathetic male officials, and a few hospitals provided medical care but could not satisfactorily reform or reclaim women. Moreover, by the end of the century the growing rigidity of sexual norms meant that a pregnancy out-of-wedlock was a mark of shame not only to middle-class families but to working-class families with social aspirations or families from conservative religious traditions.[44]

Retreat policies adapted to this new clientele. By the 1890s a minimum six-month confinement was required, and in 1902 the average stay was more than eight months. By the turn of the century, the Retreat had become a large congregate facility that could accommodate about ninety to one hundred women and children. In 1912 the facility received fifty-three girls, and fifty-four babies were born (one girl apparently had entered the previous year, or someone had twins). About half the children left the institution with their mothers, and about half were put up for adoption by the Retreat or by the Protestant Orphan Asylum. Adoption was encouraged because it would more effectively hide a woman's shame and because she was more likely to get a job if she did not have a child with her.[45]

THE PERSISTENCE OF THE RELIGIOUS IMPULSE, 1913–1936

The Retreat, and the other maternity homes, remained committed to religious goals and strategies through the Depression despite financial difficulties and criticism from social workers. In contrast, the care of children became less sectarian and less committed to institutionalization as it became publicly funded.

In 1909 the first White House Conference on Dependent Children signaled Progressive reformers' vital interest in children by setting in motion the two most significant trends of future child welfare: a shift from institutional to noninstitutional care and an increase in the public funding and management of child care. The official position of the conference was that "home life" was best for children. So that poverty would no longer compel a child to be institutionalized, many states, including Ohio, passed mothers' pension laws that were supposed to provide a widow or deserted mother with a stipend sufficient to allow her to keep her children at home rather than having to place them in orphanages. In addition, child-care agencies began to place children in foster homes rather than institutions.

During the 1920s the Cleveland orphanages responded to these trends. The three largest facilities moved to the suburbs and replaced their large congregate facilities with "home-like" cottages for fewer children. Each orphanage received a new, nonsectarian name. The Catholic orphanages merged into Parmadale, the Jewish Orphan Asylum became Bellefaire, and the Protestant Orphan Asylum became Beech Brook. Although in reality most children still were institutionalized because their parents (or more often their single mothers) were poor, the orphanages began to redefine themselves as homes for "troubled" or "problem" children. They retained religious training and financial dependence on sponsoring religious organizations, but shortened lengths of institutionalization.[46]

The Depression dramatized the high costs of these institutions. Accordingly, the policy preferences of the reformist 1910s for public, noninstitutional child care became the economic necessities of the financially strapped 1930s. By 1929 Cleveland's orphanages were already overflowing with children whose parents could not support them. When private charities ran out of funds, a public agency, the Cuyahoga County Child Welfare Board, was established to take financial responsibility. Most dependent children were cared for in foster homes or in their own homes, not in the expensive orphanages.[47] More significant public support came from the federal social insurance programs and Aid to Dependent Children, set up by the Social Security Act of 1935. These and other income maintenance measures were supposed to prevent the destitution that earlier had forced parents to place their children in orphanages.

In contrast, during these same decades maternity homes changed few policies despite their membership in the secular Federation for Charity and Philanthropy. Instead of shortening confinements, the homes adopted a mandatory lengthy stay. Reversing its practice of placing illegitimate children for adoption, the Retreat endorsed keeping both mothers and children together in the maternity home for six months after confinement, in addition to an unspecified number of months prior to childbirth. Board president Mrs. Robert D. Beatty told the Federation in

1925, "At the end of this [six-month] period, the mother will not give up her baby, and this love for her child is a big element in character-building—working for her child gives the mother an aim in life which makes her stronger."[48] This policy of redemptive maternity, best articulated by Kate Waller Barrett of the National Florence Crittenton Mission, was employed at the other maternity homes as well.

The Retreat continued to affirm its goal of spiritual reclamation: "the care and training" of unwed mothers. That care still entailed a six-month confinement; the training was still in domestic skills, which was all the home could provide. Girls were not allowed to leave the institution to take courses in secretarial work, for example. Mrs. Beatty explained that such training was impractical for a clientele that often had not even finished grade school. More important, bookkeeping and stenography classes "would interfere with our training. . . . In our institution, and we think in most of the other institutions, girls are trained in all branches of housework, such as cooking, serving, cleaning, laundry work, nursery work, and sewing." These were not simply job skills but the means of reclamation: "All [inmates] are taught to sew, . . . to darn, repair, and make their own and their baby's clothes. . . . We feel that a girl gains much in self-respect by being neatly dressed." And, Mrs. Beatty concluded, "self-respect is a great step in reformation."[49]

Among other Federation members and especially social workers, however, the financial crisis of the Depression inspired increased dissatisfaction with institutional care in general and some outspoken criticism of maternity homes in particular. A 1932 study of maternity homes in Cleveland and elsewhere criticized their rigid regimen and the limitations of exclusively domestic training: "Regularity of rising hours, say 6 a.m., early morning feeding of babies . . . 7 a.m. breakfast after which each goes to her room or dormitory and makes her own bed. This completed, each girl takes her assigned duty in the various departments of the home. Under the supervision of the staff, [the girls do] the cooking, housekeeping, laundry. The nursery usually is given to a girl who desires that work or who wants to follow nurse maid's work when she leaves the home. Those who have lighter duties assist with the ironing on laundry days."[50] A more general report in 1934 charged that homes prohibited outside excursions except occasionally to church, censored inmates' mail, limited intellectual stimulation to visits from social workers or ministers, and did not even allow women to give birth in a hospital unless absolutely necessary. This report urged "greater flexibility in planning for unmarried mothers," such as placement in foster homes.[51]

To make matters worse, the Federation's 1936 Bolt Report also uncovered disturbing rates of recidivism, which cast serious doubts upon the homes' historic claims to reclaim and reform. (See Table I.3.) Some women given maternity home care during their first illegitimate pregnancies had second illegitimate children; two even had a third. Three of the thirty-four second-time offenders so identified (but none of the third) had been first confined at the Retreat.[52]

But the homes' most serious difficulty was finances. Cleveland homes in 1935 were full and in fact recorded a slightly larger percentage of registered illegitimate births in 1935 than in 1931. Although the number of clients held steady, the homes' sources of income declined, and like other private agencies, they ran larger and larger deficits.[53] In 1919 the Retreat had built a new but smaller facility that housed only fifteen women and twelve children, and although its fees were the same as the other homes' (fifty dollars for a Cleveland resident; seventy-five dollars for a woman from outside the county), its small size meant that it could not generate much income.

Unlike the other homes, the Retreat was not part of a national agency from which it could receive referrals. (It had incorporated separately from the YWCA in 1921.) The Retreat's endowment income had begun to fail as early as 1927, forcing it to ask for contingency funds from the Federation.[54] In 1936 the president of the Retreat's board made a last plea before the Federation on behalf of the Retreat and other maternity homes where "young girls" could "receive good care, discipline, and training." If social workers did not make better use of the Retreat, she warned, it would close and its remaining endowment would go unused.[55] Three months later, the Retreat closed its doors forever, and its remaining inmates were placed in the Florence Crittenton Home.

CONCLUSION

The other maternity homes—St. Ann's Loretta Hall, Booth Memorial Hospital, Mary B. Talbert Home, and the Florence Crittenton Home—survived the Depression. In them the mission of the spiritual reclamation of fallen women, first institutionalized at the Retreat in 1869, survived into the last decades of the twentieth century.

Like those elsewhere, Cleveland's maternity homes continued to be administered and financially sustained by religious organizations—the Catholic church, the Salvation Army, and the National Florence Crittenton Mission. These three organizations still run the majority of existing maternity homes, although the National Florence Crittenton Mission has become the Florence Crittenton Services, a nominally secular agency.

Despite changes in policies and clientele, especially after World War

II, the homes remained explicit about their religious purpose. Unaffiliated with any specific church, the Florence Crittenton Home nevertheless received funds and services from the women's groups of local Protestant churches, and local ministers conducted regular church services in the home throughout its existence as a maternity home. When the home's first secular social worker was hired in 1949, she discovered that "bible study classes were a regular part of the program, and actually the only formal program functioning at that point. These were under the supervision of a young woman minister of the Pentecostal Church."[56] The home offered a spiritual life program until 1970, when it discontinued services to unwed mothers.

At the Catholic facility, even though the approach to unwed motherhood was ostensibly psychological by the 1950s, the Sisters of Charity proudly noted how many of the unmarried mothers in the home had "returned to the sacraments."[57] In 1967 the home's administrators described its goal this way: "The purpose of the spiritual or religious program of the Home is to help the unmarried mother understand and utilize the support that religious values can bring to her life. The whole program is permeated with a religious orientation since DePaul [formerly St. Ann's Loretta Hall] is a sectarian agency deeply committed to religious affiliation."[58] The farewell words written by a young woman at DePaul in 1972, more than a century after the Retreat opened its doors, would have reassured the earlier Protestant churchwomen: "All of you will remain in my thoughts and prayers as I leave. All the times we shared together will not be forgotten. Some times were good—others, not so good. But they will always be in my heart. Thanks so much for the love and care you all showed toward me. God bless you and your babies."[59]

Salvation Army colonel Jane E. Wrieden, a former head of Booth Hospital who held a master's degree in social work, spoke in 1949 of the role of religion in her maternity home work: "The important thing is not the religious services or Bible study classes. In daily living together, one personality flows into another, and with us, religion is an integral part of this process. As we try to help these girls and women rebuild their lives, we count as much on the group experience in a Christian atmosphere as on individual counseling."[60] Cleveland's last maternity home is administered by a church, the Salvation Army, which believes—in Wrieden's words—that its social work "is an expression of our devotion to Jesus Christ."[61]

Anticipating the twentieth-century welfare state, historians have generally emphasized the development of public policy and public institutions such as the Cleveland Infirmary. Consequently, they have focused on the secularization of social welfare: the partial substitution of an environmental for a moralistic outlook and of public subsidies for sermons.

51

As a result, historians of social policy have underestimated the importance of private agencies and the tenacity of the religious mission that gave birth to them.[62]

Historians of women have done likewise. Joan Brumberg argues that rescue homes became secular agencies during the Progressive period, and the home for unwed mothers in Elmira that she examined apparently did. Peggy Pascoe attributes the demise of rescue homes to the collapse of Victorian gender-based moralism in the face of the cultural pluralism of the early twentieth century. (If the Retreat's closing is illustrative, failure of funds is a readier explanation.) According to Estelle B. Freedman, the decline after 1920 of these female institutions that had empowered women in the late nineteenth century explains the post-suffrage weakness of the woman's movement.[63]

Yet maternity homes in Cleveland and their women's work for women lived for several decades past the 1920s. Overtly religious, admittedly self-interested in their proselytizing, and insular in their concern for co-religionists, the homes continued to provide shelter and care for thousands of women and infants. The strength of their religious impulse allowed maternity homes to stay their historic course for most of this century when there were pressures to do otherwise and, more important, to provide care for women pregnant out-of-wedlock when the public sector would not.[64]

This religious orientation has had several implications for that care. Because of the belief that conversion, whether religious or psychological, is best achieved within an institution, maternity homes remained committed to institutionalization long after it ceased to be standard social welfare practice. Because other dependent populations were deinstitutionalized, maternity home inmates constituted a larger proportion of the institutionalized population in 1966 than in 1923: .036 percent in 1966, compared with .011 in 1923.[65]

In 1983 the Catholic maternity home, DePaul, still preferred a three-month confinement, as did the Salvation Army facility for unwed mothers in 1989.[66] This is half the required confinement of the 1930s, but it is far longer than the forty-eight-hour recovery period permitted new mothers by most hospitals today. The escalating expense of institutionalization, particularly after childbirth became medicalized, necessitated a change in homes' clientele from working class to middle class, as will be seen in the case of St. Ann's Loretta Hall/DePaul and the Florence Crittenton Home.

The explicitly evangelical purpose of maternity homes has sustained their privatization and compounded these financial difficulties. In 1966 only 2 of 201 maternity homes in the United States were public institutions.[67] Public agencies have been understandably reluctant to grant monies that might be used for proselytizing.[68] For their part, the Salvation Army and the Catholic dioceses found it difficult to accept public funds that came with morally offensive strings attached, such as the proviso, in the late 1960s and 1970s, that the receiving agency distribute birth control or abortion information. The Salvation Army endorsed family planning in 1972, but it has continued to oppose abortion, and the National Conference of Catholic Charities has remained opposed to both. Without public funds homes were forced to raise fees and cut back residential services, and during the 1960s and 1970s, they closed in large numbers or provided only outpatient services.

The original goal of spiritual reclamation, made imperative by both past origins and present church support, has seemed increasingly irrelevant in a secular culture. And to interpret premarital sexual activity as sin appears at best strained in a society as sexually permissive as our own.

Like its mission and its female traditions, the Retreat's endowment survived the Depression. The money went to the Cleveland Foundation for use in work with unwed mothers, and the Retreat Memorial Fund from the city's first maternity home allowed the remaining homes to hire some social work staff.[69] These caseworkers and group workers, like the founders and matrons, have been women, substituting one generation of benevolent ladies for another of female social workers.

◆ 3 ◆

SOCIAL WORKERS TO THE RESCUE: THE FLORENCE CRITTENTON HOME, 1912–1970

She must be called of God to do this the greatest work to which a woman is called. . . . It should not be entered upon as other professions are, for salary, for while the laborer is worthy of her hire (and a matron earns all she can get), yet, if this is the motive which prompts her, she will be a failure.
Fourteen Years Work with Street Girls

"This greatest work" was the rescue of fallen women by the National Florence Crittenton Mission. The Mission's founder, Charles Crittenton, thus shared the goals of other maternity homes, and Crittenton matrons were chosen because they were "called of God," not because they had acquired secular social work skills. Through the 1910s and 1920s, professional social workers shared Crittenton's strategies. By the early 1940s, however, changing social work principles eroded that agreement, and in the post–World War II years, pious matrons and volunteers were partially replaced by caseworkers, and redemptive maternity by adoption. In 1970 pressure from social work professionals changed the Cleveland Crittenton Home's historic mission as well.

In response to pressures from the Cleveland federated charity organization, the Cleveland Florence Crittenton Home professionalized its staff. But the Crittenton Home, and the other maternity homes, changed slowly and reluctantly, clinging to traditions derived from decades of reclaiming fallen women. Changed policies such as the endorsement of adoption, intended to modernize maternity homes, instead made them more peripheral to the care of unwed mothers.

54

THE PROFESSIONALIZATION OF SOCIAL WORK

The professionalization of social work began as a late-nineteenth-century response to problems of urban poverty, but social work's early principles and practices developed in the child-saving decades of the early twentieth century.

The specific antecedents of social work were attempts to make charity more "scientific." The earliest was the founding in 1874 of the National Conference on Charities and Corrections, at whose annual conferences representatives from both private and public agencies exchanged ideas and data about how to improve and coordinate social services. It became the National Conference on Social Work in 1917 and in 1956 the National Conference on Social Welfare.

The charity organization societies, which arose in the 1880s in large cities, also endorsed scientific charity: a more efficient distribution of outdoor relief by private nonsectarian agencies—themselves, for example. The societies distrusted public relief such that as distributed by the Cleveland Infirmary because it encouraged corruption in the givers, who used it as political patronage, and fostered pauperism in the recipients, who relied on it so that they would not have to earn a living. The charity organization societies distrusted equally the haphazardness and proselytizing of sectarian private agencies. The Retreat might have been an example.[1] The societies, therefore, attempted systematic analyses of the causes of poverty in order to determine which of the poor were responsible for their own poverty (and were therefore responsible for its solution) and which should be relieved by others.[2] A poor relief system based upon such scientific analysis and collection of data and better coordination of agencies would also prevent the expensive duplication of private fund-raising efforts and the waste of charitable monies on the unworthy poor.

The desire for efficient and systematic relief was accompanied by the desire to professionalize those who distributed it, specifically by supplementing, if not replacing, volunteer "friendly visitors" to the poor with men and women who had specific skills and clear-cut guidelines for their work.[3] To provide this, social work education programs were established, beginning with a summer training program organized in 1898 by the New York Charity Organization Society that developed into the Columbia School of Social Work. By 1919 there were fifteen schools of social work in the United States.[4]

Most of the new social workers were women. The nineteenth-century ideology that described women as caring and nurturing, and which had encouraged them to join the Women's Christian Association and the multitude of other benevolent and evangelical activities, encouraged them to become friendly visitors for the charity organization societies or other relief organizations. Early social work combined this older gender-based tradition with scientific expertise now available at social work schools. The new profession had not developed the exclusive criteria for membership—long, expensive years of education or overtly sex-discriminatory policies—that barred women from entering law, medicine, the clergy, and to a lesser extent, academic life. Not least important, because it was in the nonprofit sector, social work did not pay well, making it less attractive to men and therefore more open to women. A growing number of college-educated middle-class women found social work an attractive career in which they could at first share leadership positions with men.[5]

The feminization of the social work profession during the early twentieth century took place simultaneously, and not coincidentally, with the development of the child-saving movement. Progressive child-savers fought for a wide variety of reforms, including child labor laws, juvenile courts, playgrounds, better schools, and public health measures such as free milk dispensaries. Child-saving was a major impetus for establishing settlement houses and for improving child-care institutions and child-placement agencies.

During the 1910s child-saving and professional social work became closely connected. The 1910 Western Reserve Conference on the Care of Neglected and Dependent Children not only reiterated the central message of the 1909 White House Conference on Dependent Children—that children should be raised by families, not institutions—but endorsed "socially trained workers . . . both in institutional and placement agencies."[6] Child welfare, therefore, became an early social work specialty.

In 1912 child-saving got another boost from the federal government with the establishment of the U.S. Children's Bureau in the Department of Labor. The bureau did invaluable investigations on child welfare, and through its vast correspondence with mothers all over the country, it became a leader in the movement for "scientific motherhood." The bureau also tried to establish professional social work standards for child care for both public and private agencies.[7]

THE NATIONAL FLORENCE CRITTENTON MISSION AND REDEMPTIVE MATERNITY

Although the founding of the National Florence Crittenton Mission (NFCM) was almost contemporaneous with the beginnings of scientific charity, the Mission was the product of the evangelical tradition that had produced the Retreat. Like the Retreat, the goal of the Crittenton homes was saving women, not children; their best-known strategy was redemptive maternity.

NFCM co-founder Charles Crittenton was a successful businessman whose religious conversion impelled him to become a street preacher and rescue worker among the brothels and saloons of New York City, in the manner of YMCA and YWCA missionaries. According to his account, he realized that it was futile to tell a prostitute to "go and sin no more" if there was nowhere for her to go. In 1883 he opened the Florence Crittenton Night Mission (named after his deceased daughter) to offer prostitutes food, shelter, and the gospel.[8] A subsequent trip around the world convinced Crittenton that rescue work was imperative everywhere, and he opened several homes on the West Coast in the early 1890s. A temperance advocate and a one-time Prohibition Party candidate for mayor of New York, Crittenton attended an 1892 national WCTU convention and met the organization's charismatic leader, Frances Willard. Crittenton pledged five thousand dollars to open five new WCTU rescue homes, and some WCTU homes later joined the Crittenton chain.[9]

Brochures for Crittenton homes bore the motto "Go and Sin No More." To Crittenton, religious conversion was the most important component of the fallen woman's rescue. He believed in a literal heaven and hell and in the "direct interposition of God and of Satan in human affairs" so that conversion (or damnation) was a likely and logical occurrence.[10] Like the founders of the Retreat, Crittenton deplored the double standard that permitted an erring man to escape his sins and left the woman to pay for them. He pointed out that if Christ enjoined human beings to be their brothers' keepers, so ought they to be their sisters'. He preferred the nickname Willard gave him, "the brother of girls," to the more commonly used "millionaire evangelist."[11]

In 1893 Crittenton was joined by Dr. Kate Waller Barrett, whose ideas about the reclamation of fallen women were to dominate Crittenton work until the 1950s. Barrett, the wife of an Episcopalian minister and the mother of six children, had attempted rescue work in Atlanta, Georgia. The obstacles she encountered encouraged her to get a medical degree so that she could better serve women and to attend a lecture by Crittenton that persuaded her to combine her efforts with his.[12] In 1895 they founded the NFCM, which received a national charter from Congress in 1898. Crittenton was NFCM president and Barrett was vice president. After Crittenton's death in 1909, Barrett was president of the national organization until her death in 1925.

The NFCM was a loose federation in which the homes remained fairly autonomous. Some were rescue missions, others served delinquent girls referred by juvenile courts, and some were maternity homes. The NCFM provided advice, direction, and sometimes funds. Homes referred to each other within the network, a valuable service to unwed mothers who did not want to give birth in their hometowns. In 1897 there were fifty-one homes affiliated with the NFCM; by 1918 there were sixty, and they cared for 8,679 women and 2,309 babies.[13]

A prominent public figure, a suffragist, and a member of the International Council of Women, Dr. Barrett was best known for her leadership in rescue work, which by the 1910s had become directed less at prostitutes than at unwed mothers. Although she was devoutly religious, like her mentor Crittenton, her most popular publication was entitled *Some Practical Suggestions on the Conduct of a Rescue Home* (1903). The rescue home she envisioned sounded much like the Retreat, with the same emphasis on religious conversion, domesticity, and discipline within a familial setting. The home's goal must be the "spiritual regeneration and industrial independence" of fallen women, Barrett believed. It should be first and foremost a home, not an institution: "A true home— God's home—where [a girl] will experience safety and love." The home's inmates should be a family, in which shared domestic tasks would teach the girls useful skills: "We believe that every lady should know how to cook, wash, and iron, if she does not know anything else, and as we expect our girls to be ladies in the highest and truest sense, they must all learn to do these things, and do them well," Barrett wrote. When one inmate's mother protested that her daughter should not have to do housework, Dr. Barrett is said to have responded: "My dear woman, if I had been so unfortunate in training my daughter that when she was eighteen years old I had to bring her to a rescue home for the cause you have brought your daughter to us, I would be very glad if someone else would try a different method in dealing with her from what I had tried." There were strict rules about visitors and mail and daily schedules for work and recreation.[14] The home, Dr. Barrett wrote, should be "a big, old-fashioned roomy house in a quiet part of the city, with large sunny bright rooms, . . . with books and magazines on hygiene, child study, and self culture" and an especially pretty room for the nursery, "for no home is complete without a baby."[15]

Dr. Barrett believed that babies and maternity played the most crucial role in an unwed mother's reclamation.[16] In 1897 she delivered a much-reprinted speech to Crittenton workers in which she stated the cardinal principle of the Crittenton homes: that motherhood itself was a "means of regeneration." The implications of redemptive maternity were practical: the unwed mother should remain in the maternity home for at least six months with her child and if at all possible keep the child with her when she left. Ideally, the father and mother should marry, but if this was not possible, the mother should raise the child alone for her own sake: "There is that God-implanted instinct of motherhood that needs only to be aroused to be one of the strongest incentives to right living." [17] Barrett's ideas rested not only upon her optimistic faith in woman's innate maternal capabilities but upon her realistic assessment of male nonsupport.

Dr. Barrett was a transitional figure in rescue and maternity home work, partially—although not completely—bridging the gap between the evangelical Charles Crittenton and the professional social workers of the twentieth century. Her principle of redemptive maternity became an article of faith for both rescue workers and child-care professionals for the next three decades. [18]

THE CLEVELAND FLORENCE CRITTENTON HOME, 1912–1937

The Cleveland Florence Crittenton Home began service in 1912, almost simultaneously with the Cleveland Federation for Charity and Philanthropy, which sought to professionalize the city's private social welfare agencies. The policies of the Crittenton Home and the other maternity homes were endorsed by the Federation.

The Crittenton Home differed from the Retreat in some significant respects. There were no wealthy philanthropists or their daughters and wives on the early Crittenton boards. The first board of trustees included three Protestant ministers and a school superintendent. [19] Unlike the Retreat board of managers, who received donations and social recognition for their work with fallen women, the Crittenton board had continual financial woes as well as difficulty finding a neighborhood that would accept the home. A site was located on Cleveland's northeast side, but the home was much smaller than the Retreat, with a capacity of about fifteen women. Photographs show a spacious, comfortable-looking home with no enclosing walls, much like the ideal home Barrett had proposed. The Cleveland facility's small size is probably explained by the presence of three established homes—the Retreat, St. Ann's, and the Salvation Army Rescue—but that may in turn explain its inmates' loyalties to it, evidenced in their frequent return visits to the home and continued correspondence with its matrons. [20]

The home began to specialize almost immediately in unwed mothers, but because its founder, Mrs. Isabelle Alexander, was a social worker attached to the juvenile court, its first inmates were girls judged delinquent or predelinquent by the court. Statistics collected by the home for

1916–17 indicate the inmates' working-class backgrounds. Twenty-five of the fifty-eight girls listed housework or factory work as their occupation; most had finished sixth grade but only one had three years of high school. They were almost overwhelmingly Protestant.[21]

Despite its twentieth-century beginning in Cleveland, the Crittenton Home shared the nineteenth-century evangelical goal and strategies of its founders and of other Cleveland maternity homes: spiritual reclamation through religious conversion and redemptive maternity. Its first annual report boasted of success in saving many a girl who had "fallen from the pathway of virtue and purity. . . . Impressing that girl with the glorious gift and responsibility of Motherhood as well as with the very highest and strict principles of morality and right, has in many cases been clearly rewarded by a complete transformation of the girl's character."[22] That sought-for transformation meant that women were required to stay with their infants for six months after confinement, which became the policy of the NFCM as well as of the Retreat and the other homes.

Crittenton work was unmistakably women's work. The homes had a volunteer medical staff to care for women who were pregnant or ill. The 1907 Crittenton guidelines on physicians advised that the doctor should be female, if possible: "This is pre-eminently woman's work to care for and succor her unfortunate sisters." A male doctor might offend "whatever of modesty" the unwed mother still possessed. The guidelines also warned against allowing a home to become a clinic for medical students.[23] The first doctor at the Cleveland home was male, but the home usually had women doctors on the volunteer staff as well.

More important than doctors were the Crittenton female volunteers. The Cleveland home, like those elsewhere, relied heavily on Crittenton "Circles" of women from church guilds, the Kings' Daughters, WCTU chapters, and the Order of the Eastern Star. The circles performed a wide variety of services for homes' inmates, both mothers and children. In 1916, for example, the Bible class of a local Methodist church presented each girl with a Christmas present of a Bible, to be used at Sunday devotions.[24]

Even after the home joined the Federation, the circles raised crucial funds with monthly luncheons at the home and an annual June Day festival where fancywork and baked goods were sold. A male board of trustees handled the money, but the female board of managers oversaw daily operation of the home, ordering food, arranging for repairs, admitting inmates, and making arrangements for them and their infants when they left. The board also hired and fired the staff. The only full-time staff person was a matron, chosen for piety and strength of character. The matron must be a Christian, Dr. Barrett had advised, "for unless she is a child of

God, she can never have [the] gift of forgetfulness" of the fallen woman's sin.[25] The Cleveland home's second matron, Mrs. Ella Jewell, was apparently such a woman. She remained at her post from 1914 until her death in 1928.

Like the Retreat, the home was a charter member of the Cleveland Federation. The Federation itself was in the vanguard of the federated charity movement, which, in the spirit of scientific charity, tried to rationalize both the fund-raising and the operations of the city's myriad social welfare agencies. The Federation's power over its member agencies derived from its ability to distribute or withhold the funds it raised from the community.[26] With the encouragement of the president of the Federation, Martin A. Marks, the School of Applied Social Sciences at Western Reserve University was opened in 1916. The school fostered close organizational and intellectual ties between professional social workers and the Federation.[27]

One of the Federation's first actions was to organize the Conference on Illegitimacy, composed of agencies that dealt with unwed mothers and their children. As the conference's name indicated, its primary interest was the children, not the mothers. The conference, like the Federation itself, was intended to make the delivery of services more efficient and professional. The Cleveland Conference soon joined the national Inter-City Conference on Illegitimacy, which was established in 1918 by a group of social workers and which until its demise in the mid-1930s held its annual meetings with the National Conference on Social Welfare.[28] Cleveland Conference members included the city's official child-placing agency, the Cleveland Humane Society; several hospitals; the juvenile court; the Babies' Dispensary; and the Retreat, St. Ann's Maternity and Infant Asylum, the Florence Crittenton Home, and the Salvation Army Rescue.

Through the Conference on Illegitimacy and the Children's Council, which superseded it in 1935, the Federation tried to impose professional social work standards on the maternity homes. In 1922, for example, the conference endorsed the position that "the principles of good social case work should be applied to every phase of [maternity home] work. The Executive head of each maternity home should have thorough social case work training."[29] However, it was easier to state a preference for professionals than to compel agencies to hire them, and in 1922 there simply were not many professionals available. The only delegates to the conference who were social work professionals in the early 1920s worked for large agencies such as the Cleveland Humane Society, the city Child Welfare Division, or Cleveland's Associated Charities. Maternity homes were represented at the conference by volunteer board members such as Mrs.

Beatty from the Retreat, by matrons such as Mrs. Jewell, or by women religious, officers of the Salvation Army, and nuns from St. Ann's.

Even those agencies that employed caseworkers provided few services for unwed mothers that required professional training. A good example is a Humane Society caseworker's description in 1921 of her own handling of a sixteen-year-old unmarried mother, which had extended over a four-year period. The society's involvement was prompted by a call from the "telephone operator at ——— Hospital" because the girl was ready to be discharged with her four-week-old baby and had no place to go. The caseworker's initial investigation revealed the client to be "an American girl; orphaned; . . . she and her brother had lived with stepmother. . . . W[oman] anxious to give child for adoption." The caseworker placed the girl temporarily in a maternity home, persuaded her to keep the baby, got her a job at domestic service, took her and her baby to the hospital on several occasions, tracked down the putative father and initiated court proceedings—only partially successful—against him for child support, took the girl into her own home when she lost her first job, found her another one, discouraged an inappropriate suitor, encouraged an appropriate one, and finally got her a third job. Final disposition: "W and Mr. W—married. . . . Both anxious to make home for child." [30] A heroic odyssey, surely, but one requiring more perseverance and strength of character and body than classroom hours or textbook technique. [31]

During the 1910s and 1920s professional social workers occasionally criticized Crittenton homes specifically and maternity homes in general. The professionals referred to the homes' practices and rationales as "backward" or "unimaginative and unprogressive" because the homes did not employ trained caseworkers. [32] Such rhetoric to the contrary, caseworkers probably would have made little practical difference in the ways that the homes operated. Lacking both trained staff and clearly defined professional policies, the Conference on Illegitimacy simply endorsed the historic practices of the maternity homes—specifically, Barrett's policy that an unwed mother and her child should remain together in the home so that the mother might be reclaimed. In 1914, the conference recommended that "in every possible case the mother be expected to nurse her child" because "maternity has no reforming impulse unless the mother has the care of the child for some time. . . . [I]f a woman does have the responsibility of motherhood, she is much sobered thereby." [33]

Thus maternity homes continued to keep women and children together for weeks or even months after confinement. The long-range goal of maternity home care, as stated by Dr. Barrett and others, was to prepare women to take care of their children permanently. If a woman was unable to take her child with her into domestic service, for example, the homes sometimes boarded the child, with the mother remaining financially responsible for it. If she was unable to pay, the Cleveland Humane Society might help. The arrangement may not fit the definition of "together," but the unwed mother at least did not officially give up custody of the child, and she might eventually be able to maintain it in her own home. A Salvation Army officer described just such a happy outcome to conference members: "A most ignorant and inexperienced girl, an orphan who had not hardly any advantage in life, became a mother at 16 years of age. Hard to handle before the baby was born, she afterward became exceedingly tractable. She was very fond of her child. After the usual stay in the . . . Home, she secured a position with her baby in a private family where she remained until the baby was more than a year old. After that she boarded the baby at the home. The child is now six years old. The mother is making $6 a week as a domestic and has a bank account. . . . She . . . has visited the child twice a week. She has improved wonderfully and is soon to marry and take her child with her."[34]

In a 1924 publication the U.S. Children's Bureau also endorsed the homes' practices: "The policy of keeping mother and child together, at least during the nursing period, has for a long time been advocated and followed successfully by many maternity homes and some child-caring agencies."[35] But the bureau was not primarily concerned with the spiritual reclamation of the mother because the staff explained pregnancy out-of-wedlock in environmental as well as moral terms: the "background of illegitimacy" was bad home conditions and "poor character." [36] Bureau investigations showed that infant mortality was higher for illegitimate than for legitimate children, and the bureau reasoned that this was because unwed mothers abandoned their children or left them in unhealthy foundling homes or "baby farms" instead of nursing and caring for the infants themselves. True to its mission, the bureau was concerned with the physical well-being of children: illegitimacy was not about fallen women but about child welfare.[37]

The bureau encouraged efforts to establish paternity and to enforce the father's financial responsibility, but because these usually failed, the bureau recognized that the mother must shoulder the parenthood alone. Well-run maternity homes, therefore, were commended for providing care for both mother and child for prolonged periods of time and encouraging the mother to be responsible for the child after she left the home.[38] Following the bureau's lead, the Cleveland Conference on Illegitimacy in 1926 noted: "There seemed to be general agreement among all agencies doing creditable work throughout the country . . . that the unmarried mother should keep her child, if at all possible, . . . instead of separating mother and child and giving child for adoption, as was formerly done by many agencies. . . . That adoption should be the last resort."[39]

WOMEN'S WORK AND SOCIAL WORK, 1938–1970

The financial crisis of the Depression created greater divergence between the policies of the social work profession and the traditions of the maternity homes. The Cleveland Crittenton Home partially professionalized its staff in the post–World War II years, but other policies remained unchanged.

In 1938, Maud Morlock of the U.S. Children's Bureau expressed the growing professional concern with the prohibitive expense of institutionalization. She urged the annual convention of the NFCM to be more flexible in its approach to unwed mothers and to consider, for example, the use of foster home care, which was becoming more widely used for dependent children.[40] By the early 1940s, social workers became convinced that adoption was preferable to keeping mother and child together, for the Depression also underscored the financial difficulty a woman supporting a child singlehandedly had. A Salvation Army officer, writing to Morlock in 1944, described this changed thinking: "The child was always discharged [from the maternity home] with the mother in the hope that its influence would better her life. . . . There was an equally sincere conviction a little later that an unwed mother, if she kept her child, had not the slightest chance and that the child so kept was overpoweringly stigmatised."[41]

Demographic changes also challenged the traditional belief that motherhood was woman's best and most useful role. Birth rates fell during the Depression, and the number of mothers in the paid labor force escalated during the early years of World War II. Recorded illegitimate births increasingly were to teenagers. Social workers like Morlock doubted that an adolescent, who "herself may feel unloved and unwanted," could make a fit parent.[42] Rejecting the idea that all women who had borne children were suitable mothers, social workers maintained that they must individualize each case, as Morlock suggested, and decide which women should or should not put their infants up for adoption.[43]

The adoption of illegitimate children was not without its own dangers. Although state laws had tightened procedures, legal adoptions tripled between 1934 and 1944 because of the low birthrate during the Depression. The demand for white adoptive infants also created a black market on which maternity homes and unwed mothers sold infants.[44] Warning that "[i]nfants of unmarried mothers are especially in danger of being exploited," the U.S. Children's Bureau advised adoptions only through a licensed agency using professional caseworkers to do thorough investigations of adoptive families and children. This position was also endorsed by the Federation.[45]

In this context, professionals now faulted maternity homes for long confinements of mothers and children. Homes kept the women and children together solely for the convenience of the institutions, argued one critic: "Back of [that practice] is the agency's need for the services of the mother, not the baby's need for the mother. The demand . . . here is for continuing penance beyond ordinary requirements, as well as an exploitation of her love for the baby."[46] Long confinements made adoption emotionally difficult: "Many maternity homes refuse to face realistically the mother's wish to place her child in adoption." Not surprisingly, the speaker concluded that skilled casework service should be available to help the mother "make this decision of major importance to her and to the baby."[47]

In response to such criticisms, the NFCM adopted some of the vocabulary of professional social work.[48] However, the organization remained extremely reluctant to endorse the use of secular social workers who might object to the homes' religious mission, especially because the NFCM had begun to train its own personnel in the 1920s. Neither of Dr. Barrett's successors, her children Reba Barrett Smith and Robert Smith Barrett, had secular social work training. (When the NFCM did begin to meet with the National Conference on Social Work in 1946, it was over the objections of Robert Smith Barrett.)[49] An NCFM committee on standards in 1934 maintained that every home should employ a caseworker but that the matron should be "an intelligent, Christian woman" and that the "superintendent should be a Protestant."[50]

By 1943 pressure from outside organizations such as federated charities and from within the NFCM itself compelled the organization to modify grudgingly and halfheartedly its opposition to adoption and secular workers. Its board of trustees urged that "the basic Crittenton principle of keeping mother and child together always be held a sacred responsibility"; however, if adoption were imperative, it should "be handled in full accordance with State laws . . . and only with legally recognized child-placing agencies," which did employ caseworkers.[51] The probable adoption of children also meant shorter confinements for the mothers and less expense for the homes, a practical advantage that may have somewhat offset the emotional and political difficulties of changing historic tradition. In addition, many states, including Ohio, required that mothers and infants stay together until arrangements could be made for the children, and this requirement could mean a lengthy confinement even if the home's policies had been modified.

The tradition of local autonomy allowed Crittenton homes to regard or disregard NCFM's pronouncements, and practices varied widely from one home to another. In Cleveland, the volunteer board of managers still ran the Crittenton Home, as it had in the 1910s, controlling its domestic routines, the admission and discharge of clients, and the hiring of staff. In 1947 Children's Services, a child-placing agency, complained that Crittenton board members, rather than caseworkers, also did the follow-up on women after they left the home.[52]

Worse, the chairman of the Crittenton board arranged "gray market" adoptions. Although legal, these were condemned by professionals as well as the NCFM because they bypassed investigation of adoptive homes by caseworkers. A Federation study of such independent placements in 1942–43 revealed that six of the sixty-two children were placed by the Crittenton Home, although it was the smallest of the maternity homes.[53] According to the *Cleveland Press*, by the end of the decade, the Crittenton Home had "a widespread reputation" as a source for gray market babies.[54] As the scandal became public, the home in 1949 hired its first full-time professional social worker, Lois Bielfelt, as home superintendent. In 1950 the board of managers was disbanded and the board of trustees, which now included women, took charge of the home's daily operation. The facility then affiliated with the newly organized Florence Crittenton Homes Association (later the Florence Crittenton Association of America). The association, formed as the result of dissatisfaction with traditional NCFM policies, endorsed professional social work standards for the care of unwed mothers, a position then reiterated by the Cleveland home's board of trustees in 1952.[55]

The Crittenton caseworker's careful records reveal how the agency, which had originally gone to great lengths and expense to compel a woman to keep her child, now applied great psychological pressure upon a mother to place her child for adoption: "[_____], age 24. . . . While with us, she fluctuated constantly in her feelings about the baby, who is now in temporary board. Her life experience has been such that we feel she needs psychiatric help, but she is not ready to accept it. Ultimate plans for the baby are uncertain. . . . [_____], age 40. . . . While with us, [she] was able to gain a more optimistic attitude toward life and is looking forward to her future plans. The baby has been placed for adoption. . . . [_____], age 34. . . . [S]he kept her baby on the basis that she is too old to expect to have another. The baby is in a temporary boarding home where [the mother] hopes to keep her indefinitely. We have been unable to get her to accept psychiatric help and her approach to her situation is most unreal. Her caseworker will continue seeing her in an effort to protect the baby."[56]

Nevertheless, the belief in redemptive maternity died hard at the Crittenton Home. Not until 1962, and only after the repeated urging of Children's Services and the Ohio Department of Health, did the home close its nursery and allow infants to be placed for adoption directly from the hospital. In the tradition of Kate Waller Barrett, the Crittenton board continued to maintain that mothers should see their babies "to impress upon them a sense of responsibility."[57]

Through the 1950s the home was able to employ a half- or full-time caseworker, although much of the casework was still done by children's agencies and concerned the child's welfare, not the mother's. With the help of Cleveland Foundation monies from the Retreat bequest, the Crittenton Home employed a part-time group worker, a practice soon followed by the other homes.[58] Although all the maternity homes consistently requested Federation funds to hire professional staff, they often were turned down.[59]

The Crittenton Home often ran a deficit, and its efforts to explain its clientele and financial picture to the Federation repeated the familiar stereotypes and realities of unwed motherhood: "Girl is 15 years old. Alleged father has left town. Mother of girl is a widow earning $280 a month to raise two children. . . . Girl is 22; works in factory. Stepfather refuses to have her in the house. Alleged father denies paternity. . . . Girl is 23 and sole support of aged parents. . . . Alleged father has disappeared." The Federation's response was to recommend better collection procedures from a clientele that was increasingly middle-class and, in the Federation's estimation, more able to pay its own way.[60]

Perennially strapped for money, the home continued to rely on volunteers to provide services and funds in the tradition hallowed by custom. In addition to the volunteers from church groups, the home had become a training site for Cleveland Junior League provisional members. In 1970 the Cleveland Crittenton Home claimed the services of seventy volunteers.

The professionalization of the Cleveland home's staff, therefore, remained only partial, and caseworkers often differed only slightly from volunteers in their care of unwed mothers. When Superintendent Bielfelt came to the Crittenton home in 1949, she discovered that Bible study classes were "actually the only formal program functioning." Although she was a secularly trained social worker, she did not halt the class but instead taught it herself for a year and a half. The homes' other programs included classes in "knitting, sewing, shell-jewelry making," which volunteers taught but which Bielfelt supervised.[61] Bielfelt left the home in 1956.

CONCLUSION

In 1970 the Crittenton Home changed its mission, partly because of its continued financial difficulties. Equally important, the social activism and political ferment of the 1960s directed the attention of the Federation and the professional social work community to the problems of the inner city and black Americans and away from the private agencies that had been the Federation's original concern.

In the early 1960s, the future of the Cleveland home had looked bright. Nationwide, sixty-nine hundred women entered the forty-five Crittenton homes in 1962. Most homes were filled to capacity; many had long waiting lists or had turned away clients.[62] Because the Cleveland facility had received its first large bequest in 1962, the board planned to expand its home, a former mansion on once-elegant Euclid Avenue in the Hough area. As late as 1965, the home was filled to capacity.[63] The neighborhood, however, had become a black ghetto that in 1966 was torn by the city's worst race riot. The home was frequently broken into (once while the board of trustees was meeting there), and the staff, the clients, and their visiting families were harassed and sometimes even attacked on the street.[64] This occasioned additional expenses for security and, most important, frightened away potential clients. After buying adjoining properties and paying an architect twenty-two thousand dollars to design an expanded facility, the board decided to move to a safer suburban location.

The proposed move was a last-ditch attempt to retain the home's changing clientele, which, like that of the national organization, was predominantly white and middle-class. As occupancy fell and deficits climbed, the Cleveland home took fewer nonpaying women.[65] The Federation, having already warned the home that taking fewer indigent clients would have serious repercussions, in 1967 cut its subsidy severely.

The cut was a response not only to the Crittenton Home's dwindling clientele but to another disagreement between the maternity homes and the social work profession. In the wake of the Hough riots, Cleveland mayor Carl B. Stokes appointed a panel headed by Dr. Herman D. Stein of the Western Reserve University School of Applied Social Science to investigate the city's welfare system. The panel concluded that much of the blame for the "crisis in welfare" lay with the public sector, especially the inadequacy of state funding for Aid to Families of Dependent Children. The panel also urged that the private agencies of the Federation increase their involvement in "the problems of public welfare" and expand programs for the poor.[66]

This was not the direction that the Crittenton and other maternity homes had been going during the previous two decades. In 1968, 66.8 percent of the Crittenton Home's clientele lived outside the county, 18.2 percent were suburban residents and only 15 percent were residents of Cleveland. When the home admitted a few black women, fights broke out between them and the white clients.[67] In March 1970 the Federation informed the Crittenton Home that it would no longer fund its program for unwed mothers. The official explanation was the "declining need for traditional maternity home services." The maternity homes were in fact about half empty.[68]

The Crittenton board did not deny the declining use of maternity homes by the "moderate- to upper-income women" who could pay for service. Nor did it deny that changing sexual norms had apparently removed "the stigma formerly attached to unwed motherhood." But there was still a need for maternity home service, the board argued, and it was the dangerous and deteriorated Hough neighborhood, not the home itself, that was responsible for its lower occupancy. In conclusion, the Crittenton board angrily charged the Federation with capitulating to "the militant and aggressive demands for services made by the inner-city residents": the home had stayed the course, but the Federation had "changed direction."[69] These were legitimate accusations. But maternity home services to a white, middle-class clientele, which the Federation itself had funded for at least two decades, no longer seemed relevant when black ghettos were going up in flames.

After some months of indecision, during which the Crittenton board asked the Federation for direction, the home acted on its own. It briefly provided temporary shelter for referrals from juvenile court, assuring itself of payment for services. The home site on Euclid Avenue was then sold, and services were transferred to two suburban sites, where in 1971 the agency opened group homes for nonpregnant delinquent girls, the Cleveland home's original clientele. Occupancy rates in all Crittenton homes fell in the late 1960s and early 1970s, and the changed nature of service had already become the practice elsewhere.[70] The Cleveland agency also changed its name to Florence Crittenton Services. In 1976 the Florence Crittenton Association of America became the Florence Crittenton Division of the Child Welfare League of America, a broadranging child-advocacy agency.

The professionalization of social work constitutes an important chapter in social welfare history. The substitution of trained, efficient, secular caseworkers for devout and earnest amateurs is usually dated from the Progressive period, particularly the first decades of this century, when the first schools of social work were established and reformers experimented with traditional means of relieving poverty.

This is not what happened at the Cleveland Florence Crittenton Home or other maternity homes in Cleveland and elsewhere.[71] Because the homes depended upon federated charities for funding, and, probably more important, because they survived into the late twentieth century, they did change some policies to conform to social work standards. But the slowness with which they capitulated is significant. Their employment of professional caseworkers began decades after schools of social work started to turn out graduates and decades after reformers had ostensibly changed institutional policies and practices. As in the case of their religious mission, maternity homes clung to their past, to customs of child care and volunteer participation initiated by the agencies' founders, sanctioned by decades of practice, and ultimately derived from the rescue of fallen women. In 1965 a national survey of maternity homes indicated that only 33 percent had professional, full-time caseworkers on their primary staffs.[72]

Within the maternity homes the conflict between two gender-based approaches to social policy was played out: the nineteenth-century tradition of the pious philanthropist and Christian matron dedicated to the rescue of women versus the twentieth-century, professionally trained expert interested in child welfare. The names of the major public assistance programs for women are symbolic of these divergent strategies. The state mothers' pensions, although dating from the 1910s and 1920s, had nineteenth-century roots and promised aid to women; the 1935 federal Social Security Act program was called Aid to Dependent Children.

On the other hand, the conflict between women's work and social work should not be overstated. As the story of the Cleveland Crittenton Home shows, there were often few practical differences between them. The social worker and the rescue worker may have had different priorities, but both were more interested in changing unwed mothers than in changing the men who impregnated them or the economic and social conditions that permitted and then punished unwed motherhood.

The reluctance of homes to employ professionals was probably matched by the reluctance of professionals to be employed there and the reluctance of the Cleveland Federation to fund the social workers it mandated. Given a choice, secularly trained caseworkers logically chose to save children rather than redeem mothers because child welfare was at least sometimes publicly funded. The slow professionalization of maternity homes is further evidence of the low status of the clientele, a status confirmed by the lack of public subsidy and dwindling interest on the part of the Federation during the 1960s.

The Federation's halfhearted efforts to compel maternity homes into the social work mainstream had unintended and ironic consequences. Professional staff, even if female, was more expensive than volunteer staff, and the requirement that homes hire caseworkers necessitated higher fees and a middle-class clientele that could afford to pay them. When the professionals urged that illegitimate children be placed for adoption, the maternity homes, whose raison d'être in the early twentieth century had been to keep mother and child together, became used almost exclusively by women who wanted to put their children up for adoption or who were persuaded to do so by staff at the homes.[73] Maternity homes became shelters for women whose children were adoptable—white children. Black women were excluded by the shortage of adoptive homes for black infants and most maternity homes' written or unwritten policies of segregation. By the mid-1960s, the social work profession was no longer interested in the homes whose white, middle-class clientele the Federation's own policies had encouraged.

The professionalization of maternity home staff may have meant better services, but it also meant services for fewer women. The medical profession and the medicalization of childbirth would take maternity homes even further in the same direction.

◆ 4 ◆

FROM HOME TO HOSPITAL: ST. ANN'S INFANT AND MATERNITY ASYLUM, 1873–1983

The majority come to us not only to be fed and cared for, but even to be clothed as well. Often, if the family of the unfortunate girl be in a position to provide for her, it, as frequently in a time of trouble and disgrace, abandons her, and thus, she becomes an outcast.
Cleveland Catholic Diocese Archives, *1904*

Sister Superior M. Peter may have exaggerated the destitution of these "unfortunate girls" in hopes of an increased subsidy from the Cleveland bishop, but as she suggested, the first patients at St. Ann's Infant and Maternity Asylum were not only pregnant out-of-wedlock but dependent on Catholic charity. By the 1910s this asylum for outcasts spawned two separate facilities: a maternity hospital for married women and a separate facility for unmarried mothers, where the primary goal was spiritual and then psychological rehabilitation. The hospital closed in 1973. Ten years later the small home for unwed mothers did the same.

Like other hospitals, St. Ann's began as a social welfare institution for the poor and became a medical facility for the middle class. But as married motherhood became a medical event, unwed motherhood retained spiritual rather than medical significance. The physical and moral segregation of unmarried women at this Catholic facility reinforced the definition of their motherhood as illegitimate.

HOSPITALS AND CHILDBIRTH

Until the very end of the nineteenth century, voluntary hospitals were religious or charitable enterprises, less medical than social service institutions, intended for and used primarily by the indigent.[1] Most health care, including childbirth, took place at home.

In their pre-industrial origins, hospitals were largely controlled by nonmedical entities—religious orders or boards of trustees and philanthropists. These men raised the funds, made policies, and admitted patients. Consequently, except for the presence of doctors on their staffs, hospitals resembled poorhouses and maternity homes in significant ways. Some public hospitals, like Cleveland City Hospital, began as the medical department of the poorhouse. "Dependence as much as disease" was the criterion for admission.[2] The destitution and probable homelessness of its patients meant that a hospital's primary function was often simply providing long-term shelter.

Hospitals played a marginal role in the health care of most Americans for much of the century. Before the Civil War a doctor could practice his whole life without ever going into a hospital.[3] Further, because doctors knew little about aseptic techniques and nothing about germs, hospitals were unhealthy places. Lacking the facilities and the expertise to diagnose and treat most illnesses, hospital staffs could provide little more care than most patients could receive at home.

In the last decades of the century, hospitals underwent significant changes. As doctors realized that hospitals could provide them with desirable clinical practice on poor patients, as was the custom in the great European medical universities, larger hospitals became teaching facilities, often affiliating with the proliferating medical schools. The employment by the 1890s of aseptic techniques made hospitals safer and more convenient sites for major surgery, the employment of new diagnostic tools like the X-ray, and the treatment of acute illnesses. These new medical strategies enhanced the role of doctors even as the rising costs of equipment and staff, especially during the hard times of the 1890s, diminished the ability of churches or pious philanthropists to pay the bills and control policies. At private hospitals medical purposes supplanted historic charitable functions, and hospitals sought to replace their indigent clientele with patients who could pay escalating medical costs.[4]

Childbirth—considered a natural, although sometimes dangerous, female function—was slower than general medicine to move into a hospital setting. During the colonial period American women gave birth in their own homes and were assisted by midwives, whose approach to child-bearing was noninterventionist because they had few tools with which to hasten or ease the process. Even as fertility rates fell throughout the nineteenth century, middle-class women gradually replaced midwives with male doctors. Because few women could attend the medical schools in this country or abroad, only men could boast of university-acquired obstetrical training and specialized skills, especially with forceps, which might make birthing quicker and safer. For their part, male doctors were anxious to claim obstetrics as their own because it was steady work. The home remained the childbirth setting preferred by both patients and doctors.[5]

The only institutionalized childbirths took place in poorhouses like the Cleveland Infirmary, the few private lying-in hospitals, or the maternity homes. The women patients were always destitute and sometimes unmarried, and therefore subject to discipline and moral reformation.[6] The Cleveland Maternity Home, for example, although originally intended for "worthy women," served unmarried women as well, and its matron was required "to exert a religious influence over the inmates and hold some religious service each day," like the matrons in the maternity homes.[7] Hospital childbirth consequently bore the double stigma of destitution and immorality.

Hospital childbirth was dangerous due to frequent outbreaks of puerperal fever, caused by doctors' carelessness about antiseptic techniques combined with their tendency to use instruments. Doctors themselves sometimes attributed high maternal mortality rates to the low morals of their patients, as one doctor explained to an 1877 meeting of the American Gynecological Society: "The majority of patients who seek the lying-in asylums are unmarried, and it cannot be doubted that this circumstance has a bad influence on their chances of recovery" from the ravages of puerperal fever. Little wonder that the doctor did not recommend hospital childbirth except "if the women are very poor, if they have filthy homes, if there are many children, a drunkard for a husband, or other disturbing influences." And less wonder that in 1900 only 5 percent of American women bore their children in hospitals.[8]

CATHOLIC CHARITIES AND CATHOLIC SISTERS

Hospitals were among the scores of Catholic social welfare institutions founded in the nineteenth century. Within the Catholic church, most social welfare activities became the women's work of Catholic sisters.

Fleeing the economic and political woes of their homelands, Catholic immigrants to the United States became disproportionately dependent on public and private relief. Because relief was often accompanied by a strong dose of Protestant proselytizing, Catholic charity sought not only to rescue fellow human beings from destitution but fellow Catholics from Protestantism. Catholic dioceses sponsored scores of institutions for their dependent co-religionists, especially hospitals and orphan asylums.[9]

The primary dispensers of Catholic charity were the religious communities of sisters. Although almost invisible in standard histories of the Catholic church in the United States, sisters "outnumbered male church workers in the last half of the century in almost every diocese. . . . [T]here were almost four times as many nuns as priests by the century's close"—more than forty thousand.[10] Few male religious orders immigrated to the United States, but Catholic patterns of settlement spawned more than a dozen American communities of nuns, including the Sisters of Charity of Emmitsburg (known after 1850 as the Daughters of Charity of St. Vincent de Paul), the Sisters of Charity of Nazareth, and the Dominican Sisters. From 1830 to 1860 these women were joined by fifteen European orders.[11]

Nuns came at the urging of local bishops to serve as missionaries to the heathen or caretakers of the dependent. In 1851, for example, the Sisters of Charity of St. Augustine were invited to Cleveland by its first bishop, Amadeus Rappe, to administer the city's first Catholic hospital. Uprooted from European communities, emigrating nuns braved the trans-Atlantic passage, the hostility of American Protestants, and the necessity of supporting themselves. The cloistered life of European orders did not prepare them for earning a living in the United States. For a few the challenge was too great: two of the original Sisters of Charity returned to their native France, overwhelmed by the foreign customs and speech of Americans and the enormity of their task.

Most nuns taught in the growing number of Catholic schools, but they also staffed the Catholic orphanages, homes for the aged and working women, and mental institutions. Nuns became best known to Protestant Americans as nurses: four hundred served on both sides of the Civil War. The Daughters of Charity opened the first Catholic hospital in the United States in 1832 in St. Louis, and by mid-century, as nursing began to professionalize, the care of the sick became an increasingly popular ministry for nuns. In the course of the nineteenth century, nuns administered 2,645 hospitals in the United States.[12] The hospitals appealed particularly to a Catholic clientele fearful of the alternatives—the poorhouse or a Protestant voluntary hospital—and some were designed for a specific Catholic ethnic group.[13]

American Protestants were suspicious of nuns (as well as priests) not only because of their Catholicism and their peculiar garb, but because they rejected marriage and motherhood, central to American definitions of gender.[14] The nonconformity of nuns was more apparent than real. Catholics who had joined, or aspired to join, the American middle class shared its admiration for the cult of true womanhood and for its female virtues of piety, domesticity, and subordination. Life in the convent "institutionalized the true woman's attributes." Although celibate, nuns exemplified "maternity of the spirit" as "brides of Christ" and, like Protestant matrons, played their own spiritual roles as teachers and moral exemplars. Like housewives, nuns provided domestic services like cleaning, cooking, and sewing for priests.[15] Many areas of nuns' lives were controlled by priests, bishops, or the pope. When lines of authority were not clearly drawn—and sometimes when they were—nuns and male clergy struggled over property ownership, the management of institutions, or the choice of religious superiors within communities. Cleveland bishop Richard Gilmour interfered in the election of the mother superior of the Sisters of Charity of St. Augustine in 1883–84, placed disobedient nuns under ecclesiastical censure, and deprived them of some of the sacraments; the sisters appealed to Rome but ultimately capitulated.[16] But cooperation, not conflict, between nuns and male clerics was the norm, and nuns, like Protestant women, seldom challenged—indeed, probably revered and sustained—the male religious hierarchy.[17]

CLEVELAND'S ST. ANN'S INFANT AND MATERNITY ASYLUM, 1873–1909

In various versions of the story of the opening of St. Ann's in 1873, the leading role is played by a worthy widow, turned away from the Catholic hospital in the last throes of labor, or a Catholic girl, sequestered in the Retreat and refused the ministrations of a priest.[18] Although neither tale may be strictly accurate, both reveal the asylum's sectarian beginnings.

Bishop Gilmour, head of Cleveland's Catholic community from 1872 to 1891, was at first reluctant to provide shelter for unwed mothers, fearing that this would imply diocesan sanction for illegitimate pregnancy. Pressing moral and practical considerations overcame his reluctance. Like the founders of the Woman's Christian Association homes, Catholic clergy feared for the bodies and souls of young women in the city. The poverty and sexual vulnerability of Catholic women immigrants—for example, the Irish in the Cleveland poorhouse—made these fears well founded. Consequently, by 1870 every major diocese had built institutions where "the virtue and innocence of destitute females of good character might be shielded from the snares and dangers to which their destitution exposes them."[19] For women who had already succumbed to vice, the Sisters of the Good Shepherd opened nine convents before 1870, including one in Cleveland, where erring and wayward women were encouraged to repent and join the order of Magdalenes.[20]

Exterior of the Cleveland Infirmary, 1855. Courtesy of the MetroHealth Medical Center Archives

"Fallen women" sewing at the Retreat. Courtesy of the Western Reserve Historical Society, Cleveland

Exterior of the Cleveland Retreat, 1899. Courtesy of the Western Reserve Historical Society, Cleveland

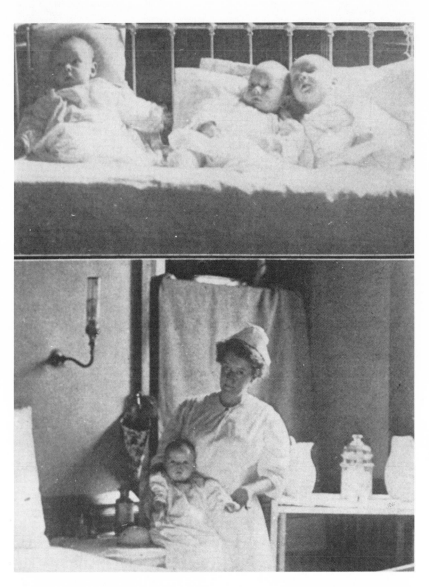

Infants and nurse at the Retreat, 1913

Exterior of the Cleveland Florence Crittenton Home, 1915. Courtesy of the Western Reserve Historical Society, Cleveland

Infants at the Cleveland Florence Crittenton Home. Courtesy of the Western Reserve Historical Society, Cleveland

"Hop Right In, Sis. I'm Goin' Your Way."
—Cartoon by Donahey, in the Plain Dealer

Promotional material for the Cleveland Federation for Charity and Philanthropy, 1913

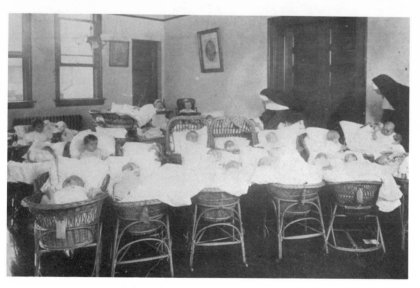

Infants and Sisters of Charity of St. Augustine at St. Ann's Infant and Maternity Asylum. Courtesy of the Sisters of Charity of St. Augustine Archives, Richfield, Ohio

Artist's depiction of "the challenge of the city," which the Cleveland
Federation was designed to meet

Salvation Army staff and volunteer doctor at the Rescue. Courtesy of the Western Reserve Historical Society, Cleveland

Salvation Army staff and infants and children at the Rescue

Mary B. Talbert Home, the former site of the Salvation Army Rescue, 1925. Courtesy of the Salvation Army, Greater Cleveland Headquarters

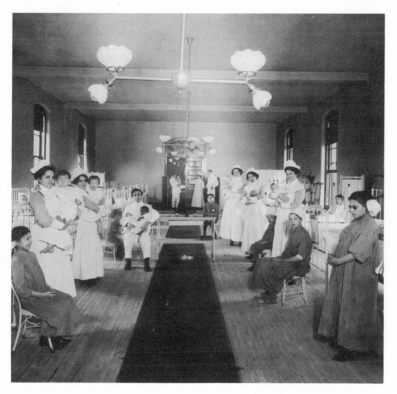

Ward at Cleveland City Hospital, ca. 1890. Courtesy of the Metro-Health Medical Center Archives

Dr. Frederick Douglas Stubbs, the first black intern at Cleveland City Hospital. Courtesy of the Metro-Health Medical Center Archives

Grace Rice Wilkes, R.N., left; Edna Wolley Austin, R.N., top right; and Dorthea Davis Walker, R.N., bottom right; the first three black women admitted to Cleveland City Hospital's nursing school in 1930. Courtesy of the MetroHealth Medical Center Archives

Cleveland MetroHealth Medical Center Towers, 1988. Courtesy of the
MetroHealth Medical Center Archives

Catholic proscriptions against birth control and abortion also strengthened arguments for an asylum for unwed mothers. The number of abortions in the United States peaked in the 1870s, and abortionists and abortifacients became so readily available that they were advertised in popular magazines, including Protestant journals.[21] Abortion until the time of quickening was legal in most states until a wave of anti-abortion legislation began in the 1860s. The Catholic church (in 1867), the orthodox medical profession, and organized women's groups also opposed legalized abortion.

Illegal or self-induced abortions, however, remained a dangerous possibility. Contraceptives such as pessaries or douches were used by the middle class, but when the 1873 Comstock Law made distributing contraceptives or information about contraception illegal, these became even less accessible to working-class women. Until the 1910s, there was in fact little public support for the greater availability of contraceptives, and the Catholic church also opposed their use.[22] With neither abortion nor birth control readily available, a woman pregnant out-of-wedlock might abandon or kill her infant to hide her shame. Several Catholic dioceses therefore opened foundling homes and, after 1870, homes for both mothers and children.[23]

The perennial anxiety about Protestant proselytizing also encouraged the opening of a diocesan home for unwed mothers. The many Irish women in the Cleveland Infirmary, sometimes pregnant out-of-wedlock, were easy prey for Protestant missionaries from the WCA. Some did end up in the Retreat, susceptible to its evangelicalism.

Pressured by sectarian competition, by the welfare needs of the rapidly growing Catholic population, and by the church's prohibitions against family limitation, the bishop gave permission to the Sisters of Charity to establish St. Ann's Infant and Maternity Asylum. This nursing order already administered several hospitals around the country, including St. Vincent Charity Hospital in Cleveland, behind which the asylum was built.

The rationale for St. Ann's resembled that of other Cleveland maternity homes. The official historian of the Cleveland diocese, George F. Houck, explained the home as Charles Crittenton had his: "A censorious world may say, this is fostering crime; but no, it is the Savior's own method: 'Woman, neither will I condemn thee. Go, and now sin no more.'"[24] With spiritual reclamation its goal, the asylum's means included regular masses, special services on Catholic holy days, and visits and confessions by priests. As at the other homes, reclamation was women's work under male direction. The nuns were spiritual exemplars, as were the volunteers and matrons at the Protestant homes. The *Catholic Universe* explained: "The patients are served by the Sisters, who not only bestow upon them temporal blessings, but also fervently and silently pray that the fallen one like Magdalene, may repent and return to grace."[25]

The medical staff was all male and was appointed by the bishop, although the mother superior occasionally challenged an appointment. Doctors and medical students from Western Reserve University School of Medicine served at St. Ann's without pay to gain valuable clinical experience, professional status, and possibly paying patients. Students needed the permission of both the house physician and the mother superior to examine patients. Unlike other Cleveland maternity homes, St. Ann's did not allow women doctors to deliver patients there, at least through the mid-1920s.[26]

Despite the free services of student nurses and doctors, nuns, and volunteers, the expenses of maintaining a growing physical plant and acquiring new medical technology continued to rise, and in the first decade of the twentieth century, St. Ann's, like other private hospitals, began to seek paying patients. From 1888 to 1900, only 39 of the 249 women admitted to St. Ann's were able to pay even part of their fees. By 1906, fully a third of the 365 patients were full-pay patients.[27] Bishop Ignatius Richard Horstmann then approved the expansion of St. Ann's facilities to accommodate those "who would be glad to pay a good sum" so that the institution might become more self-supporting.[28]

Persuading respectable women to give birth in a hospital was not easy, and like maternity hospitals elsewhere, St. Ann's began a campaign to recreate its public image. In 1910 the St. Ann's house physician announced in the *Cleveland Medical Journal* that the hospital now welcomed private patients and their doctors. For many years, he conceded, St. Ann's purpose had been "to care for unfortunate girls only . . . but in time the advantages of hospital care in confinement began to be recognized," and married women sought admission as well. Anxious to disassociate the hospital from the stigma of unwed motherhood, he claimed that in the previous year, half the patients had paid full rates and that most of these were married. The article cited several advantages of hospital birth to doctors and patients. Doctors could conduct "labor cases of whatever nature, with . . . strict regard for cleanliness," and could better control both patient and environment without the interference of midwives, family members, or domestic routines. "To the woman about to pass through the perils of childbirth," St. Ann's offered "not only all the safeguards of a completely equipped hospital but also all those home comforts which seem to be essential to this class of patients." What class the doctor referred to is implicit in the comforts he described: twenty private rooms, each of which had furnishings valued at five thousand dollars.[29]

HOSPITAL VERSUS HOME, 1910–1973

After 1910 married and unmarried women were housed in separate buildings at St. Ann's. In 1918 St. Ann's Infant and Maternity Asylum was renamed St. Ann's Maternity Hospital, the "hospital" indicating its new medical mission, and the building for unmarried women became Loretta Hall. The physical separation of the two groups of women emphasized the growing differences in their treatment.

St. Ann's Maternity Hospital flourished as middle-class women increasingly became persuaded that hospital childbirth was safe and less painful than birth at home without anesthesia.[30] Only 26 percent of all registered births in Cleveland took place in hospitals or maternity homes in 1919; in 1930 that number increased to 60 percent. (See Table 4.1.)[31] St. Ann's Maternity Hospital's 141 beds made it the second largest maternity facility in the city (Maternity Hospital was the largest), and the vast majority of St. Ann's patients were married women—90 percent in 1930.[32] After the lean years of the Depression, the hospital enjoyed rising occupancies, and in 1951, filled to capacity by baby-boom births, St. Ann's moved to a handsome building on a new site near Cleveland's eastern suburbs, closer to the hospital's potential clientele. This facility changed its name to St. Ann's Hospital and in 1952 incorporated separately from the facility for unwed mothers and infants. The hospital had also become an important medical teaching institution with a large staff of interns, residents, and student nurses. In 1965, with the help of a large federal grant, the hospital added a 135-bed wing.

Loretta Hall, meanwhile, remained a social service agency directed by nuns, and one of forty-four Catholic homes for unwed mothers administered according to guidelines established by the National Conference of Catholic Charities.[33] Founded in 1910, the conference was intended to bring Catholic social welfare agencies and institutions into line with professional social work standards.[34] For example, it endorsed the policy of keeping mother and child together, using the rationale of Dr. Kate Waller Barrett and the Cleveland Conference on Illegitimacy.[35] The National Conference, however, continued to stress the spiritual causes and cures for illegitimate pregnancy: "Many of these girls have become careless in their religious obligations, neglecting confession and Holy

TABLE 4.1
PLACES OF BIRTH, CLEVELAND, 1930

	Living Births
Total for the City	17,895
Total Home Cases	7,416
Total Hospital Cases	10,479
Maternity Hospitals	3,732
Booth Memorial	64
Florence Crittenton	15
Mary B. Talbert	55
Maternity	2,293
Retreat	20
St. Ann's Maternity	1,285
Cleveland City Hospital	836

Source: City of Cleveland, Department of Public Health, *Annual Report*, 1930 (Cleveland, 1930), 36.

Communion, but after they have made their peace with God . . . then they are ready to begin the uplift in their lives," the director of a maternity home in Pittsburgh told her conference audience in 1931.[36]

In Loretta Hall the religious mission remained paramount. An unwed mother received spiritual instruction, attended evening chapel, and was encouraged to join the Sisters of the Good Shepherd as a Magdalene. Even if she was not a charity patient, she was required to work in the home and the infant nursery. As at the Retreat and the Florence Crittenton Home, these domestic chores were justified as essential to moral rehabilitation, but the work also helped pay for a woman's six- to eight-month confinement. Visitors were limited to family and "young men if marriage [was] imminent."[37] In 1939 Sister Annette, director of Loretta Hall, told the annual Conference of Catholic Charities that although patients at the home received the same medical care as did the patients at St. Ann's Hospital ("some of our finest married women in Cleveland"), at Loretta Hall "the real work is in that invisible world of human souls where only God Himself can estimate its value."[38]

However, like the hospital three decades earlier, the home began to change its clientele in the wake of the Depression. In 1935, the great majority of the inmates at Loretta Hall were domestic servants, with a few factory workers and waitresses. This working-class profile corresponds with data in the Federation's 1936 Bolt Report and with information collected in 1914 and 1923 by the Federation. (See Table I.2.)[39] This clientele could not pay for or even work off its lengthy confinements in the maternity homes. Because Ohio did not fund maternity home care for dependent or medically indigent women, all homes remained entirely privately funded.

By the early 1940s, the Federation, as a primary source of funds, began to pressure the homes to raise rates—which were then fifty dollars for women from within the county, seventy-five dollars for out of county, and $100 for out of state (Mary B. Talbert Home charged less)—and to collect more money from clients. The homes, accustomed to behaving like charitable institutions, protested but eventually acquiesced.[40] The homes did not exclude women who could not pay because the Federation required them to take dependent clients. However, the rising fees obviously limited the number of women who would be likely to apply.

This trend toward a middle-class clientele, noted already at the Florence Crittenton Home, was encouraged by two other factors. First, private health insurance, which helped to cover rising medical costs, was available primarily to middle-class clients. In addition, the new insistence by social workers that maternity homes encourage adoption made them attractive to middle-class women, who were often more reluctant than working-class mothers to keep their illegitimate children. Consequently, by the late 1950s, the inmates of the Catholic home, like those at the Florence Crittenton Home, were no longer working-class dependents but middle-class paying clients: "middle-middle"-class women, "90 percent white Catholic," from families who preferred placing an illegitimate child for adoption to an early and unsuitable marriage.[41] The two Salvation Army homes in Cleveland had a similar clientele.[42]

Despite their middle-class backgrounds, unmarried women remained physically and morally segregated from married patients. When St. Ann's Hospital moved to the suburbs, the facility for unwed mothers, now DePaul Infant and Maternity Home, stayed in the old central city location. At DePaul, women were still treated as though they were charity patients, required to work in the home and nursery. There were sound economic reasons for this because maternity home confinements were still long: in 1960 the average length of stay at DePaul was three months, and many clients stayed longer.[43]

More significant was the cruel difference in the definitions of married and unmarried motherhood, especially in the context of the postwar baby boom. Making up for time lost during the Depression and World War II, Americans rushed to marry and have families. Birth rates reversed a century-and-a-half-long decline as married women had third and fourth children. Although women continued to enter the paid work force in record numbers, the nineteenth-century cult of domesticity enjoyed a revival as the "feminine mystique," the belief that marriage and motherhood defined woman's identity.

Affirming its historic conservative position, the Catholic church had opposed both woman suffrage and then the Equal Rights Amendment when it was first introduced to Congress in 1923 on the grounds that they would endanger home life and women's traditional roles. In the postwar period, Catholics, like other Americans, sought to reassert the importance of family and female domesticity, founding, for example, the Christian Family Movement. In 1948 and 1949 pastoral letters from the American bishops described the family as "a divine institution that human will cannot alter or nullify."[44]

In this context, motherhood without marriage represented shocking deviance. Accordingly, the Catholic maternity homes found particularly congenial the new medical definition of pregnancy out-of-wedlock as symptomatic of psychiatric disorder. As the psychiatric consultant to DePaul explained in the early 1960s, many of the middle-class "girls" came from families that had a "history of internal conflict. . . . Some girls verge on the psychopathic and others, at least on the surface, appear to be . . . well controlled with their essential problem appearing in the area of the management of their sexual impulse." An unwed pregnancy, he concluded, "might be equated with suicide."[45]

The psychiatrization of unwed motherhood had its origins in the 1910s, when illegitimacy was occasionally blamed on the feeblemindedness of immigrant or working-class women who did not score well on the IQ tests administered sporadically by maternity homes and other social agencies. In 1917 a psychologist reported to the annual gathering of the National Conference on Social Work that unwed mothers were far more likely than a "law-abiding group of working women'" to score badly on a "card sorting test" or an "easy opposites test."[46]

During the 1920s, influenced by the work of Mary E. Richmond and Mary C. Jarrett and the popular vogue for Freudian psychiatry, social casework moved in the direction of psychological diagnosis and treatment and placed renewed emphasis on psychological services to unwed mothers. In 1928 the Cleveland Conference on Illegitimacy heard a psychiatrist recommend both psychological testing and psychiatric counseling for unwed mothers.[47] However, none of the maternity homes employed a psychologist during the 1920s.[48] In the post-Depression period, as psychiatric social work became a prestigious specialty, psychodynamic casework was especially recommended for child-placing and child-guidance agencies, and psychiatric or emotional problems became almost the only professional justification for institutionalizing children, as the Cleveland orphanages had realized some decades earlier.[49]

By the mid-1950s, psychodynamic interpretations had finally come to dominate social workers' thinking on unwed motherhood, for two reasons.[50] First, such interpretations explained the otherwise inexplicable behavior of the illegitimately pregnant white, middle-class women who had become the clients of maternity homes and social agencies. Secularly trained professionals could hardly rely on the nineteenth-century interpretation of illegitimate pregnancy as a fall from God's grace. Environmental explanations relying on cultural deviance or economic deprivation, such as those advanced by the U.S. Children's Bureau in the 1920s, did not seem to work either.

From the new psychoanalytical perspective, sex without marriage could be attributed to a woman's personality disorders. The caseworker at the Florence Crittenton Home explained some of her clients' pregnancies this way: "———— has been an unhappy person who feels that neither of her parents really care what happens to her. . . . ———— is a typical product of county child welfare homes, a very passive, conforming youngster, who has had little in life and is uncertain as to how she can get anywhere," or "———— had a very unfortunate marriage that ended in divorce soon after the birth of her daughter. She has never since then been able to get hold of herself or put any real direction in her life. She is very sorry for herself and bursts into tears at the least provocation."[51]

Second, although phrased in scientific terminology, the psychiatric approach was by no means antithetical to the traditional religious approach to illegitimate pregnancy and in fact provided added justification for traditional treatment: the lengthy confinements, now described as necessary for therapy; the separation of mother and child and subsequent adoption; and the use of professional social workers.

The psychological diagnosis of unwed motherhood received the enthusiastic endorsement of Catholic and lay professionals in the *Catholic Charities Review* as well as secular social work journals. Writing in the *Review*, DePaul director Sr. M. deMontfort explained "pregnancy out-of-wedlock as a result of symptomatic behavior" and the DePaul program as "a constructive treatment for the illness of which sexual behavior is the symptom."[52] In 1965 Sr. Joseph Marie, the director of social services at DePaul, stressed the "changed philosophy" of maternity home care. In 1920, she said, the home's purpose was "to care for unmarried mothers and their more unfortunate offspring"; today, however, "since science is beginning to understand more clearly the psychological patterns which often lead to pregnancy out-of-wedlock, the entire living experience at DePaul is focused on treatment."[53]

Exactly as in professional casework, there was probably more lip service than application of modern policies. An account of daily activities at DePaul suggests that little had really changed. On Easter Sunday in

1960, the "girls all wore becoming Easter hats and corsages. . . . Sister and girls sang hymns all through Mass."[54] DePaul and the other maternity homes added psychiatrists to their consulting staffs and psychiatric consultation to their list of available services, but the psychiatrists actually spent little time at the homes and gave primary assistance and direction to the staff rather than to the mothers. The DePaul psychiatrist was usually on site only an hour and a half a week. A 1965 survey of maternity homes across the country revealed that in only 5.7 percent of the institutions did all inmates receive psychological testing and in only 2.1 percent did all inmates receive psychiatric evaluation at admission. In 59.5 percent of the homes, no inmates received evaluation.[55]

The psychiatric approach also had the allure of being potentially publicly funded because of federal legislation in 1966 that provided monies for the building or maintenance of state mental health programs. In 1969 DePaul joined with the Florence Crittenton Home and Booth Hospital in the Maternity Home Mental Health Consortium. The consortium was supposed to provide new psychiatric, psychological, and group therapy to unwed mothers, putative fathers, and families.[56] The project received one year's funding from the Cuyahoga County Board of Mental Health and Retardation and operated for a second year with funds from the Cleveland Foundation. Even with this financial support, the consortium could employ only two part-time and one full-time psychologists to conduct personality inventory testing and group therapy. There was never enough money to hire even a part-time psychiatrist for the consortium's clients, most of whom were white, middle-class, Catholic, and probably from DePaul.[57]

The ineffectiveness of this approach, or at least of its implementation at DePaul, is illustrated in an article in a DePaul newsletter probably written in 1972. The writer, a young mother, described "group counseling every week to help us help each other so that we may be able to make the decisions that are best for us." This meant the decision to put their infants up for adoption. The writer, however, had not internalized—or at least could not verbalize—the psychiatric explanation of her pregnancy: "Expecting and bringing a child into the world is the most wonderful experience in life. Because it is happening at an unfortunate time, I am thankful I found DePaul."[58]

In 1969 annual admissions to DePaul dropped to 138 after holding steady at about 170 from 1961 to 1968. Home administrators blamed the decline on higher fees mandated by the Federation.[59] Pressured itself by social welfare activists to provide more services for the poor but caught in budget shortfalls of its own, the Federation in 1971 turned over responsibility for the allocation of monies to the United Torch. United

Torch was not any more interested than the Federation had been in supporting services for middle-class white women, and in 1972 it cut its allocation to DePaul because "it is not appropriate to continue allocation of scarce community resources to low and declining community needs."[60]

Conclusion

In 1973, a century after the founding of St. Ann's Maternity and Infant Asylum, St. Ann's Hospital closed its eight-year-old building. Its sister facility for unwed mothers survived for another decade, but ultimately neither could outlast changing sexual behavior and birth control technology.

In 1973 the DePaul Home became DePaul Family Services. It retained twenty beds for unwed mothers but offered primarily outpatient services such as day care, health care, and counseling. In 1976 the residential unit admitted only forty-two women.[61] In 1983 this small facility at DePaul, once part of the city's second largest maternity hospital, also closed. The Catholic diocese continued to offer unmarried mothers outpatient medical care and counseling in Cleveland or maternity home care elsewhere in one of the few remaining Catholic homes for unwed mothers.

Loretta Hall/DePaul had flourished partly because of the large Catholic population of northeastern Ohio and partly because of close identification with the medical services of St. Ann's Hospital. Although the treatment of married and unmarried mothers became different, both facilities initially benefitted from the medicalization of childbirth that began at the turn of the century. In the 1960s, both became victims of the medicalization of family planning as birth control devices became widely available and widely used. During the 1920s and 1930s the laws prohibiting the distribution and sale of contraceptives were modified in many states in response to legal challenges from feminists like Margaret Sanger, the acceptance of birth control by the medical community, and Americans' Depression-born desire to limit family size. After the baby boom, however, the middle class opted again for smaller families, an option made easier by the availability of the contraceptive pill. Birthrates dropped as rapidly in the 1960s as they had risen through the 1950s. The emerging women's movement made reproductive rights a key demand, and a sexual revolution, evidenced in rising rates of premarital intercourse, made legal means of family limitation a necessity.[62] There was also growing public concern about a rapidly increasing world population and about poverty in the United States.

Family planning, in short, became viable social policy. In 1965 federal legislation provided funds for family planning programs, and the 1973 Supreme Court decision *Roe v. Wade*, permitting abortion under certain conditions, was followed by the establishment of abortion counseling facilities and clinics. The Cleveland Federation first supported family planning in 1966 and in 1971 endorsed "programs of effective contraception for unmarried women" and "abortion on request for those who wish it and have no religious or other moral objections" as means to "reduce illegitimacy."[63]

The Catholic church did not alter its opposition to birth control or abortion. The Florence Crittenton Association waived its original objections to family planning and abortion in the late 1960s, and the Salvation Army okayed birth control in 1972 but has remained opposed to abortion. Opposition to family planning had historically provided one of the significant intellectual and moral justifications for maintaining Catholic maternity homes and outpatient services such as those at DePaul. By the early 1970s, the prohibitions against family planning that had sustained the maternity homes made them irrelevant to their secular funding sources such as the Federation or state and federal governments.

More important, maternity homes became irrelevant to the middle-class clientele they had cultivated. These women—even Catholic women—had easy, legal access to birth control and abortion, and married or unmarried, could effectively control pregnancy. According to John d'Emilio and Estelle B. Freedman, although 70 percent of American Catholics conformed to church teachings on birth control in 1955, by 1970, encouraged both by the theological ferment of the period and the growing availability of birth control, "nonconformity among Catholics had jumped to 68 percent."[64]

Historians have documented the movement of childbirth from the home to the hospital and its results: the "masculinization" of childbirth as female midwives were driven out of business by male obstetricians; the increased use of intrusive medical techniques in delivery; the necessary rationalization of the hospital setting to prevent infection; and the patient's loss of control over the birthing process to the doctor and the institution.[65]

These mixed reviews most accurately describe childbirth for middle-class married women, for unlike the nuns at St. Ann's Infant and Maternity Asylum or the pious matrons of the Retreat and the Florence Crittenton homes, historians have assumed that all child-bearing women had husbands. For unwed mothers the hospitalization of childbirth had different implications. Maternity homes, like hospitals, may have changed from charitable to for-profit institutions, but homes never became medical institutions, and childbirth out-of-wedlock never became a wholly medical event but remained charged with spiritual significance. The moral and physical segregation of these mothers, like their early removal from the poorhouse, the lack of public funds for their institutional care, and the lack of professional staff, was further punishment for their sexual misconduct. Sexual deviance even outweighed class differences, as illustrated by middle-class women's treatment as charity patients.

In the longer run, the demarcation between married and unmarried received dramatic definition in the changed meaning of motherhood. Although considered a lapse from grace, unwed motherhood had been credited with having redemptive powers by rescue workers like Kate Waller Barrett and social workers at the Cleveland Conference on Illegitimacy in the 1910s and 1920s. In 1933, at the sixtieth anniversary of St. Ann's, Cleveland bishop Joseph Schrembs eulogized the unwed mother, "who has enough of the truth in God in her, enough of the spirit of faith in her, she [would] sooner bear the scar on her breast than to stain her hands with the blood of her unborn child."[66] In the psychiatric vocabulary of the postwar years, however, an unwed mother was no longer a lapsed saint but a disordered personality, and moreover, one that there was not time or money enough to heal.

Finally, the expenses of medicalization, far greater than the expenses of professional social work, meant that after the Depression maternity home services would be available to fewer of the charity patients for whom St. Ann's and the other homes were founded. By the late 1960s, women who became pregnant out-of-wedlock were most often those who had less access to birth control or abortion, the poor and black women whom the private sector had served least.

◆ 5 ◆

CHANGING FACES OF UNWED MOTHERHOOD: THE SALVATION ARMY RESCUE AND MARY B. TALBERT HOME, 1892–1990

*[Salvation Army] Major Van Der Schouw says she has a colored girl only
14 years old with a baby eight months old. Her mother . . . cannot take the
baby into her home but will take her daughter back. She wants the girl to wean
the baby and find a boarding place for it.*

In 1915, when the matron of the Salvation Army Rescue presented this unusual case to the Federation Conference on Illegitimacy, the Rescue was the only Cleveland maternity home that admitted black women, and very few applied. A decade later, the Army opened its second Cleveland facility, Mary B. Talbert Home, for black women only. This segregated and inadequate facility became less able to serve its growing clientele in the post–World War II period. Talbert Home closed in 1960, replaced by an outpatient clinic. In 1990, the Army maintained the city's last home for unwed mothers at its Booth Hospital; its small size represented an effective end to maternity home care in Cleveland.

Cleveland's Talbert Home is a striking illustration of the separate and unequal provision for black Americans by white social policymakers. At this home, inequities were guaranteed when racist assumptions about black illegitimacy were combined with gender-derived traditions of caring for unwed mothers. Ultimately, a black clientele would change those traditions.

BLACK AMERICANS AND SOCIAL WELFARE

After emancipation, social welfare policies provided little for freed blacks. White neglect was countered by black self-help, often initiated by black, middle-class women whose welfare goals resembled those of their white counterparts.

As federal reconstruction ended in 1877, historic American racism revived. The belief in the inherent superiority of whites was behind a foreign policy that expanded beyond the territorial boundaries of the United States at the expense of nonwhite populations in the Pacific and around the Caribbean. Domestic policies excluded Orientals, segregated American Indians on western reservations, and ghettoized southeastern European immigrants in urban slums.

Racism also shaped social welfare practices. In the South, where most blacks lived, local officials provided separate and unequal poorhouses and insane asylums and minimal outdoor assistance. In the North, public poorhouses only occasionally admitted blacks: very few appear on the registers of the Cleveland Infirmary or elsewhere.[1] There were striking disparities in the provisions for black and white children. In 1883, 78 percent of child-care institutions admitted only white children; 19 percent of the total claimed to take both white and nonwhite children, but probably sheltered no more than one nonwhite child. Only 9 of the 353 institutions were for black children.[2] By 1910 there had been little improvement: only 52 of 1,151 child-care institutions across the country were for nonwhite children; the few integrated institutions were probably public facilities such as the Ohio county children's homes.[3]

Blacks, therefore, organized their own social services. As was the case for whites and especially for Catholics, churches and church-related organizations such as benevolent societies were the most important welfare providers, distributing relief to members, doing mission work in slums and jails, and supporting a few institutions such as orphanages, hospitals, and homes for the aged. Institutions, however, were expensive, and the great untaxed fortunes of men like Charles Crittenton had few counterparts among blacks.[4]

By the early twentieth century, black charity work was dominated by the black women's club movement, particularly by members of the National Association of Colored Women (NACW), founded in 1896. The impetus for the NACW lay partly in the segregationist policies of national women's organizations such as the General Federation of Women's Clubs or the YWCA, but also partly in the years of experience and expertise gained by black women in charitable and benevolent activity within their local churches.[5] The NACW's leadership, drawn from the black elite, was well-educated and at least middle-class; many had wealthy husbands and some, although married, had careers or professions.

The NACW shared with the YWCA the conventional beliefs in women's moral superiority and social responsibilities.[6] The first NACW president, Mary Church Terrell, told the organization's 1897 convention that black women should aid their own people because they were "the mothers, wives, daughters and sisters of [the] race."[7] Consequently, NACW clubs sponsored a wide variety of welfare activities and institutions, including homes for the aged, orphanages, kindergartens, day nurseries, vocational classes, and employment bureaus.[8] In 1896, black women in Cleveland established the Home for Aged Colored People (later renamed the Eliza Bryant Home).

Of particular concern to middle-class clubwomen was the protection of black working women, who were far more likely than white women to be sexually exploited. Their exploitation was rationalized by prevalent stereotypes about black female sexual promiscuity and immorality, openly expressed in the racist climate of the turn of the century. An American journalist's characterization of all black women as prostitutes inspired the first national black women's conference in 1895, which proclaimed: "Now with an army of organized women standing for purity and mental worth, we in ourselves deny the charges . . . not by noisy protestations of what we are not but by a dignified showing of what we are."[9] This conference laid the groundwork for the NACW, which always felt compelled to defend the black woman's reputation against charges of sexual immorality.

Like white women's groups—and with much of the same elitist desire to impose their own sexual norms on lower-class women—NACW clubs founded agencies and institutions to provide safe shelter for black women, especially those new to city life. An early example was the White Rose Industrial Association of New York, whose purpose was "to establish and maintain a Christian non-sectarian Home for Colored Working Girls and Women, where they may be trained in the principles of practical self-help and right living." The National League for the Protection of Colored Women had branches in several eastern cities, and other women's organizations founded homes for working women who were excluded from local YWCAs. In 1898 black women in Atlanta organized a segregated Florence Crittenton Home, which received enthusiastic support from a local minister: "The shameless districts should be regularly canvassed and a way of escape be made for every erring girl that wants to lead a pure life."[10]

THE SALVATION ARMY AND "HALLELUJAH FEMALES"

The Salvation Army's attempts to proselytize black Americans made it unique and innovative among late nineteenth-century evangelical Protestant churches. However, its attempts to rescue unwed mothers, black and white, remained traditional women's work.

From its American beginnings the Army made ambitious efforts to recruit black members, launching in 1885 a "Great Colored Campaign and Combined Attack upon the South." [11] Although black indifference and white hostility prevented much success during these years, the Army persisted in its mission. Black leader Booker T. Washington praised the Salvation Army: "I have always had the greatest respect for the work of the Salvation Army, especially because I have noted that it draws no color line in religion." [12]

Like the YWCA, the Army was the creation of British evangelical benevolence. And like the National Florence Crittenton Mission, its founder, William Booth, was a city missionary who inadvertently became a social worker. But Booth had a more compelling vision than Charles Crittenton or the WCA prayer groups. The church Booth founded in 1865 in London—first called the Christian Mission and renamed the Salvation Army in 1878—actually fulfilled the dream of late-nineteenth-century missionaries to "evangelize the world" in his own lifetime. By 1900 there were Salvation Army corps in Wales, Scotland, Ireland, France, Switzerland, Australia, India, South Africa, Ceylon, and the West Indies. Cleveland was the site of the first Salvation Army attack on American sin. The small mission established by British cabinetmaker James Jermy, an associate of Booth's in the London Christian Mission, survived only from 1872 to 1876. [13]

Four years later, when Commander George Scott Railton and seven "Hallelujah females" disembarked in New York City, conditions in the United States were ripe for the Salvation Army. [14] The street preaching of American evangelicals such as the YMCA and the city missions of established Protestant denominations had left much of the urban population untouched and unchurched. The cities' dispossessed, the tramps, vagabonds, and alcoholics, eagerly listened to the Army's message that Christ would save their souls while the Army saved their bodies. The Army's colorful uniforms and lively bands attracted crowds and converts to the "Great Salvation War." [15] After the Army returned to Cleveland in 1883, its open-air meetings were described with amused condescension by the *Cleveland Plain Dealer*: "A tall, stout man, fantastically attired, was exhorting sinners to repentance at the top of a powerful pair of lungs, and drawing the most lurid pictures of the place of everlasting torment." However, the Army quickly won over several corps of recruits and established its social service programs of street preaching, jail visitation, and outdoor relief. By the end of the 1880s the Army had gained a foothold in forty-three states.[16]

The Salvation Army's solution to all secular problems was, and is, religious conversion. Booth maintained: "Our specialty is getting saved and keeping saved and then getting somebody else saved" so that an intensely personal religious experience assumes a larger social purpose, "religious salvation through social service."[17]

Because Salvationists believed that sin and error originated in human nature, not in the external world, they had no quarrel with the economic or political status quo. The Army's mission of saving the poor without damaging the rich appealed to many American philanthropists and politicians. Although the Army's symbol was the "lassie" with the Christmas kettle for small contributions, the organization also got financial support from wealthy men such as Clevelanders John D. Rockefeller, Mark Hanna, and Myron T. Herrick, as well as political endorsements from prominent public figures like Theodore Roosevelt ("I thoroughly believe in a brass band").[18]

Women always outnumbered men in the Army, both as officers and as foot soldiers.[19] "My best men are women," Booth admitted. He had been surprised in 1860 when his wife, Catherine, persuaded of her own call to preach, unexpectedly rose and took over the pulpit from her husband, her first step on a long and successful career as a preacher. Catherine Booth, convinced even as an adolescent of women's spiritual and intellectual equality, was inspired in 1859 by American evangelist Phoebe Palmer to write her own influential pamphlet, "Female Ministry; or, Woman's Right to Preach The Gospel." In it she attempted to refute arguments against women's preaching derived from the Bible and from custom by invoking familiar and reassuring ideas about womanhood: "We have numerous instances of [woman] retaining all that is most esteemed in her sex and faithfully discharging the duties peculiar to her own sphere, and at the same time taking her place with many of our most useful speakers and writers. . . . [Women ministers] have been amongst the most amiable, self-sacrificing, and unobtrusive of their sex."[20]

The rare opportunity to preach as well as practice the gospel may explain the preponderance of women in the Army: in 1896, at least one thousand of the Army's 1,854 officers were female.[21] Two of William Booth's daughters were commanders of the American Army: Emma Booth-Tucker, "the Consul," with her husband, Frederick St. George deLautour Booth-Tucker; and Evangeline Booth, commander of the American organization from 1904 to 1934.

Evangeline Booth, the symbol of the Army to much of the American public, became so prominent a female evangelist that she delivered the invocation at the 1932 Democratic convention. Like her mother an advocate of sexual equality, Evangeline also entertained conventional ideas about women's work. "In the Salvation Army," she wrote in 1930, "we see the summation of the woman's movement, her equal status with man in social and spiritual and intellectual responsibility, her readiness to find a greater happiness in service than any selfish pleasure could have afforded. . . . The hospitals and homes for mothers, deserted by those who should have been at their side as partners in parenthood, the hotels for working women, the visitation of women in prisons, the bureaus of employment, the young women's residences . . . , these are only some of the agencies which are conducted by the women officers of the Salvation Army."[22]

In 1934 Evangeline became the fourth general of the Army and the first woman to hold the post, illustrating Army women's important but still secondary role. Even today, although they receive similar training, women do not receive equal pay and have been less likely than men to be promoted to leadership positions. Army officers, male and female, can marry only other officers, and female officers assume their husbands' ranks and are expected to follow their husbands' assignments rather than their own.[23]

Women directed many of the Army's social service programs and headed the Women's Social Service Department. (There was also a Men's Social Service Department.) In the United States and Britain, the Women's Social Service Department grew out of the Army's rescue work, which became the department's chief responsibility, although it also administered day nurseries and homes for children and working women. Female officers headed the Army's homes for unwed mothers (and later hospitals), serving, like Protestant matrons and Catholic nuns, as spiritual exemplars for fallen women.

The rescue homes were the Army's most successful institutions. Its first home, in New York City, announced this intention in 1886: "The Rescue Home for the fallen and the falling is now opened for young women who desire and are earnestly seeking the salvation of their bodies and souls."[24] By 1920 the Army administered twenty-six such homes.[25]

The Army opened its Cleveland home, the Rescue, in 1892 when Colonel Mary Stillwell made an impromptu but successful plea for funds after the brass band scheduled to entertain a mass meeting was detained.

Pairs of female officers, emboldened by their faith that "God has given his angels charge concerning them," then searched through the city's slums and red-light districts, finding many women in desperate straits. "One young girl, 17 years of age, wept bitterly when the Rescuers prayed behind a saloon, and said it reminded her of her childhood days."[26]

Beneath the Army's religious rhetoric, its annual reports provide some empirical evidence of the poverty and family disruption of urban working-class women: "The average age of the 12 girls now in the Home is 21 years. One girl, 17 years of age, has been in the workhouse twice, and in the dungeon of the workhouse several times for bad conduct while in there. Another fell at 13: has been in jail several times. Married at 15. Can neither read nor write. Another fell at 17. Her family deserted by her father when she was only 8. Mother a drunkard." This 1893 report also included a rare public allusion to abortion: "[The young woman] was a very bright girl, 20 years of age; deceived under promise of marriage and cruelly deserted. . . . She had determined to take her own life but delayed and consulted a physician as to a criminal operation. He very wisely advised her to come to our Home." (The story ended happily when the young woman converted and later married her deceiver.)[27]

Like the other homes, the Rescue sought the fallen woman's conversion to Christ, glorying in the women who became Army recruits, "workers for the Master" and "dedicated to God and the Army."[28] The Rescue also employed the traditional strategies for reclamation: prayer meetings, Bible readings, the Christian example of matrons (who were Army officers), training in domestic skills, and lengthy confinement of mother and child.

The institutional development of the Cleveland Rescue also parallelled that of other homes. Its first inmates probably were prostitutes or would-be prostitutes. Many of the rescued women stayed only briefly at the home, and many were not pregnant. By 1907, however, the home, describing itself as a maternity home as well as a rescue, boasted of its hospital department with a generous doctor who donated his services. Like St. Ann's, the home then became a hospital, in 1923, with the new medical orientation acknowledged by a name change to Booth Memorial Home and Hospital. The hospital took paying patients by 1929, but most mothers paid little or nothing.[29] In 1930 the Army moved the hospital to East Cleveland. The old building became the site for the Talbert Home.

The Army's social service institutions for blacks were generally segregated.[30] In 1917 the Army opened the Evangeline Booth Home for black unwed mothers in Cincinnati, where the Army already maintained a home for white women. Evangeline Booth Home, although intended for charity patients, also gave black physicians a place to deliver their private patients. This segregated home would be a model for Cleveland's Talbert Home.

CLEVELAND'S MARY B. TALBERT HOME, 1925–1939

Despite the efforts of welfare reformers during the Progressive period, institutions were still a chief means by which Cleveland's private agencies coped with dependency. When the Army opened the Talbert Home in 1925, most Cleveland welfare facilities did not admit blacks.

Most Cleveland institutions were sectarian, founded before the turn of the century when the city's small black, middle-class population— slightly more than 1 percent of the city's total—was of little concern to social agencies.[31] Through the 1920s thousands of Southern black immigrants migrated to Cleveland and other northern cities. Unused to urban life and often destitute, they found that private agencies made few efforts to help them. For example, in 1923, although 20 percent of private child-care agencies across the country had a policy of admitting children of both races, no private child-care institutions in Cleveland admitted black children, and there was no public children's home in Cuyahoga County.[32] As late as 1930, Cleveland's noted black author Charles Chesnutt reported: "No colored children are received at any Cleveland orphan asylum. . . . None of the 'old folks homes,' male or female, are open to Negroes, except the Cleveland Home for Aged Colored Persons [the Eliza Bryant Home]."[33] Exclusion from private institutions meant hardship when the private sector still spent little on outdoor relief and the public sector spent almost nothing.

For a number of reasons the city's black community did not establish its own institutions, except for the Eliza Bryant Home. Some black leaders opposed separate black facilities, preferring to push for integrated facilities. Two separate attempts to open a settlement house for blacks failed because of disagreement within the black community over whether the facility should be segregated. In addition, institutions may have cost too much. Efforts to raise money for a black hospital failed, even with the endorsement of black leaders.[34]

The problem of providing services for blacks without integrating white facilities was solved by the establishment of separate institutions for blacks such as Cleveland's Phillis Wheatley Association. This residence for black working women, named for the first American black poet, was opened in 1911 by Jane Edna Hunter, a Southern migrant and an admirer of Booker T. Washington's philosophy of self-help. When Hunter discovered that black women were not permitted to live at the YWCA, she founded this separate facility over the protests of some black leaders. She received funds from the white community, particularly from YWCA board members, and in return was forced to include whites on Phillis Wheatley's board of trustees.[35] The Phillis Wheatley Association would be the local model for Mary B. Talbert: a segregated institution, financially controlled by whites, with nominal aid from the black community.

Hunter realized, as had the black clubwomen, that black women migrants to the city experienced the same cultural and familial dislocation that had made earlier newcomers sexually exploitable. Rural customs of premarital intercourse persisted without guarantees of marriage or even stable cohabitation with male sexual partners, who often were unable to find steady work. Women's sexual vulnerability was further compounded by the prevalent stereotypes about their promiscuity and especially by their poverty. The safe and inexpensive housing at the Phillis Wheatley Association would shield women from premarital sexual activity and unwed motherhood.

Rising illegitimacy rates accompanied the black urban migration. The U.S. Children's Bureau in 1920 found that illegitimacy rates for black women in cities like Baltimore, Washington, D.C., and Philadelphia were higher than the national average.[36] However, the Cleveland Conference on Illegitimacy displayed little interest in black women in its early years. Summary data conscientiously reported "nativity" of unwed mothers served at member agencies in 1914, but there is no mention of "colored" women.[37] In 1921 and 1922, the conference noted uneasily the growing numbers of illegitimate births to black women, and in 1923 recorded that 100 of 446 registered illegitimate births were to black women. (See Table 5.1.) Only fourteen were delivered at maternity homes: five at St. Ann's and nine at the Rescue. Neither the Florence Crittenton Home nor the Retreat accepted black women.[38]

The conference was torn between accepted ideas about black illegitimacy and accepted ideas about maternity home care. On the one hand, conference members shared the popular belief that shaped policy for another four decades: that illegitimate pregnancy was more readily accepted by blacks than by whites and that black unwed mothers therefore were less in need of the sheltered setting of the maternity home.[39] Stereotypes about the sexual permissiveness of black women may have been implicit, but assumptions about black illegitimacy seemed to be supported both by the available Cleveland data and by the 1920 statistics and analysis of the U.S. Children's Bureau. The authors of the analy-

TABLE 5.1
REGISTERED ILLEGITIMATE BIRTHS, BY RACE,
CLEVELAND, 1922 AND 1923

Year	Total Illegitimate Births Registered	White	Colored
1922	372	297	75
1923	446	347	99

Source: Conference on Illegitimacy, June 21, 1924, FCP MS 3788, container 30, folder 739, WRHS.

sis, respected child welfare experts Emma O. Lundberg and Katharine E. Lenroot, explained black illegitimacy rates in environmental terms: "laxness of marriage relations among the Negroes" stemmed from poverty, the disruptive impact of urban life, and lack of educational opportunities. But the authors also noted that illegitimate black children were customarily cared for by mothers or relatives.[40] These data made it easy for white social workers, like those at the Cleveland Conference, to conclude that no maternity home care was necessary and to ignore or overlook contrary evidence.

Almost simultaneously with the debate at the conference, Elsie Johnson McDougald, a black social worker and high school principal, challenged the Children's Bureau conclusions in an article published in *Survey Graphic*: "Contrary to popular belief, illegitimacy among Negroes is cause for shame and grief. When economic, social and biological forces . . . bring about unwed motherhood, the reaction is much the same as in families of other racial groups. Secrecy is maintained if possible. . . . Stigma does not fall upon the unmarried mother, but perhaps in this matter the Negroes' attitude is nearer the modern enlightened ideal for the social treatment of the unfortunate."[41]

The conference still endorsed the policy of keeping unwed mother and child together in the maternity home for her reclamation, which was difficult to implement when no homes except the Rescue (and infrequently St. Ann's) took black women. This awkwardness was compounded when the Cleveland Council of Colored Women, an affiliate of the NACW, asked the Federation for funds to open a home for black women. The council's president, Cora Boyd, was a former schoolteacher active in the local PTA and in the state and national NACW and the wife of Elmer F. Boyd, a funeral director and a member of the NAACP and the Phillis Wheatley board of trustees.[42]

The Federation was not willing to support a black-run home, and it certainly was not willing to urge the integration of existing homes. Since the Army already maintained the Cincinnati home for black women, the Federation asked the Army to administer a similar home in Cleveland, with some financial support from the council. The Army officer in charge of the Cincinnati home advised the conference in 1924 that it was "unwise for any large number of colored girls to be cared for in the same building with the white girls."[43] In Cleveland, the Army, therefore, rented a separate building for black women from 1925 to 1929. When Booth Memorial moved to East Cleveland, the Talbert Home moved into the older facility.

The Mary B. Talbert Home was named for the second president of the National Association of Colored Women, an anti-lynching activist and the recipient of the Spingarn award from the National Association for the Advancement of Colored People. The Cleveland Council of Colored Women made an initial donation of one thousand dollars and gave occasional other gifts, but left the management of the home to the Salvation Army.[44] The regimen at the Talbert Home was established by the Army, not the council, and resembled that of the other maternity homes. There was religious training and instruction in "plain sewing, cooking and general housework."[45]

Having agreed to establish the Talbert Home, the conference and the Army continued to assume that private maternity homes should not even try to serve the great majority of black women. In 1925 only two of the Army's homes were for blacks—Evangeline Booth in Cincinnati and the Talbert Home, which had only twelve beds, some reserved for private, paying patients of black physicians. Clearly a facility this small could care for very few women.[46]

A decade after the Talbert Home's opening, the inadequacies of private services to black women were even more obvious. According to the Federation's Bolt Report, in 1935 private agencies provided 50.6 beds per 100 white illegitimate births and 24.6 beds per 100 black illegitimate births. Prior to the Retreat's closing, there were four homes open to white women with a total capacity of 156 beds and 134 bassinets, and one home open to black women with a capacity of 32 beds and 30 bassinets.[47]

In 1935, 10.2 percent of black births were illegitimate, compared to 3.0 percent for whites. Black women were more likely to have multiple illegitimate pregnancies.[48] The Bolt Report nevertheless concluded that there was enough residential care for black women. The reasoning was familiar: "It is easier to get colored unwed mothers back in their homes after the birth of their babies as illegitimacy is not regarded as so much of a disgrace among the colored. The demand for maternity home care . . . is therefore not so great."[49]

Talbert's services were in fact cut. Its occupancy dropped to 60 percent in 1933, and one floor was closed. Its capacity was reduced to thirty-two, and four of those beds were for private patients. (The Army provided forty beds for white women at Booth.)[50] Social workers had become reluctant to refer black women to the Talbert Home because they felt that the facility did not have "sufficient funds to care for all the girls for whom it has room."[51] The result was predictable: in 1935 almost half of all unwed mothers with registered births bore their children in private maternity homes. But although 29.7 percent of registered illegitimate births were to black women, they constituted only 15 percent of those receiving maternity home care.[52]

More Separate and More Unequal, 1940–1969

The opportunities for jobs created by World War II accelerated the movement of blacks to heavy-industry towns such as Cleveland. Blacks also became a larger proportion of the city's population as the white middle class moved to the suburbs, abandoning older neighborhoods in the central city. Cleveland's black population grew from 85,000 in 1940 to 251,000 in 1960.[53] The second great migration of the postwar period worsened the problems of illegitimacy. Like the first, the migration was accompanied by family disorganization and poverty, and it widened the gap between provisions for black and white unmarried mothers.

Cleveland's private agencies still did not integrate their facilities. Although services for black children were inadequate in all cities, in Cleveland the private agencies received no public subsidies and consequently were under no public pressure to integrate. Black children in Cleveland "were excluded from virtually every residential facility that existed." Adoption services, provided primarily by private agencies, were almost nonexistent for black children.[54] These exclusionist practices embarrassed the Federation, then under pressure from the local chapter of the American Association of Social Workers to provide equal access to child-care institutions. But the Federation did allow sectarian agencies, which meant almost all of them, to give priority to co-religionists, a policy that continued to exclude black children. In 1949, although most black children were Protestant, the largest Protestant orphanage, Beech Brook, took only white children.[55]

The institutionalization of dependent populations, however, had become the exception rather than the rule. This was in small part because of social workers' dislike of institutions and in large part because the Depression had underscored their cost and the New Deal had provided federally funded social insurance and outdoor relief programs that allowed dependent people to remain in their own homes. These alternatives to institutionalization for dependent children limited the impact of the exclusionist policies of private agencies. Dependent black children could be placed in foster homes by the Cuyahoga County Child Welfare Board, if not by private agencies, or at the very worst, could be sheltered at the county detention home, where they would be cared for at public expense until they could be returned to their families.[56]

For unwed mothers, institutionalization in a maternity home remained a preferred—although inadequate, for some black unwed mothers—practice. In 1944 Maud Morlock of the U.S. Children's Bureau, addressing the annual conference of the National Florence Crittenton Mission, criticized private agencies for not providing services to black women. (Crittenton homes did not accept black women at this time, at least not in Cleveland.) Morlock attacked the racial stereotypes repeatedly expressed in Cleveland and elsewhere: "In many communities the idea prevails that Negroes are tolerant of illegitimacy and that the Negro unmarried mother and child are accepted by family and friends. Because of this supposed acceptance, social service for the mother and foster care for the baby are considered unnecessary." These reasons for withholding service, she continued, were "fallacious." She asked for "more casework service and maternity home care for Negro unmarried mothers."[57]

Morlock's pleas went unheeded in Cleveland even as black illegitimacy rates continued to rise. Registered illegitimate births in Cleveland increased from 500 in 1940 to 898 in 1946; by that year, 47.2 percent were to nonwhite women, a number greatly disproportionate to the number of blacks in the city. All Cleveland maternity homes were full and accepted only about 50 percent of their applications. The "total demand for service exceeded the total available facilities," said a 1948 Federation report.[58]

The Talbert Home was particularly hard-pressed because it was the only home that received significant numbers of black women. The Federation pressed for integration of child-care facilities, but not of the white maternity homes, and it did not plan to expand Talbert.[59] Moreover, at the Talbert Home, confinements were lengthened by a state requirement that an unwed mother stay in the home until her child was placed, and agencies that readily placed white children were unwilling or unable to find adoptive homes for black children.[60]

Because casework at maternity homes was concerned primarily with child placement, Talbert's clients got little help from professional social workers.[61] Talbert's clients were younger than those of other maternity homes (most were between fourteen and seventeen years of age), but almost all kept their infants, in sharp contrast again to the other homes, where adoption had become preferred policy.[62] The long confinements of black women who did wish to put their children up for adoption and the low average income received per case made the Talbert Home the least cost-efficient of the maternity homes.[63] To try to compensate, the facility took greater numbers of paying, married patients and fewer women who could not pay, as did St. Ann's and the Crittenton Home. In 1952, Talbert's 528 private patients received 2,829 days' care; its 178 unwed mothers received 10,142 days' care. The result was a $40,557 deficit.[64]

In that same year independent consultants hired by the Army to chart the future course of Booth and Talbert pointed out the medical shortcomings of both, and particularly of Talbert. Booth was faulted for facilities "inadequate for modern obstetrical care," but Talbert was described as "a hazard and beyond reclamation and . . . inadequate for comprehensive maternity care." The medical staff at Booth was rated good, but the staff at Talbert was "not the highest" because none had completed internships at accredited hospitals and none had obstetrical specialties. Patients at Booth were from higher income groups than those at Talbert, even though the latter were from the black middle class.[65]

The consultants' recommendations, like those of the Federation, affirmed existing racial policies with the standard argument. Because blacks attached less stigma to illegitimacy, black unwed mothers needed fewer services than whites: "Social workers have indicated that for ideal planning, one-sixth of the non-white unwed mothers require sheltered care or other intensive assistance, and three-fifths of the white unwed mothers require sheltered care or other intensive assistance."[66] Moreover, only 16 percent of the city's black unwed mothers were delivered at the Talbert Home, even though it had the lowest fees.

Despite the negative evaluation, the Army kept Talbert open, probably because of what had happened when the Evangeline Booth Home in Cincinnati had closed. Cincinnati's black facility had become so obsolete that the state would no longer license it. However, when its patients were integrated into the white Army hospital, white doctors refused to refer patients there even though black women were in a separate ward. The consequent declining use by paying white clients created grave financial difficulties for the hospital and the Army.[67]

In 1960 the Federation withdrew its subsidy to the Talbert Home despite the fact that black women accounted for the great majority of Cleveland's illegitimate births.[68] Talbert closed, and its remaining patients were placed at Booth Hospital.

In the context of the emerging civil rights movement, Federation social workers had become sharply critical not only of the segregation at Talbert but of the racist practices of all private maternity homes. The

Army, after publicly endorsing the 1954 Supreme Court desegregation decision, in 1956 had urged "immediate plans to provide additional facilities to help to meet the urgent needs of Negro unmarried mothers and their babies." Cleveland's Booth Hospital had been integrated in 1959, but seven of the thirty-four Army homes, all in the South, were still for whites only.[69] Critics also argued that black women had higher illegitimacy rates not because unwed motherhood was acceptable behavior but because they had less access to birth control or abortion and fewer means of concealing illegitimate pregnancies and births. Further, marriage was less likely to bring respectability or economic security for a black woman, whether or not she was pregnant.[70] Accepting an illegitimate child into the family when there were no options did not imply acceptance of illegitimacy.[71]

Critics pointed to race-specific diagnoses and treatment of illegitimacy: a white, middle-class girl's pregnancy was explained in terms of psychological difficulties, but a black girl's might be explained in terms of a sexually permissive and disorganized culture.[72] Private agencies, therefore, geared their psychiatric services to white, middle-class women who could afford them. Black women, discouraged by agency fees, outright discrimination, or the insistence on adoption when there were no adoptive families for black children, were shunted off to public agencies. These agencies in turn acted punitively, compelling identification of the putative father before assistance was made available, providing inadequate casework, or applying a double racial standard.[73] What had evolved was a "two-track system of social services for unmarried parents and their children. For a few thousands of white girls there [was] shelter, medical care, and a therapeutic, helping approach. For the rest there [was] little or no service, or a punitive, demoralizing, disabling system of relief."[74]

By 1965 the national nonwhite illegitimacy rate was almost ten times that of whites (22.9 per thousand for whites; 215.8 per thousand for nonwhites), and it continued to rise. Of particular concern to policymakers were black teenagers aged fifteen to nineteen, whose illegitimacy rates rose from 76.5 per thousand to 90.8 per thousand from 1960 to 1970, again about ten times the rate of white teenagers.[75] Cleveland figures for 1969 compiled by the Federation revealed that half of all unwed pregnancies were to teenagers and that "the highest rates of out-of-wedlock pregnancies occur[red] in inner-city, low-income areas to non-white mothers."[76]

These women were not served by maternity homes. The percentage of black women in maternity homes administered by all private agencies across the country rose only slightly, from 12 percent in 1960 to 17.1 percent in 1969.[77] This was partly the result of deliberate desegregation of the institutions, but also the result of their diminished use by whites. In 1966 Army major Mary E. Verner, a nationally recognized expert on the care of unwed mothers and an administrator at Booth Hospital, conceded, "Providing services to the unmarried mother today is no longer the apparently simple matter it once seemed to be. . . . [O]nly about one in ten unmarried mothers receives maternity home service . . . and of these only one out of 50 is nonwhite."[78]

The Army replaced the Talbert Home with Booth-Talbert Clinic in the Hough neighborhood, not far from the besieged Florence Crittenton Home. After the 1966 riots destroyed the original facility, the Army relocated the clinic in the new Hough MultiPurpose Center. Verner described the neighborhood as having a "high rate of delinquency, financial dependency, and unemployment" and the clinic's clientele as having "a low self-image, lack of motivation and apathy. A majority of the girls are nonwhite, are between the ages of 11 and 19, are pregnant for the first time, and are considering keeping their babies."[79] Administered by a black officer, Brigadier Dorothy Purser, the clinic offered a wide variety of medical and social services on an outpatient basis until it closed in 1976.[80]

During the 1960s, these comprehensive services—including medical care, vocational and psychological counseling, casework, and compensatory programs such as high school equivalency classes—replaced maternity homes as the policymakers' response to unwed motherhood for two reasons. First, comprehensive services seemed to best meet the multiple needs of young, black unwed mothers. The Child Welfare League of America, for example, emphasized the "complex framework of health care, education, welfare, and legal resources" required by unmarried parents and established professional standards for these specialized services.[81]

Second, comprehensive services were much cheaper than maternity homes, especially because the public sector would now pay some of the bills. Lyndon Johnson's War on Poverty expanded local and federal funds for a wide variety of social welfare programs, some of which made it easier for a single mother to care for her child in her own home: expanded Aid to Families of Dependent Children, food stamps, rent supplements, and job training.[82] Medicaid might pay for the hospital delivery of an unwed mother although it would not pay for maternity home confinements.

In 1969 Cleveland maternity homes, now only about half-full, cared for only about 20 percent of unwed mothers. (See Table 5.2.)[83] Since 1913 the Federation had provided both financial and moral support for the proposition that the best treatment for pregnancy out-of-wedlock was

TABLE 5.2
MATERNITY HOME OCCUPANCY RATES, CLEVELAND, 1968–1970

	1970	1969	1968
Booth Memorial Hospital	56%	74%	81%
DePaul Maternity and Infant Home	60%	80%	91%
Florence Crittenton Home	60%	63%	79%

Source: Report of the Unmarried Parents Planning Committee, 1971, 13, FCP MS 3788, container 49, folder 1171, WRHS.

maternity homes. Now, having endorsed legalized birth control in 1966, the Federation, bowing to economic and demographic imperatives, endorsed comprehensive services and recommended further cuts in maternity home beds.[84]

CONCLUSION

The Army home for unwed mothers survived the Federation cuts. The tradition of lengthy sheltered care, which had once supported five maternity homes in Cleveland, did not.

During the 1970s maternity home use continued to decline across the country. Bed capacity in all Army maternity homes fell by 55 percent; some homes closed, and some were adapted for other uses such as midwives' training.[85] In Cleveland, far more unwed mothers were seen at the Army's outpatient clinics than were housed in the Army maternity home at Booth Hospital: in 1976 average occupancy of the home ranged between twelve and seventeen, although it could accommodate fifty to sixty women.[86] When DePaul closed its residential unit in 1983, the Army home became Cleveland's last residential facility for unwed mothers.

Despite rising costs and dwindling clientele, the Army maintained this home through the 1980s because of its century-long tradition of caring for unwed mothers and because of its continued opposition to abortion. The home's eighteen beds served only a tiny fraction of the city's unwed mothers: a total of 6,525 in 1989.[87] For all practical purposes, the private sector's historic solution to unwed motherhood—spiritual reclamation through long-term residential care—ended.

Awakened by the visible and militant civil rights movement of the 1960s, historians—like social workers—condemned separate and unequal opportunities for black Americans not just to make a decent living but to be cared for if they could not.[88] From this perspective, it is easy to conclude that the Army's accommodationism legitimized race-specific ideas and policies toward unwed motherhood and that its inability or unwillingness to challenge stereotypical ideas gave them added credibility. Certainly the Army's traditions of reclaiming fallen women—when applied to black women—exacerbated existing racial inequities in Cleveland, compounding the segregation, the underfunding, and the underprofessionalization of services.

Yet, of the private agencies that administered maternity homes, the Army tried hardest to serve black women. Its theology was colorblind even though its practices were not. The Army was forced to operate within a racist social welfare system. The failure of private child-care agencies to place black children for adoption and the reluctance of the Federation to expand or improve Talbert were beyond the Army's control and greatly compounded the difficulties of providing first-rate care for black women. The Army chose to maintain a separate and unequal home for black women because, as it had learned in Cincinnati, the option was no home at all.

The story of the Talbert Home is one of white Army officers, Federation administrators, and public officials making decisions about black women, but the fate of Talbert also illustrates the impact of black Americans on white policymakers. When the number of blacks to be served became too great, the practice of institutionalizing unwed mothers simply ended and the tradition of homes for fallen women, nurtured by post–Civil War female benevolence, energized by evangelicalism, and subsidized by great white fortunes, collapsed. Although maternity homes had been under fire by professional social workers for several decades, under duress because of their cost since the Depression, and threatened most recently by changing sexual norms and behavior, it was the changing faces of unwed mothers that finally brought to a close a century-long tradition of institutional care and spiritual reclamation.

Because of declining occupancy and escalating insurance costs at Booth Hospital, the Army sold the medical facility (but not the home for unwed mothers) in 1987 to Cleveland Metropolitan General Hospital. The former City Hospital, offspring of the old Infirmary, used this once-private hospital for its own maternity patients, many of them unmarried and black.

BACK TO THE POORHOUSE: CLEVELAND CITY/ METROPOLITAN GENERAL HOSPITAL, 1889–1990

City Hospital does not receive the more intelligent American girl who journeys from her native town to the city where she can remain in a safe retreat, but instead gathers largely the less experienced girls of foreign parentage who work up to the last minute in pregnant conditions and then in desperation turn to the city for help.

This comment in a 1914 City Hospital annual report is obviously about unwed mothers, the desperate and "less experienced" mothers delivered at this public facility. The "more intelligent," although probably no less desperate, women might have found shelter at one of the maternity homes or hospitals. But as these private facilities provided services to fewer and fewer dependent women, the public hospital, once the city poorhouse, again became Cleveland's largest single provider of medical services to unwed mothers.

Throughout the twentieth century responsibility for poor relief and health care shifted from the private to the public sectors, a change accelerated by the Great Depression. All relief programs were designed to penalize unmarried mothers, but Cleveland's City Hospital best illustrates the public intolerance for women who were not only sexually delinquent but poor and black.

As the story of Cleveland's unwed mothers returns to this public institution, all the familiar themes reappear. This hospital's poorhouse beginnings survived in its continued financial problems and the stigma attached to its use. Its care for unwed mothers, although publicly funded, retained the intrusive moralism of the private maternity homes. Its few social workers struggled to serve growing numbers of women. Initially the beneficiary of the hospitalization of medicine, City Hospital was the loser after the Depression, when the expense of hospital childbirth compelled once-charitable private maternity homes and hospitals to search for paying clients and to shift indigent patients to City. In the postwar years, growing numbers of black women, denied services by private child-placing agencies and segregated maternity homes, gave birth at this public hospital. And despite increased public spending since the mid-1960s, unwed mothers here received what Harry F. Dowling has called "under-care for the underprivileged." [1]

THE RELIEF OF MOTHERHOOD

Their ever-growing numbers in the work place did not prevent women from simultaneously joining the growing number of those in poverty in the late nineteenth and early twentieth centuries. In response, the public sector expanded its welfare role even though private agencies in Cleveland, as elsewhere, still bore considerable responsibility for dependent mothers and children.

Cleveland's female labor force mirrored national trends. In 1900, almost 30 percent of working women (14,246) were domestic servants; more than 10,000, however, worked in manufacturing, most probably in the clothing industry, and they represented almost 20 percent of the manufacturing work force.[2] A 1912 investigation by the Consumers' League of Ohio, the local chapter of the National Consumers' League, provided more detailed information: twice as many women (7,000) worked in garment-making as in the next largest job category, retail stores; 2,500 worked in "knit goods and weaving"; and 2,000 worked in laundries. Light manufacturing like cigar-making and the hardware industry also employed several thousand. (The Consumers' League did not concern itself with domestic servants.) The best-paid women earned nine dollars a week as milliners; the vast majority earned six dollars to seven dollars a week. All earned less than what the league considered adequate to support a single woman.[3] A working woman who could barely support herself certainly could not support herself and any offspring for whom she was the primary caretaker.

The solution to the growing destitution and dependence of women and children was mothers' pensions. The first innovation in public out-door relief since the seventeenth century, the state-funded pensions were initiated during the 1910s by a generation of policymakers, men and women, who revered motherhood above all female roles. The pensions also gathered wide support from some private charities, women's organizations, and settlement house workers, who wished to remedy the obvious failure of local governments to provide for women and children.[4] For example, in 1910, after Cleveland mayor Tom L. Johnson left office, women without husbands (widows and grass widows) and children remained the vast majority of the city's dependents. Since their forced exodus from the Infirmary, they received only outdoor relief—no cash, and only such groceries, shoes, and fuel as officials thought appropriate, always subject to cutbacks when times were bad or when public corruption was unearthed. Such skimpy and uncertain relief meant that mothers entered the work force and their children entered orphanages, for as welfare reformers well knew, many "orphans" had one or two living parents who were simply too poor to support their own children.

State mothers' pensions were small stipends to allow "suitable" mothers deprived of their "natural [male] breadwinners" to stay at home and raise their children. Pensions could thus be rationalized as payment for a mother's services. Echoing the recommendations of the 1909 White House Conference, a U.S. Children's Bureau pamphlet explained that mothers' pensions would preserve the child's "home life [,] . . . the highest and finest product of civilization." Since private orphanages were often subsidized with public monies, mothers' pensions had an added economic advantage: "It is actually cheaper in dollars and cents to maintain children in their own homes than to support them in institutions," the pamphlet pointed out.[5]

The intended beneficiaries were widows indigent through no fault of their own, not unwed or otherwise unfit mothers. Only three states specifically authorized aid to unmarried mothers, and according to a U.S. Children's Bureau official, the fitness of the mother became a crucial criterion in most states, with the result that unmarried mothers were seldom accepted.[6] In order to reassure taxpayers that recipients would be deserving and that no male breadwinner would escape his familial obligations, there was supposed to be careful screening of mothers. In Ohio an applicant's home was investigated to ensure that "the mother [was] the proper person morally, physically, and mentally to bring up the children."[7]

The pensions had greater political than economic significance: their recognition of public obligation for the welfare of mothers and children was more important than the amount of monies distributed or the number of recipients. Most states by 1921 had passed mothers' pension laws, but less than half of the counties in the United States actually distributed the stipends, and few women actually received them.[8] The pensions were too small to allow a woman, married or unmarried, to support herself and her children, and they probably became merely supplements to other forms of outdoor relief. In 1920 the Cleveland Hospital Council Survey judged mothers' pensions "a partial approach. . . . [T]hey are most inadequate . . . so inadequate that in numbers of cases, the pension must be supplemented by Associated Charities."[9]

In 1914 Cleveland's Associated Charities (AC), the descendant of the Cleveland charity organization society and a charter member of the Federation, had a bigger and better trained staff than either the mothers' pension program, administered by the juvenile court, or the city outdoor relief department. Although AC spent less on relief—including food, fuel, shoes, and the Wayfarers' lodge (a shelter for men)—than did the mothers' pensions program, the private agency spent almost as much as the city's outdoor relief department did and served three times as many clients.[10] Like other charity organization societies, AC was committed to stable family life as a way of preventing destitution and was by no means free of moralistic analyses of dependence: its 1921 annual report listed "character defect" among several causes of poverty.[11] The organization did not condone illegitimate pregnancy and doubtless made energetic efforts to keep unwed mothers from receiving aid. Nevertheless, most recipients of AC relief were husbandless mothers who described themselves as deserted, divorced, separated, and even unmarried.[12]

PUBLIC HOSPITALS

Like public outdoor relief, public hospitals expanded during the first three decades of this century. Yet, like private relief agencies, private hospitals, still charitable enterprises, also played a significant role in the medical care of indigents. Cleveland institutions illustrate these national trends.

From 1873 to 1889, the number of beds in public hospitals more than doubled, responding to rapid urbanization and the growing demand for medical services. Simultaneously, public "hospital units emerged from their poorhouse shells and evolved into general hospitals."[13] Cleveland City Hospital officially separated from the Infirmary in 1889.

City Hospital, adjoining the poorhouse buildings, shared the inadequacies of the old facility. Not until 1892 were the open drains for sewage in the basement of the Infirmary's main building replaced by flush toilets. The hospital staff was responsible for the inmates of the Infirmary, which in 1901 housed almost nine hundred persons, both indigent and insane.[14] Only in 1909, when the city moved the dependent populations of the Infirmary to Warrensville Township, did the hospital unit become a free-standing facility, still located on the site of the old poorhouse.

In the late nineteenth century, public hospitals struggled to medicalize their staffs and services. In 1891 a full staff of physicians and surgeons replaced the one doctor at Cleveland City Hospital who since 1878 had served both the hospital and the Infirmary patients for twelve hundred dollars a year. The hospital opened its own nursing school in 1897, intending that medical expertise should replace the "slip-shod methods derived from an entire lack of proper nursing education in an institution generally referred to as a poorhouse." Student nurses served without pay, and the senior nurse earned only twenty dollars a month. The nurses lived in the basement of the Infirmary until a nurses' home was provided in 1909.[15] In 1914 City Hospital affiliated with the Western Reserve University School of Medicine, which then became responsible for staff appointments.

Although public hospitals were, in theory, medical facilities, their patients' poverty and serious illnesses meant that these facilities could not abandon their original almshouse functions. They still provided medical care for the most indigent urban dwellers, the chronically ill, and the most contagious patients, including those with venereal diseases and tuberculosis. If patients could pay anything, Cleveland City Hospital sent them elsewhere.[16] In 1920 the hospital superintendent claimed that almost half of its patients "have no homes and must be kept in hospital until ready for work, the only alternative being the Warrensville Infirmary." Almost 30 percent of its patients remained hospitalized for more than two months.[17]

The public facilities could not take private patients whose fees might cover the rising expenses of the new medical technology and professional staff. Moreover, as with the old poorhouse, taxpayers were reluctant to help those who seemingly were too lazy to help themselves, and hospital administrators, like poorhouse superintendents, had to promise that no undeserving pauper would get free medical care. The resident house physician at City Hospital reported in 1911: "There is no justification or excuse in misplacing dispensation of charity. . . . [The irresponsible poor] will not prepare for a rainy day if someone else furnishes the umbrella."[18] The most important job of the hospital's first social worker was to ensure that patients were eligible for free care.

Public hospitals could spend far less per patient than private hospitals. Consequently, "most [hospitals] were deficient in several or many areas. In a few the buildings were . . . old, dilapidated, and poorly kept, the wards . . . crowded, unkempt, and disorganized, the drugs and supplies . . . scantily provided, the equipment . . . deficient, outmoded, and outworn, and the doctors, nurses, and attendants . . . overworked."[19] At City, nurses, house physicians, and staff frequently complained about low salaries, and in 1920, the Hospital Council Survey charged that City was so short of nurses that "the conditions amount to a serious neglect by the city of its solemn responsibility for the humane care of sick and helpless citizens."[20] Three smaller Cleveland hospitals had well-organized social service departments, but City Hospital had "a single worker, who without any definite policy or guidance, has endeavored to mitigate personal or other problems for those few patients she could reach among the thousands passing through that institution yearly."[21] In 1924 the hospital opened a social service department with one professionally trained caseworker.

In 1920 City's 785 beds made it by far the largest hospital in Cleveland.[22] Throughout the decade, City Hospital's occupancy rose steadily, and under an innovative director of public welfare, Dudley S. Blossom, the hospital added several new buildings.

Like other public hospitals and like the poorhouse from which it came, City Hospital also served unwed mothers. The hospital belonged to the Federation Conference on Illegitimacy and attempted to follow acceptable social work procedures. In 1914 the social worker complained about the sexual double standard, as rescue workers often had, but also about current Federation policies: "It seems a strange travesty of justice that we force the woman to keep her child, lest she make the same mistake again, nurse the baby, lest it not have a fair physical start in life; work for less than any minimum wage board ever dreamed of lest our institutions become overcrowded with nameless infants; while the man walks away unmolested." Nevertheless, the worker also believed the mothers were ignorant and irresponsible: "These girls have not made preparation for the coming child or considered its future destination or support. Rather, they have a vague idea that they can leave their babies in the hospital and return soon to their former position."[23] The hospital consequently had few qualms about attempting to discipline these patients.

City Hospital was not primarily a maternity facility. Hospital births were more likely to be at private hospitals or at the maternity homes. The largest of the private hospitals was Maternity Hospital, which opened in 1891 as the Maternity Home, a homeopathic teaching institution specializing in obstetrics, and whose first patients were indigent married and unmarried women. The facility had moral and religious as well as medical goals. The matron was required to "exert a religious influence over the inmates and hold some religious service each day."[24] In 1917 the institution, now an allopathic hospital, not a home, formally affiliated with the Western Reserve University School of Medicine and expanded its twelve maternity beds to sixty. The hospital also operated several out-patient maternity clinics on the city's East Side, and hospital physicians delivered many of the city's home births.[25] Difficult cases or women who could pay part of their medical fees were referred to Maternity Hospital for delivery.

Throughout the 1920s City Hospital and Maternity Hospital delivered about equal numbers of unwed mothers. However, the differences in treatment and cost indicated that City took the poorest women. Maternity Hospital provided prenatal care through its clinics; City Hospital did not. Maternity charged $4 to $8 a day for private patients; City charged $2.90 "if able to pay." Maternity provided a three-week stay after confinement; City, two weeks.[26]

In 1925 Maternity Hospital enhanced its prestige as a teaching facility and its respectability for middle-class patients when it moved to University Circle on Cleveland's far East Side and merged with Lakeside and Babies and Children's hospitals, creating a large, multiple-service university-affiliated hospital. In 1927 its social service department noted that a "greater number of unmarried mothers [had] been given prenatal care and instruction than in any previous years—53 white patients and 73 colored." The department referred a handful to maternity homes (nine to Talbert) and forty-five to City Hospital. These referrals help to explain why 47 percent of City's 801 deliveries in 1928 were of black women, even though the facility was far from East Side black neighborhoods. By the end of the decade, Maternity Hospital's clinics referred more and more women, probably the poorest patients and many probably black, to City Hospital.[27]

CLEVELAND CITY HOSPITAL, 1930–1959

The Great Depression revealed that neither private relief nor private hospitals could care for dependents during serious and prolonged economic disaster. Public agencies came to the rescue, and Cleveland City Hospital became a major maternity facility for unwed mothers.

The Depression came as no surprise to private agencies like Cleveland's Associated Charities. The city's heavy-industry economy had begun to sag and the agency's relief rolls had begun to rise in 1927 and 1928. But forewarned was not necessarily forearmed. By the winter of 1929, the organization, despite its professional staff and its long years of dealing with economic downturns, could not keep pace with the rapidly escalating number of unemployed and destitute people. An estimated forty-one thousand Cleveland workers were jobless in April 1930; by the following January the number was one hundred thousand. The city of Cleveland had stopped distributing outdoor relief altogether in 1922, leaving it to AC and two other private relief agencies. But as endowment incomes fell, annual gifts disappeared, and the Federation fund drives fell short, private agencies realized that only government had enough resources to provide relief and urged that the city again assume this responsibility. AC declared that its own resources were exhausted and that its debts totaled $600,000.[28] Local public efforts at relief were futile. A city public works program was ineffectual, as was a one-mill tax levied in 1932 by Cuyahoga County.[29]

Like other cities, Cleveland was rescued by the federal government. Public works projects became the major conduit for federal funds, but the assumption that men were primary breadwinners meant that there were few private or public works programs for women. From 1928 to 1934 the number of recipients of mothers' pensions in Cleveland had more than doubled, and by 1938, 42 percent of all the city's families on relief were headed by women.[30] The hardship of women and their children was acknowledged by the inclusion of Aid to Dependent Children in the 1935 Social Security Act. Like the mothers' pensions, ADC was inspired by the U.S. Children's Bureau and was supposed to allow mothers and children to remain together in their homes.

ADC broadened the categories of parents eligible for aid, but the stipulation that homes be "suitable" and the latitude given to states to establish eligibility meant that mothers of illegitimate children were less likely than married women to receive relief, or that the relief came attached with harsh conditions such as the requirement that the putative father be named. In 1938–39, only 5 percent of the children receiving ADC benefits were illegitimate.[31]

There are no Cleveland figures from this period indicating that unwed mothers got less ADC than other dependent women. But in correspondence with the Cleveland Federation, U.S. Children's Bureau official Maud Morlock expressed concern that unmarried mothers were being shortchanged. The Federation's response was not reassuring: funding was short, casework services were practically eliminated, and local staff used their own discretion in determining a mother's fitness.[32]

As private hospitals accelerated the change from charitable to for-pay facilities, public hospitals were compelled to provide more health care for growing numbers of medical indigents. In 1930 City Hospital admitted a record 11,066 patients, its occupancy rate was 95.1 percent, and its outpatient clinic recorded more than 50,000 visits. Fallling tax revenues exacerbated the hospital's perennial financial difficulties, and

TABLE 6.1
PLACE OF BIRTH OF ILLEGITIMATE CHILDREN,
CLEVELAND, 1931 AND 1935

	1931		1935	
Total	No.	%	No.	%
Place of birth	480	100.0	496	100.0
Maternity Homes	209	43.5	238	48
Booth	41	8.5	62	12.5
Crittenton	10	2.1	12	2.4
Talbert	27	5.6	36	7.2
Retreat	12	2.5	9	1.9
St. Ann's	119	24.8	119	23.9
Hospitals				
City Hospital	67	14	101	20.3
Maternity Hospital	59	12.3	29	5.8

Source: Bolt Report, Nov. 30, 1936, 4, FCP MS 3788, container 33, folder 829, WRHS.

hospital facilities and equipment deteriorated. An advisory committee investigated charges of political patronage and made administrative changes, but in 1938 six departments had to be closed for lack of funds.[33]

City Hospital's maternity ward soon felt the Depression's impact. In 1930 City delivered 8 percent of all hospital births, with only 6 percent of all maternity beds. The indigence of its patients is suggested by the hospital's puerperal death rate: 20.3 per 1,000 live births, more than six times that of Maternity Hospital and more than three times the city average of 6.6 per 1,000. The total number of births doubled from 1931 to 1935.[34]

City Hospital also delivered growing numbers of unwed mothers. (See Table 6.1.) In 1931 the hospital delivered 8 percent of all institutional births and 14 percent of all illegitimate institutional births; in 1935 it delivered 15 percent of all institutional births and 20 percent of all institutional illegitimate births. In 1935, 10 percent of all City Hospital births but only .048 percent of births in all institutions were illegitimate.[35]

The maternity homes continued to care for about 45 to 48 percent of unwed mothers during these years, so the increase in illegitimate births at City was probably the result of referrals from private hospitals, especially Maternity Hospital. In 1931 Maternity delivered 12.3 percent of institutional illegitimate births, less than 3 percent of the women delivered at the private facility. In 1935 it delivered only 5.8 percent of institutional illegitimate births, about .015 percent of its total deliveries. That

114

year, 69 percent of unwed mothers for whom City had any social service records had been referred by Maternity.[36] Those referrals probably were black and probably were the most indigent of Maternity Hospital's outpatient clients.

Their poverty is illustrated in a comparison with other maternity facilities. In 1935 City Hospital had the highest infant and maternal mortality rates, the highest rate of venereal patients, the highest rate of unemployed patients, and the largest number of unwed mothers known to the public relief agency. City also had the highest proportion of black women: 55 percent of its unwed mothers whose case files were examined by the Federation were black.[37]

The number of births at City Hospital dropped during World War II, probably because of a wartime personnel shortage at the hospital and war-induced prosperity, which allowed women to make the more attractive choice of birth at a private facility.[38] In the immediate postwar years, both numbers of births and shares of births at City Hospital rose again.[39] Probably many were to black women because private hospitals did not welcome either black patients or black doctors.

As had public hospitals elsewhere, City Hospital had integrated its medical staff earlier than private facilities. In 1928 City had appointed a black doctor to its outpatient staff, and in 1930, as the result of political pressure from black councilmen, it admitted three black nurses to its teaching program. The next year the hospital hired a black intern with degrees from Dartmouth and Harvard Medical School, Frederick Douglas Stubbs, the first black to receive an appointment at a major teaching institution. Black staff obviously attracted black patients.[40]

A 1948 Federation study found that City had a higher-than-average proportion of black unwed patients and that its social service department was "obviously unable to serve all its unmarried mothers." Because of the lack of adoptive homes for black children, the hospital social workers were unable to close cases as rapidly as the private facilities. Although the maternity homes turned down more cases than they took, City Hospital had to take almost all those who applied.[41] The social service department conceded that "for a number of months the department did not attempt to know the unmarried pregnant patient."[42]

During the next decade, as the baby boom peaked, private maternity homes and hospitals filled their beds with paying patients. Of particular significance to City Hospital, so did Mary B. Talbert Home, still the only facility that admitted significant numbers of black unwed mothers. Accordingly, in 1952 the City Hospital annual report noted: "In the past two years our service to obstetrical patients has increased nearly one hundred percent. . . . There is every reason to believe that the restriction of staff and charity beds by other hospitals in the community has created additional demands on City to accept an increasing responsibility for indigent obstetrical patients." Although Maternity Hospital was not mentioned by name, it had discontinued its home delivery service, which had been used primarily by blacks, in 1951. According to the 1952 Salvation Army study, most of the "lower and lower middle income non-white maternity patients are admitted to City Hospital."[43]

During the 1950s City Hospital's financial woes were worsened by the accelerating flight of middle-class, white taxpayers to the suburbs. In 1958, in an effort to broaden the hospital's revenue base, Cleveland turned over to Cuyahoga County the administration of the medical facility that the city had maintained for more than a century. City Hospital then became Cleveland Metropolitan General Hospital (CMGH).

Almost simultaneously, the hospital released figures that revealed the growing inability or unwillingness of private homes and hospitals to serve black unwed mothers. In slightly more than a year during 1957–58, the hospital delivered "940 illegitimate births to single women; 665 to separated women; 150 [women] were divorced and 63 widowed. Of the total 1,818, 168 patients were white and 1,650 [90 percent] were Negro." In words that echoed City's 1914 annual report, the hospital social service department expressed its concern: "Most of the patients are admitted to the hospital in labor with little if any prenatal care. . . . Many others are without any exhibited interest from parents, relatives, or friends. . . . Physicians are concerned about the lack of postnatal follow-up as well as prenatal care." The department was clearly not able to provide casework and had contact in one six-month period with only 170 cases out of 675.[44] The Talbert Home's closing in 1960 worsened the situation.

POORHOUSE ENDINGS, 1960–1980

Public spending on relief and health care continued to rise, but at Cleveland's public hospital, which became the major provider of services for unmarried mothers, those services remained inadequate.

The first significant expansion of the New Deal welfare state began in the early 1960s. In the wake of Michael Harrington's publicity about "the other America," and in the midst of the growing militance of the civil rights movement, federal spending on social welfare rose rapidly, especially under the auspices of Lyndon Johnson's War on Poverty. The fastest growing program was ADC, now Aid to Families of Dependent Children, as residency requirements were relaxed and families with unemployed fathers were included. This outdoor relief program, designed in the 1910s to support a modest number of "worthy" widows deprived of their male breadwinners, came in the 1960s to serve huge numbers of widowed, deserted, or never-married women, many of them black. Recipients of AFDC nearly doubled from 3.1 million in 1960 to 6.1 million in 1969, even though the suitable home requirement remained.[45] In Cleveland the number of people on AFDC increased fourfold from 1957 to 1967.[46]

In 1966 the U.S. Commission on Civil Rights found that AFDC payments in Ohio were "grossly inadequate to provide support and care requisite for health and decency," a judgment seconded by the panel on welfare appointed by Mayor Carl B. Stokes.[47] Despite these realities, taxpayers and politicians responded to AFDC as they had to providing public shelter for unwed mothers in the 1880s—with hostile attempts to provide less service for less money. In 1967 welfare amendments restricted AFDC benefits and added a mandatory work-training program as an incentive.[48]

The delivery of health care services at CMGH dramatized this public unwillingness to provide for dependent and husbandless women. CMGH's maternity services were so deficient that they were not accredited by the state of Ohio until 1963. The hospital's own 1962 annual report singled out the department of obstetrics as one of "the most inadequate areas [in the hospital]. Conditions in the labor and delivery suite, built for 1800 deliveries but now taking care of over 3600, are probably the most distressing at [CMGH]. . . . [E]very year, women labor in beds in corridors. There is constant traffic of maternity patients past the cystoscopy rooms, which is in violation of . . . accreditation requirements. . . . The premature nursery is very poor, and the other nurseries are inadequate."[49]

The commission also emphasized the negative impact of the city's segregated residential patterns on health care, pointing out that in 1963 the fetal and infant death rates for nonwhites in Cleveland were 50 percent higher than for whites, at least partly due to the inaccessibility of prenatal care for black women: "In 1963, CMGH delivered more Negro babies than any of the other hospitals serving low-income families, although they [were] close to Cleveland's ghetto areas." Black women, most of them living on the East Side, had to travel miles to get prenatal care at CMGH.[50]

Also in 1963, the only year for which these data are available, CMGH was the largest single medical care-giver to black unwed mothers. (See Table 6.2.) The hospital delivered only 10 percent of all births in Cuyahoga County but 36 percent of all black births and 47 percent of

TABLE 6.2
RESIDENT BIRTH STATISTICS
ACCORDING TO HOSPITAL OR INSTITUTION, CLEVELAND, 1963

Hospital	Births			
	Total	White	Non-white	Illegitimate
MacDonald House	3544	1780	1764	258
Cleveland Metropolitan				
General Hospital	3435	764	2671	958
Booth Memorial	768	600	168	162
DePaul Infant and				
Maternity Home	1810	1584	226	80

Source: City of Cleveland, Department of Health and Public Welfare, *Vital Statistics, 1963* (Cleveland, 1963).

all illegitimate births—958 babies. Twenty-seven percent of all births at CMGH were illegitimate. In contrast, MacDonald House (the former Maternity Hospital) delivered slightly more than 10 percent of all births, 24 percent of all black births, and only 12 percent of illegitimate births—258 babies. DePaul Infant and Maternity Home delivered 80 unwed mothers, and Booth Hospital delivered 162, the vast majority of whom were white.[51]

In 1965 CMGH became the primary site for the federal Maternity and Infant Care Project, which provided comprehensive services and medical care to high-risk mothers—teenagers or those in poverty. The descendant of the 1921 Sheppard-Towner Act, the project was funded initially by the U.S. Children's Bureau and carried on one of the bureau's chief missions—to lower maternal and infant mortality.[52] The project funded pre- and postnatal health care at three clinics in East Side neighborhoods and at the public hospital itself. Other hospitals took project clients, but most were delivered at CMGH. Medicaid, newly established, helped to bear the expense.

Although there were social workers on the staff, the project was almost exclusively a medical service and referred clients to other public and private agencies for casework, primarily adoptive services, which were useful to very few mothers. In 1969 there were only 660 adoptions of the 3,884 out-of-wedlock children born in Cuyahoga County.[53] Although by 1969 the project cared for more unwed mothers than did the Booth Hospital, DePaul Infant and Maternity Home, and the Florence Crittenton Home combined, it still delivered only 836 of the city's 3,019 illegitimate births in that year.[54] The project expanded its outpatient programs during the 1970s and established several new clinics, most on the city's predominantly black East Side. The number of clients rose steadily, but public subsidies did not keep pace.[55]

Medicaid initially encouraged private hospitals to take indigent maternity cases, probably accounting for the drop in births at CMGH in the late 1960s. A comparison of comparable private and public hospitals in Boston in 1967–68 suggests that private hospitals provided unwed mothers with better care.[56] As hospital costs escalated nationally and Ohio's share of Medicaid payments stalled, Cleveland's private hospitals became less enthusiastic about treating the medically indigent. Like the Maternity and Infant Care Project, CMGH had to provide expanded services without commensurately increased funds. By 1972 CMGH was the state's largest Medicaid facility.[57] Beginning in the mid-1970s, "the hospital increased its out-patient clinics as a result of cutbacks in indigent care in other hospitals."[58] Throughout the decade, the financially straitened hospital restructured. It became a complex of county health services and facilities, including a chronically ill center, which had once been the tuberculosis unit, a large East Side clinic, and a hospital for the chronically crippled.

CONCLUSION

As at the beginning of the century, social welfare strategies were in flux in the late 1980s. Again, unwed mothers bore the brunt of financial and policy changes.

As deindustrialization and middle-class flight continued, Cleveland's population, disproportionately black and disproportionately female, fell upon harder and harder times. By 1980, one-third of Cleveland's children lived in poverty, and the number continued to climb. In 1981 Cleveland had the second-highest infant mortality rate and the highest black infant mortality rate of any major city.[59]

Simultaneously, federal policies shifted from the War on Poverty to the war on welfare, and funding for public assistance was slashed.[60] Although AFDC constituted only a very small proportion of monies spent on public assistance and social insurance programs, it was a special target of the Reagan administration's Omnibus Budget Reconciliation Act of 1981 because the public associated the program with black, illegitimately pregnant women.[61] A 1987 study done for the Cuyahoga County Department of Human Services (formerly the county welfare department) found that the number of Ohio children who received AFDC rose 30 percent from 1979 to 1986, "with smaller benefits in 1986 than in 1979."[62]

The new federal policies also boded ill for public hospitals and medical services. In 1980 CMGH's annual report boasted that the hospital had not changed its "long-standing commitment to accept patients on the basis of their need for medical care . . . regardless of their financial ability. It continued to be the only hospital in this area to have an open-door admissions policy. . . . It is the leading provider for indigent care locally." [63] Two years later, the annual report worried about "the nation's commitment to quality medical care to its elderly and poor" as the federal government, in an effort to "disengage itself" from providing health care, changed its rates of payment and the state of Ohio threatened further cuts in its share of Medicaid.[64] The Maternity and Infant Project received proportionately less funding in 1987 than it had in 1975.[65]

CMGH became the largest single provider of institutional medical care for unwed mothers: in 1986, 2,419 unmarried women, 1,572 of them nonwhite, gave birth at the former poorhouse.[66] Private services for unwed mothers were almost nonexistent. The Florence Crittenton Home did not take unwed mothers after 1970, and the DePaul facility had closed in 1983. Only the eighteen beds at the Army's Booth Home remained. In 1987 CMGH bought the Booth Memorial Hospital facility, once the Salvation Army Rescue, to complement its East Side outpatient clinic and the Maternity and Infant Project clinics. In 1988 CMGH won an award from the American Hospital Association for its community outreach programs, including its best known, the Maternity and Infant Project.

Yet the future of the old poorhouse and the largest remaining home for unwed mothers remained in doubt. Medicaid cuts and pressures from private health insurance companies continued to make health care for the indigent more costly, and by 1986 CMGH had the largest uncompensated care spending of Cleveland hospitals. Consequently, in 1988 hospital officials considered leasing all or part of the hospital to a for-profit corporation, a trend that was apparent in other cities as well.[67] The contemplated privatization was further evidence of the historic public distaste for providing health care for the poor. As Harry F. Dowling has noted, and as this local history has shown, "In good times [voluntary hospitals] have held out a hand to the poor; during hard times, when their help was needed the most, they have tended to close their doors to those who could not pay." [68]

In 1990, on the Scranton Road site of the old Infirmary, home to forty inmates in 1855, stood a $40 million, twelve-story building with 558 beds, the central component in a complex of public health facilities now called MetroHealth Services. The public facility was also a significant teaching facility affiliated with a dozen universities and medical schools. Its Department of Obstetrics and Gynecology alone included twelve M.D.s and four Ph.D.s. This multimillion-dollar building symbolized Cleveland's growth from a mid-nineteenth-century village to a sprawling postindustrial metropolis.

More important, the hospital symbolized the expanded public commitment to the health and welfare of the American people, the central chapter in American social welfare history. The public hospital has provided care for those about whom the public has cared least—not only the poor, but blacks, females, and the sexually delinquent. It has provided that care by overcoming great difficulties: the least staff, the least adequate facilities, the least funding. Cleveland's public hospital is a reminder that the government has been less concerned about the welfare of some of its citizens than about others. As the country apparently moved away from health and relief provisions created by the New Deal and the War on Poverty, and as public officials discussed returning to the private sector the responsibilities that it had carried during the nineteenth century—and dropped in the 1930s—this home for unwed mothers was a reminder also of the impermanence of the welfare state that we have taken for granted for the last half-century.

LAST AND LEAST

May, 1976. 23-year-old—living on the East Side—7 months pregnant. . . .
Trying to get on welfare, but they advised her [they] must know where
[alleged father] is. [DePaul Family Services] directed her to individual
at the County Welfare Department and indicated to her if [she]
received no satisfaction to come back.

This memo records a telephone response to an advertisement placed by
DePaul Family Services in 1976 as the agency initiated a last-ditch campaign to recruit clientele. There is a dreary timelessness about the plight
of this woman soon to give birth out-of-wedlock. Like the unwed mother
in the 1893 sketch that opens this study, she turned to both public and
private agencies and probably got little help from either.

Nevertheless, the memo illustrates the usefulness of local history. In
it we catch glimpses of people who otherwise remain statistics: this 23-
year-old East Side woman; the "Maggies" seduced and abandoned in the
Infirmary; the newcomers to the city who fell victim to its vices; the
Protestant and Catholic girls who feared that their souls were lost because their bodies had been exploited; the working-class mothers who
toiled as domestic servants to keep their illegitimate infants with them;
the middle-class mothers who struggled to give their children up for
adoption; the black women who rode the bus four miles to get to City
Hospital; the teenagers who arrived there, eight months pregnant and
without husbands, families, or funds.

Local history also reveals the practical and concrete meanings of
trends that remain abstractions at the national level. "Deinstitutionaliza-
tion" meant the removal of women and children from the Infirmary;
"professionalization" of staff at the Florence Crittenton Home meant
further curtailment of services to a dozen women and their infants;
"evangelicalism" meant providing shelter and medical care for indigent

women; and "separate and unequal" in a Northern city meant inadequate health care in a private or public facility.

Cleveland history also allows us to trace the development of national social welfare policy. As we follow unwed mothers from the Infirmary in 1855 to MetroHealth Services in 1990, we can see that great changes have occurred in the care of all dependent populations, male and female, old and young, black and white. In the mid-nineteenth century, institutionalization in the Infirmary replaced the earlier tradition of outdoor relief. Outdoor relief in the form of state mothers' pensions became again a preference of welfare reformers in the Progressive period and an economic imperative during the Great Depression, when Aid to Dependent Children and social insurance programs replaced costly residential care. As the services for dependent persons specialized in the late nineteenth century, the all-purpose Infirmary was replaced by City Hospital and an old-age home; amateur and volunteer caretakers were replaced by trained caseworkers and medical professionals at maternity homes and hospitals.

Perhaps most important has been the shift in financial responsibility for those who could not take care of themselves. During the nineteenth century, the obligation was borne by both the public and private agencies. During the Depression, however, Cleveland's private institutions, including maternity hospitals and to a lesser degree maternity homes, gave up their significant welfare role to the public sector, with public hospitals like Cleveland's again picking up the slack. Today responsibility may be shifting again in response to political and budget priorities.

During this same century and a half, the definition of pregnancy out-of-wedlock as personal sin and community expense has meant that the public sector provided least and last for unwed mothers. The chief means of sustaining the indigent has been public outdoor relief, distributed by the local government at the back door of the Infirmary in the mid-nineteenth century and by the Cuyahoga County Department of Human Services today. Although they may not have succeeded, public agencies tried to distinguish which mothers were suitable—that is, married—so that they could provide less for those who were not. The public sector has funded institutional care for the elderly, children, the insane, and the delinquent, but not for most unwed mothers since their removal from the poorhouse. Outdoor relief, mothers' pensions, and ADC/AFDC have been cheaper ways of caring for women and their children than poorhouses or orphanages.

The private sector also has provided last and least. Within the maternity homes, care of unwed mothers changed with extraordinary slowness. Closely tied to established churches, the homes never lost their nine-

teenth-century evangelical mission or their primary goal of spiritual reclamation, and remained committed to lengthy institutionalization long
after it ceased to be preferred treatment for other dependent groups.
Staffed and directed by female religious, maternity homes only reluctantly participated in the secularization of social welfare practice. Despite
the efforts of the Cleveland Federation, much of the institutional care of
unwed mothers and their children in maternity homes was left to volunteers, partly because of the homes' origins in voluntarism, partly because
volunteers were cheaper than professionals, and partly because illegitimate pregnancy created a low-status clientele that did not interest the
social work profession. When the maternity homes built new facilities or
moved to affluent suburbs to cultivate a paying clientele, as did St. Ann's
and Booth Memorial hospitals, unwed mothers stayed behind in the central city, housed in the older buildings. When the care of unwed mothers
became too expensive, as in the 1930s and 1960s, the private institutions
abandoned their historic commitment to these indigent women, returning them to the underfunded public facility.

Until the last decade, social welfare history has been the story of
progress: growing public and private responsibility for social welfare,
better services, and more generous benefits for dependent Americans.
Such progress has never been a sure thing for women pregnant out-of-
wedlock, for whom the uncertainties and inequities of social policy in the
late 1980s have been the rule, not the exception.

In the final analysis, the care of those who cannot care for themselves
is the creation of the larger American society: a society that allocates
opportunities to succeed on the basis of class, race, and gender and then
punishes those who fail. The class differences endemic to American life
are apparent here. Although premarital or extramarital sexual activity
has never been restricted to working-class Americans, poor women got
pregnant most often. With less access to contraceptives or abortion, without the economic resources to avoid sexual exploitation, without family
to shelter them, these women ended up in the Infirmary or City Hospital
or in the private maternity homes. Further, the evidence suggests that
those women who received help from private or public agencies were the
"working poor," the domestic servants of yesterday and today. They were
not even the poorest of the poor, the underclass, who probably gave
birth, at least until the 1960s, unnoticed, unaided, and uncounted even
by public officials and institutions.

The disabilities of poverty have been compounded by pervasive racism. The sexual deviance of black women was taken for granted by white
social workers who assumed that it was in turn taken for granted by
blacks. Unequal recipients of separate private care—as at Mary B. Tal-

bert—black women were the most quickly consigned to inadequate public facilities and services in the postwar period. When class, race, and gender have combined, when moral and racial segregation have reinforced one another—as in the case of unwed mothers at the public hospital—the care of these women has been precarious at best, terrible at worst.

The disadvantages of gender, the powerlessness of women, appear clearly in this story. Women do not get pregnant by themselves, but their lack of economic and political resources has meant that male sexual partners could abandon them with impunity. When women consequently became dependent on public or private aid, policymakers, like sexual partners, could afford to ignore them. Admittedly, unwed mothers have sometimes been more than victims. Often risking the scorn of family and community by giving birth out-of-wedlock, they most often supported their children alone. When they asked to be admitted to homes and hospitals, or escaped them, unwed mothers acted independently to direct their own lives. But most expressions of power were small, private, and sometimes self-destructive: another illegitimate pregnancy, for example. Hardly more powerful were the female caretakers: Catholic nuns, Protestant churchwomen, "Hallelujah females," professional social workers and nurses, and pious volunteers. Mostly, they were modest and self-effacing, doing unrewarded women's work. If they had power, it was only over other, even less powerful women.

Most important, women pregnant out-of-wedlock have been living proof of the American belief that dependence is caused by sin, by personal and moral failure—in this case, the failure to conform to cultural definitions of womanhood that require that women choose celibacy or marriage. Regardless of time period, a woman pregnant out-of-wedlock has been the most easily disciplined of dependent populations. The rigid rules, the religious indoctrination, and the regimen of pre–World War II maternity homes illustrate in vivid and exaggerated form social policymakers' desire to control behavior. Unwed mothers have been the most resented and most politically vulnerable recipients of public assistance. Their financial aid has been the most easily cut, whether politicians were looking for scapegoats in the 1880s or posing as welfare reformers in the 1980s. Predictably, Charles Murray, conservative apologist for a new "poorhouse," uses an unwed mother and her boyfriend as symbols of the waste, corruption, and moral decay of the welfare system.[1]

Murray also reminds us that the social policies and practices of the last century and a half did not solve the problems of unwed motherhood. When Heather Kurent, a worker on the Federation Task Force on Teenage Pregnancy, was asked by a newspaper reporter what should be done about unwed mothers, she responded, "Everything." She meant an end to poverty, racial prejudice, gender inequities, the commercialization of human sexuality, the public's failure to provide sex education, and probably more.

The Cleveland private and public institutions described here never intended to do "everything." At best, they hoped to prevent a reoccurrence of illegitimate pregnancy by encouraging or forcing a woman to conform to gendered definitions of sexual respectability. These institutions did not challenge that definition, and only the late-nineteenth-century rescue homes raised questions about male sexual behavior and dominance—and then only halfheartedly. Neither poorhouses, private maternity homes, nor hospitals sought to redistribute economic resources or political power. The men who controlled the institutions had no desire to do so; the women who administered them had no power to. Social policy that seeks to change unwed mothers or other dependent groups without changing the larger society must fail.

Today, however, when politicians and the American public display at best apathy and at worst hostility toward the poor and dependent, it is less easy than it was twenty years ago to find fault with Cleveland institutions for unwed mothers. Today, even conceding the institutions' cautious meliorism, their attempts at social control, and their racism, it seems better to do good than to do nothing; better to provide shelter than to leave a woman and her children homeless; better to assume that a woman will sin no more than to assume that she deserves to remain poor.

◆ Notes ◆

Introduction

1. Mimi Abramowitz has referred to these beliefs as the "family ethic," the belief that a woman's "primary place is marriage and home," that women are "guardians of family and community morality, expected . . . to remain pious and chaste and to tame male sexuality . . . weak and in need of male protection and control." In *Regulating the Lives of Women: Social Welfare Policy from Colonial Times to the Present* (Boston: South End Press, 1988), 2–3, and "The Family Ethic: The Female Pauper and Public Aid, Pre-1900," *Social Service Review* 59 (March 1985): 121–35. See also Linda Gordon, ed., *Women, the State, and Welfare* (Madison: University of Wisconsin Press, 1990), especially Gordon's essay, "The New Feminist Scholarship on the Welfare State," 9–35, and Dorothy C. Miller, *Women and Social Welfare: A Feminist Analysis* (New York: Praeger, 1990), 2–23.

2. Several historians have noted the use of social welfare institutions by dependent populations. See Michael B. Katz, *In the Shadow of the Poorhouse: A Social History of Welfare in America* (New York: Basic Books, 1986); Barbara M. Brenzel, *Daughers of the State: A Social Portrait of the First Reform School for Girls in North America, 1865–1905* (Cambridge: MIT Press, 1983); Peggy Pascoe, *Relations of Rescue: The Search for Female Moral Authority in the American West, 1874–1939* (New York: Oxford University Press, 1990).

3. *Cleveland Plain Dealer*, Sept. 24, 1990, 4A.

4. Marian Wright Edelman, *Families in Peril: An Agenda for Social Change* (Cambridge: Harvard University Press, 1987), 52–53.

5. Charles Murray, *Losing Ground: American Social Policy, 1950–1980* (New York: Basic Books, 1984), and in *Commentary*, May 1985, quoted in Jonathan Kozol, *Rachel and Her Children: Homeless Families in America* (New York: Ballantine, 1988), 236.

6. *Cleveland Plain Dealer*, June 23, 1990, 12A; *New York Times*, May 11, 1990, 1, 22; July 23, 1, 25. These numbers are not precise: the June 23 *New York Times* article says an estimated 2 million women became pregnant out-of-wedlock in 1990, but according to the *Cleveland Plain Dealer*, June 15, 1991, 1, 18, the latest statistics, from 1988, say 1,005,299 babies were born out-of wedlock that year.

7. U.S. Government Printing Office, *Children Under Institutional Care, 1923* (Washington, D.C.: U.S. GPO, 1927), 14.

8. On prostitutes, see, for example, Barbara Berg, *The Remembered Gate: Origins of American Feminism; The Woman and the City, 1800–1860* (New York: Oxford University Press, 1978); Carroll Smith-Rosenberg, *Religion and the Rise of the American City: The New York City Mission Movement, 1812–1870* (Ithaca: Cornell University Press, 1971); Ruth Rosen, *The Lost Sisterhood: Prostitution in America, 1900–1918* (Baltimore: Johns Hopkins University Press, 1982); Mark Thomas Connelly, *The Response to Prostitution in the Progressive Era* (Chapel Hill: University of North Carolina Press, 1980); Steven Ruggles, "Fallen Women: The Inmates of the Magdalen Asylum of Philadelphia, 1836–1908," *Journal of Social History* 16 (Summer 1983): 107–35.

9. Susan Tiffin, *In Whose Best Interest? Child Welfare Reform in the Progressive Era* (Westport, CT: Greenwood Press, 1982), 168. Historical treatments of illegitimacy include Maris A. Vinovskis, *An "Epidemic" of Adolescent Pregnancy* (New York: Oxford University Press, 1988), and Peter Laslett et al., eds., *Bastardy and Its Comparative History* (Cambridge: Harvard University Press, 1980).

10. City of Cleveland, Department of Public Health and Welfare, *Annual Report, 1925* (Cleveland: DPHW, 1925), 18; Daniel Scott Smith, "The Long Cycle in American Illegitimacy and Prenuptial Bastardy," in Laslett et al., *Bastardy and Its Comparative History*, 364.

11. Michael B. Katz, *The Undeserving Poor: From the War on Poverty to the War on Welfare* (New York: Pantheon, 1989), 68–69, and Fred Block et al., *The Mean Season: The Attack on the Welfare State* (New York: Pantheon, 1987), 48, describe the 1980s attack on AFDC. On the differential treatment of unmarried women by the public sector, see Abramowitz, *Regulating the Lives of Women*, 2–3, and "The Family Ethic"; Gordon, "The New Feminist Scholarship," 9–35; Ruth Sidel, *Women and Children Last: The Plight of Poor Women in Affluent America* (New York, Penguin, 1986). Linda Gordon, *Heroes of Their Own Lives: The Politics and History of Family Violence. Boston, 1880–1960* (New York: Viking Press, 1988), 82–89, points out that single mothers had the hardest time meeting contemporary definitions of womanhood and consequently were penalized by family agencies. Leslie Reagan found that unwed mothers received the roughest treatment by police in Chicago when suspected of having had illegal abortions. See "'About to Meet Her Maker': Women, Doctors, Dying Declarations, and the State's Investigation of Abortion, Chicago, 1867–1940," *Journal of American History* 77 (March 1991): 1254.

12. Studies of private agencies for unwed mothers include Annette K. Baxter and Barbara Welter, *Inwood House: One Hundred and Fifty Years of Service to Women* (New York: Inwood House, 1980); Michael W. Sedlak, "Youth Policy and Young Women, 1870–1972," *Social Service Review* 56 (September 1982): 448–64; Donnell M. Pappenfort et al., eds., *A Census of Children's Residential Institutions in the United States, Puerto Rico, and the Virgin Islands*, vol. 6 (Chicago: Aldine, 1970); and Marian J. Morton, "Fallen Women, Federated Charities, and Maternity Homes, 1913–1973," *Social Service Review* 62 (March 1988): 61–82, "'Go and Sin No More': Maternity Homes in Cleveland, 1869–

1936," *Ohio History* 93 (Fall 1984): 117–46; "Seduced and Abandoned in an American City: Cleveland and Its Fallen Women, 1869–1936," *Journal of Urban History* 11 (August 1985): 443–69. Pascoe in *Relations of Rescue* describes the complex relationships between white Protestant churchwomen and Asian and Indian women in other institutions, but the Colorado Cottage Home for unwed mothers had only white inmates. Full-length studies of the National Florence Crittenton Mission are Martha Morrison Dore, "Organizational Response to Environmental Change: A Case History Study of the National Florence Crittenton Mission," Ph.D. dissertation, University of Chicago, 1986; Katherine G. Aiken, "The National Florence Crittenton Mission, 1883–1925: A Case Study in Progressive Reform," Ph.D. dissertation, Washington State University, 1980. On the decline of female traditions of benevolence, see the influential article by Estelle B. Freedman, "Separatism as Strategy: Female Institution Building and American Feminism, 1870–1930," *Feminist Studies* 5 (Fall 1979): 512–29; Pascoe, *Relations of Rescue;* Joan Jacobs Brumberg, "'Ruined Girls': Changing Community Responses to Illegitimacy in Upstate New York, 1890–1920," *Journal of Social History* (Winter 1984): 246–72; Regina G. Kunzel, "The Professionalization of Benevolence: Evangelicals and Social Workers in the Florence Crittenton Homes, 1915–1945," *Journal of Social History* 22 (Fall 1988): 26; Lori D. Ginzberg, *Women and the Work of Benevolence: Morality, Politics, and Class in the Nineteenth-Century United States* (New Haven: Yale University Press, 1990), 174–213.

13. Examples include Raymond Mohl, *Poverty in New York, 1783–1825* (New York: Oxford University Press, 1971); Katz, *In the Shadow*, which focuses on New York poorhouses; Brenzel, *Daughters of the State*; Smith-Rosenberg, *Religion and the Rise of the American City*; Priscilla Ferguson Clement, *Welfare and the Poor in the Nineteenth-Century City, Philadelphia, 1800–1854* (London: Associated University Presses, 1985).

14. Zane L. Miller, *The Urbanization of Modern America: A Brief History* (New York: Harcourt Brace Jovanovich, 1973), 25; Carol Poh Miller and Robert Wheeler, *Cleveland: A Concise History, 1796–1990* (Bloomington: Indiana University Press, 1990), 53. See also David D. Van Tassel and John J. Grabowski, eds., *The Encyclopedia of Cleveland History* (Bloomington: University of Indiana Press, 1987), xvii–lv.

15. Miller and Wheeler, *Cleveland*, 78, 100, 121.

16. Miller and Wheeler, *Cleveland*, 131, 134, 136.

17. Claudia J. Coulton et al., "An Analysis of Poverty and Related Conditions in Cleveland Area Neighborhoods" (Cleveland: Case Western Reserve University, Center for Urban Poverty and Social Change, Mandel School of Applied Social Sciences, January 1990), 15; Miller and Wheeler, *Cleveland*, 168.

18. This was the finding of the U.S. Commission on Civil Rights after a 1963 visit to Cleveland. Herman D. Stein, ed., *The Crisis in Welfare in Cleveland: Report of the Mayor's Commission* (Cleveland: Case Western Reserve University Press, 1969), 65.

19. City of Cleveland, *Annual Report, 1857* (Cleveland: 1857), 41–42; Salvation Army Rescue Home, *Diamonds in the Rough: Annual Report, Salvation Army Rescue Work in Cleveland, 1905*, 4, Western Reserve Historical Society (hereafter WRHS). Federation for Community Planning, Conference on Illegitimacy, Nov. 30, 1936, 12–13, MS 3788, container 33, folder 829, WRHS. (Hereafter this collection will be FCP MS 3788.)

20. Cleveland Workhouse and House of Refuge and Correction, MS 3681, microfilm reels 1, 2, WRHS; City of Cleveland, Department of Public Health and Welfare, *Annual Report, 1905* (Cleveland: DPHW, 1905), 21.

21. Board of Managers minutes, Florence Crittenton Services, MS 3910, container 1, folder 11, and Board of Trustees minutes, Jan. 22, 1968, container 1, folder 9, WRHS; letter, Oct. 31, 1903, from Bishop Ignatius F. Horstman, Horstman folder 11, Cleveland Catholic Diocesan Archives (hereafter CCDA).

22. Correspondence, Nov. 19, 1937, FCP MS 3788, container 30, folder 742, WRHS.

23. Committee on Unmarried Mothers, Oct. 19 and Nov. 30, 1936, FCP MS 3788, container 33, folder 829, WRHS.

24. This is commonly lamented among historians of social welfare: Robert H. Bremner, "The State of Social Welfare History," in Herbert J. Bass, ed., *The State of American History* (Chicago: Quadrangle, 1970), 89–98; Michael B. Katz, *Poverty and Policy in American History* (Philadelphia: Academic Press, 1983), 183–218; Clarke A. Chambers, "Toward a Redefinition of Welfare History," *Journal of American History* 73 (September 1986): 411–12.

25. Percy G. Kammerer, *The Unmarried Mother: A Study of Five Hundred Cases* (Boston: Little, Brown, 1918), 303; Morton, "Seduced and Abandoned," 443–69.

26. See, for example, the discussion of the race, educational background, occupation, and source of funding of unwed mothers in Florence Crittenton Association of America, *Unwed Mothers* (Chicago: FCAA, 1967), 5–9.

27. Emma O. Lundberg, *Children of Illegitimate Birth and Measures for Their Protection* (Washington: Government Printing Office, 1926), 13; Emma O. Lundberg and Katherine F. Lenroot, *Illegitimacy as a Child-Welfare Problem, Part 1* (Washington: Government Printing Office, 1920), 22.

28. Mabel H. Mattingly, *The Unmarried Mother and Her Child: A Fact-Finding Study of Fifty-three Cases of Unmarried Mothers Who Kept Their Children* (Cleveland: Western Reserve University, School of Applied Social Sciences, 1928), 20–26, 49; Salvation Army Rescue Home, *Diamonds in the Rough*, 13; scrapbooks, Florence Crittenton Services, MS 3910, WRHS; "De Scoop," probably 1972, DePaul Printed Materials, 1949–77, folder, Federation of Catholic Community Services/Catholic Charities Corporation, box 14, CCDA.

29. For a discussion of this technique for giving the inarticulate a voice, see Gordon, *Heroes of Their Own Lives*, 18–19.

30. Conference on Illegitimacy, June 3, 1933, FCP MS 3788, microfilm reel 33, WRHS.

31. Katz, *In the Shadow*, xi.

32. Young Women's Christian Association, Annual Report, 1872, 3, MS 3516, container 8, folder 2, WRHS; Conference on Illegitimacy, April 19, 1915, FCP MS 3788, container 30, folder 738, WRHS.

33. Committee on Unmarried Mothers, Oct. 19, 1936, FCP MS 3788, container 33, folder 829, WRHS.

34. Salvation Army Rescue Home, *Links of Love, Annual Report, Salvation Army Rescue Work in Cleveland, 1904* (Cleveland: Salvation Army, 1904), 10; Laura S. Parmenter, "The Case of an Unmarried Mother Who Has Cared for Her Child, and Failed," in *Proceedings of the National Conference on Social Work, 1917* (Chicago: NCSW, 1917): 285; Helen A. O'Rourke, "A Social Agency as Seen Through the Eyes of an Unmarried Mother," 1967, typescript in author's possession.

35. Conference on Illegitimacy minutes, Dec. 5, 1921, FCP MS 3788, WRHS.

Chapter 1

1. Cleveland Workhouse and House of Refuge and Correction, MS 3681, roll 1, vol. 2, Western Reserve Historical Society (hereafter WRHS). The registers of Infirmary inmates appear to be complete from 1855 to May 1867 (roll 1, vol. 2) and from 1872 to 1882 (roll 2, vol. 5). However, the records are extensively water-damaged and for most years, inmates' first names and the disposition of their cases are illegible, as are page numbers and occasionally dates.

2. Overviews of the evolution of social welfare include Walter I. Trattner, *From Poor Law to Welfare State: A History of Social Welfare in America* (New York: Free Press, 1984); James Leiby, *A History of Social Welfare and Social Work in the United States* (New York: Columbia University Press, 1978); June Axxin and Herman Levin, eds., *Social Welfare: A History of the American Response to Need* (New York: Harper and Row, 1975). An invaluable review of both general and specialized studies is Clarke A. Chambers, "Toward a Redefinition of Welfare History," *Journal of American History* 73 (September 1986): 407–33.

3. Mimi Abramowitz, *Regulating the Lives of Women: Social Welfare Policy from Colonial Times to the Present* (Boston: South End Press, 1988), 81.

4. Mimi Abramowitz, "The Family Ethic: The Female Pauper and Public Aid, Pre-1900," *Social Service Review* 59 (March 1985): 121–35.

5. Aileen E. Kennedy, *The Ohio Poor Law and Its Administration* (Chicago: University of Chicago Press, 1934), 216.

6. Michael B. Katz, *Poverty and Policy in American History* (New York: Academic Press, 1983), 58–59.

7. David J. Rothman, *The Discovery of the Asylum: Social Order and Disorder in the New Republic* (Boston: Little, Brown, 1971), 80–81, 130, 185, 207.

8. Michael B. Katz, *In the Shadow of the Poorhouse: A Social History of Welfare in America* (New York: Basic Books, 1986), 19–24.

9. Priscilla F. Clement, *Welfare and the Poor in the Nineteenth-Century City: Philadelphia, 1800–1854* (London: Associated University Presses, 1985), 110; Katz, *In the Shadow*, 41. Abramowitz, *Regulating the Lives*, 76, dates the "povertization" of women from the colonial period.

10. Clement, *Welfare and the Poor*, 120.

11. Michael Grossberg, *Governing the Hearth: Law and the Family in Nineteenth-Century America* (Chapel Hill: University of North Carolina Press, 1985), 303–9; Robert Wells, quoted in John D'Emilio and Estelle B. Freedman, *Intimate Matters: A History of Sexuality in America* (New York: Harper and Row, 1988), 49.

12. Report of the Committee on the Infirmary, 1856, MetroHealth Medical Center Archives (hereafter MHMC).

13. City of Cleveland, *Annual Report, 1857* (Cleveland, 1857), 41.

14. City of Cleveland, *Annual Report, 1873* (Cleveland, 1873), 473.

15. Quoted in James E. Pelikan and Rebecca Pelikan, eds., *The History of City Hospital and the Discovery and Interpretation of a Hospital's Past* (Cleveland: Cuyahoga County Hospital Archives, 1981), 90.

16. Cleveland Workhouse, MS 3681, roll 1, vol. 2, and roll 2, vol. 5, WRHS.

17. William Ganson Rose, *Cleveland, The Making of a City* (Cleveland: World Publishing, 1950), 296, 361.

18. Kennedy, *Ohio Poor Law*, 20–38.

19. Pelikan and Pelikan, *History*, 39.

20. Cleveland Centennial Commission, *A Centennial History of Cleveland's Charities, 1796–1896* (Cleveland: CCC, 1896), 10.

21. *Cleveland Leader*, Feb. 29, 1864, 4.

22. Cleveland Workhouse, MS 3681, WRHS; see especially vols. 1 and 2.

23. Report of the Committee on the Infirmary, 1856, 2–3, MHMC.

24. Quoted in Pelikan and Pelikan, *History*, 87.

25. City of Cleveland, *Annual Report, 1857*, 38.

26. Quoted in Pelikan and Pelikan, *History*, 86.

27. *Cleveland Leader*, June 5, 1875, 2.

28. Quoted in Pelikan and Pelikan, *History*, 28, 97.

29. Quoted in Pelikan and Pelikan, *History*, 105.

30. *Cleveland Medical Gazette* 2 (1887): 138.

31. Cleveland Workhouse, MS 3681, roll 1, vol. 2, WRHS.

32. Cleveland Workhouse, MS 3681, roll 1, vol. 2, and roll 2, vol. 5, WRHS.

33. Report of the Committee on the Infirmary, 1856, MHMC.

34. Cleveland Workhouse, MS 3681, roll 1, WRHS.

35. Report of the Committee on the Infirmary, 1856, MHMC.

36. Cleveland Workhouse, MS 3681, roll 1, WRHS.

37. Virginia Anne Metaxas Quiroga, "Poor Mothers and Babies: A Social History of Childbirth and Child Care Institutions in Nineteenth-Century New York City," Ph.D. dissertation, State University of New York, Stony Brook, 1984, 5.

38. City of Cleveland, *Annual Report, 1880* (Cleveland, 1880), 682–83. These characteristics are also found by Katz, *In the Shadow*, 86–89, and *Poverty and Policy*, 76–83, and Clement, *Welfare and the Poor*, 107–14.

39. Cleveland Workhouse, MS 3681, roll 1, WRHS.

40. Cleveland Workhouse, MS 3681, roll 1, WRHS.

41. Katz hypothesizes that men could support themselves longer and that elderly women were more likely than elderly men to be cared for by their children; *In the Shadow*, 86–89.

42. Cleveland Workhouse, MS 3681, roll 1, WRHS.

43. Cleveland Workhouse, MS 3681, roll 1, WRHS.

44. City of Cleveland, *Annual Report, 1873* (Cleveland, 1873), 403. This imbalance and the differing lengths of stay are also noted by Katz, *In the Shadow*, 86–88, 110–12.

45. Cleveland Workhouse, MS 3681, roll 1, WRHS. In the Buffalo poorhouse, too, women were far more likely than men to have "relatives"—that is, children in the almshouse—underscoring "the continued use of the poorhouse as a home for unmarried mothers and a maternity hospital"; Katz, *Poverty and Policy*, 80–81.

46. Cleveland Workhouse, MS 3681, rolls 1, 2, WRHS.

47. City of Cleveland, *Annual Report, 1867* (Cleveland, 1867), 92. Katz argues that such child placement is evidence that "family breakup was one goal" of poor-relief officials, but he does not take into consideration the difficulty that an unmarried or deserted woman had supporting a child by herself; Katz, *In the Shadow*, 105.

48. Cleveland Workhouse, MS 3681, roll 2, WRHS.

49. City of Cleveland, *Annual Report, 1858* (Cleveland, 1858), 38.

50. City of Cleveland, *Annual Report, 1878* (Cleveland, 1878), 531.

51. D'Emilio and Freedman, *Intimate Matters*, 150–59.

52. A. O. Wright, "Employment in Poorhouses," in *Proceedings of the Na-*

tional Conference on Charities and Corrections, 1889 (Chicago: NCCC, 1889), 200. Charles Murray in *Commentary*, May 1985, quoted in Jonathan Kozol, *Rachel and Her Children: Homeless Families in America* (New York: Ballantine, 1988), 236.

53. Mary Vida Clark, "The Almshouse," in *Proceedings of the National Conference on Charities and Corrections, 1900* (Chicago: NCCC, 1900), 146–58; Amos G. Warner et al., *American Charities and Social Work* (New York: Thomas Y. Crowell, 1930), 90–103.

54. City of Cleveland, *Annual Report, 1899* (Cleveland, 1899), 35, 71, and *Annual Report, 1904* (Cleveland, 1904), 28–32.

55. Susan Whitelaw Downs and Michael W. Sherraden, "The Orphan Asylum in the Nineteenth Century," *Social Service Review* (June 1983): 273; Homer Folks, *The Care of Destitute, Neglected, and Delinquent Children* (New York: Macmillan, 1902), 104.

56. City of Cleveland, *Annual Report, 1887* (Cleveland, 1887), 469.

57. The 1875 New York Children's Act, which required the removal of children from poorhouses, was accompanied by the declining use of the Buffalo facility by women as well until the 1880s, when there was a brief revival of its use by unmarried women; Katz, *Poverty and Policy*, 76, 87.

58. City of Cleveland, *Annual Report, 1857*, 44; *Annual Report, 1880*, 681; *Annual Report, 1893*, 18 (Cleveland, 1857, 1880, 1893).

59. City of Cleveland, *Annual Report, 1861* (Cleveland, 1861), 33; Report of the Committee on the Infirmary, 1866, CMGH.

60. City of Cleveland, *Annual Report, 1883*, 578–79; *Annual Report, 1890*, 499, 928; *Annual Report, 1893*, 10 (Cleveland, 1883, 1890, 1893).

61. See, for example, Susan Tiffin, *In Whose Best Interest? Child Welfare Reform in the Progressive Era* (Westport, CT: Greenwood Press, 1982), 61–87, or, for a more negative evaluation, Steven L. Schlossman, *Love and the American Delinquent: The Theory and Practice of "Progressive" Juvenile Justice, 1825–1930* (Chicago: University of Chicago Press, 1977).

62. City of Cleveland, *Annual Report, 1902* (Cleveland, 1902), 6.

63. City of Cleveland, *Annual Report, 1905*, 20; *Annual Report, 1909*, 21 (Cleveland, 1905, 1921). I am also indebted to my student Theresa Wohlgemuth for compiling helpful statistics on this point.

64. City of Cleveland, *Annual Report, 1903* (Cleveland, 1903), 16, 21. Comparable costs are difficult to figure since they were calculated differently in different years.

65. City of Cleveland, *Annual Report, 1910* (Cleveland, 1910), 60. Katz finds this changed age and sex ratio in New York, Massachusetts, and Ohio poorhouses; *In the Shadow*, 88–91.

66. David J. Rothman, *Conscience and Convenience: The Asylum and Its Alternatives in Progressive America* (Boston: Little, Brown, 1980), 10.

67. Katz, *In the Shadow*.

Chapter 2

1. Carroll Smith-Rosenberg, *Religion and the Rise of the American City: The New York City Mission Movement, 1812–1870* (Ithaca: Cornell University Press, 1971).

2. Ray Allen Billington, *The Protestant Crusade* (New York: Macmillan, 1938).

3. George M. Marsden, *Religion and American Culture* (San Diego: Harcourt Brace Jovanovich, 1990), 115.

4. Marsden, *Religion and American Culture*, 115–16.

5. LeRoy Ashby, *Saving the Waifs: Reformers and Dependent Children, 1890–1917* (Philadelphia: Temple University Press, 1984), 226.

6. Marian J. Morton, "Homes for Poverty's Children: Cleveland's Orphanages, 1855–1933," *Ohio History* 98 (Winter–Spring 1989): 5–22.

7. Martha Tomhave Blauvelt, "Women and Revivalism," in Rosemary Radford Ruether and Rosemary Skinner Keller, eds., *Women and Religion in America. Volume 1: The Nineteenth Century* (San Francisco: Harper and Row, 1981), 2, 5–6.

8. Fifty-seven percent of all foreign missionaries in the 1880s were female, according to Barbara Welter, "She Hath Done What She Could: Protestant Women's Missionary Careers in Nineteenth Century America," in Janet Wilson James, ed., *Women in American Religion* (Philadelphia: University of Pennsylvania Press, 1980), 119. According to Rosemary Skinner Keller, more women "became involved in women's missionary society work after the Civil War than in all areas of the social reform and woman's rights movement combined. Between 1861 and 1894, foreign missionary societies were organized by and for women in thirty-three denominations, and home missionary societies in seventeen." See Keller, "Lay Women in the Protestant Tradition," in Ruether and Keller, *Women and Religion*, 242–43.

9. Elizabeth Wilson, *Fifty Years of Association Work among Young Women, 1866–1916* (New York: Young Women's Christian Association, 1916), 23; Mary S. Sims, *The Natural History of a Social Institution: The YWCA* (New York: Woman's Press, 1936), 5, 7.

10. Charles H. Hopkins, *A History of the YMCA in North America* (New York: Association Press, 1951), 25–29, 192–94.

11. Sims, *Natural History*, 7.

12. Nancy Woloch, *Women and the American Experience* (New York: Alfred A. Knopf, 1984), 543.

13. Joan Jacobs Brumberg, "'Ruined' Girls: Changing Community Responses to Illegitimacy in Upstate New York, 1890–1920," *Journal of Social History* (Winter 1984): 252.

14. On early attempts to rescue prostitutes, see Smith-Rosenberg, *Religion and the Rise of the American City*, 98–113; Barbara Berg, *The Remembered*

Gate: Origins of American Feminism: The Woman and the City, 1800–1860 (New York: Oxford University Press, 1978), 177–93; Nancy Hewitt, *Women's Activism and Social Change: Rochester, New York, 1822–1872* (Ithaca: Cornell University Press, 1984), 35–41; Kathleen D. McCarthy, *Noblesse Oblige: Charity and Cultural Philanthropy in Chicago, 1849–1929* (Chicago: University of Chicago Press, 1982), 11; Steven Ruggles, "Fallen Women: The Inmates of the Magdalen Asylum of Philadelphia, 1836–1908," *Journal of Social History* 16 (Summer 1983): 107–35. The English antecedents of American societies are described in Martha Morrison Dore, "Organizational Response to Environmental Change: A Case History Study of the National Florence Crittenton Mission," Ph.D. dissertation, University of Chicago, 1986, 5–7. Annette K. Baxter and Barbara Welter describe the evolution of such an asylum into New York City's Inwood House, which became first a reformatory and then a home for unwed mothers in the twentieth century, in *Inwood House: One Hundred and Fifty Years of Service to Women* (New York: Inwood House, 1980).

15. Colleen McDannell, *The Christian Home in Victorian America, 1840–1900* (Bloomington: Indiana University Press, 1986), xiii, xv; Peggy Pascoe, *Relations of Rescue: The Search for Female Moral Authority in the American West, 1874–1939* (New York: Oxford University Press, 1990), xix, 6.

16. Mildred Esgar, "Women Involved in the Real World: A History of the Young Women's Christian Association of Cleveland, Ohio, 1868–1968" (1968), 35, 41–42, unpublished typescript, WRHS.

17. Newspaper clipping, 1869, in scrapbook, Young Women's Christian Association, MS 3516, container 11, WRHS. The collection is titled after the group's later name.

18. Works Progress Administration of Ohio, *Annals of Cleveland, 1818–1935*, vol. 52 (1869), 614, and vol. 48 (1865), 60, 68, 83 (Cleveland: WPA, 1937).

19. Mrs. Howard Ingham, "After Twenty-Five Years, 1868–1893," 8, YWCA MS 3516, container 8, folder 6, WRHS.

20. David D. Van Tassel and John J. Grabowski, eds., *The Encyclopedia of Cleveland History* (Bloomington: Indiana University Press, 1987), 1058.

21. Annual Report, 1891, 20, YWCA MS 3516, WRHS.

22. Van Tassel and Grabowski, *Encyclopedia of Cleveland History*, 762–63; Ingham, "After Twenty-Five Years," 9; John D. Rockefeller Papers, Financial Materials, Charity index, ca. 1879–1906, Rockefeller Family Archives, Tarrytown, NY.

23. Annual Report, 1891, 16, and Annual Report, 1893, 7, YWCA MS 3516, container 8, folder 4.

24. Annual Report, 1873, 21, YWCA MS 3516, container 8, folder 3.

25. Annual Report, 1873, 21, YWCA MS 3516, container 8, folder 3.

26. Two WCTU homes for unwed mothers—the Anchorage in Elmira, New York, which opened in 1890, and the Colorado Cottage Home in Denver, which

opened in 1886—were studied extensively by Joan Jacobs Brumberg and Peggy Pascoe and serve as useful comparisons for the Cleveland Retreat. See Brumberg, "'Ruined Girls,'" and Pascoe, *Relations of Rescue*.

27. Pittsburgh and Allegheny Women's Christian Association, *Annual Report* (Pittsburgh: PAWCA, 1874), 27; *International Messenger* (March 1901): 188–89.

28. *Earnest Worker*, August 1874, 5.

29. Salvation Army Rescue Home, Annual Report, 1893, WRHS.

30. Board minutes, March 4, 1879, YWCA MS 3615, container 1, WRHS.

31. Pittsburgh and Allegheny Women's Christian Association, *Annual Report*, 27.

32. Scrapbook, 1873, YWCA MS 3516, container 11, WRHS; McDannell, *Christian Home*, 45.

33. Annual Report, 1895, 23–24; Board minutes, Aug. 5 and Oct. 7, 1879, YWCA MS 3516, container 1, WRHS; Pascoe, *Relations of Rescue*, 80.

34. Annual Report, 1891, 16, YWCA MS 3516, container 12, WRHS.

35. Annual Report, 1907, 22, YWCA MS 3516, container 12, WRHS.

36. *International Messenger*, 189.

37. Sheila Rothman, *Woman's Proper Place: A History of Changing Ideals and Practices, 1870 to the Present* (New York: Basic Books, 1978), 75.

38. *Earnest Worker*, June 1873, 5, and November 1875, 2; Van Tassel and Grabowski, *Encyclopedia of Cleveland History*, 802.

39. Minutes, Aug. 5, 1879, YWCA MS 3516, container 1, and Annual Report, 1872, 3, YWCA MS 3516, container 8, folder 2, WRHS.

40. *Earnest Worker*, February 1875, 5.

41. *Earnest Worker*, July 1874, 5.

42. This is similar to the arrangement described by Barbara M. Brenzel, *Daughters of the State: A Social Portrait of the First Reform School for Girls in North America, 1865–1905* (Cambridge: MIT Press, 1983), 119–21.

43. Annual Report, 1879, 6, YWCA MS 3516, container 1, WRHS.

44. Brumberg, "'Ruined Girls,'" 249; Pascoe, *Relations of Rescue*, 91.

45. Annual Report, 1902, 22, YWCA MS 3615, container 8, folder 15, and Annual Report, 1912, 39, YWCA MS 3615, container 9, folder 10, WRHS.

46. Morton, "Homes for Poverty's Children," 16.

47. Lucia Johnson Bing, *Social Work in Greater Cleveland* (Cleveland: Welfare Federation of Cleveland, 1938), 56–57.

48. Federation for Community Planning, Conference on Illegitimacy, Dec. 14, 1925, MS 3788, container 30, folder 739, WRHS. (Hereafter this collection will be FCP MS 3788.)

49. Conference on Illegitimacy, Dec. 8, 1930, FCP MS 3788, container 30, folder 740, WRHS.

50. Conference on Illegitimacy, Jan. 23, 1932, FCP MS 3788, microfilm reel 33, WRHS.

51. Conference on Illegitimacy, May 14, 1934, FCP MS 3788, microfilm reel 33, WRHS.

52. Committee on Unmarried Mothers, Oct. 19, 1936, FCP MS 3788, container 33, folder 829, WRHS.

53. Bolt Report, Nov. 30, 1936, 4, FCP MS 3788, container 33, folder 829, WRHS.

54. Budgets and Budget Policies, FCP MS 3788, container 8, folder 187, WRHS.

55. Committee on Unwed Mothers, Feb. 5, 1936, FCP MS 3788, container 33, folder 829, WRHS.

56. Cleveland Foundation, "Program Contents Used in the Past," Sept. 8, 1952, MS 3627, container 4, folder 17, WRHS.

57. Diary for the Annals of the Sisters of Charity, June 10, 1960, Archives of the Sisters of Charity of St. Augustine, Mount Augustine, Richfield, Ohio.

58. Periodic Review, 1966–67, DePaul Maternity and Infant Home folder, Cleveland Catholic Diocesan Archives (hereafter CCDA).

59. "De Scoop," probably 1972, DePaul Printed Materials, 1949–77, folder, Federation of Catholic Community Services/Catholic Charities Corporation, box 14, CCDA.

60. Quoted in Beulah Amidon, "Front Line Officer," *Survey Graphic*, October 1948.

61. Jane E. Wrieden, "The Social Work of the Salvation Army in the United States," pamphlet printed by the Salvation Army, probably in mid-1960s, 11, photocopy in author's possession.

62. Early examples include Grace Abbott, *The Child and the State: Select Documents*, 2 vols. (Chicago: University of Chicago Press, 1938), and Edith Abbott, *Public Assistance: American Principles and Policies* (Chicago: University of Chicago Press, 1940). Following that tradition are Walter I. Trattner, *From Poor Law to Welfare State: A History of Social Welfare in America* (New York: Free Press, 1984); Michael B. Katz, *In the Shadow of the Poorhouse: A Social History of Welfare in America* (New York: Basic Books, 1986).

63. Brumberg, "'Ruined Girls,'" 262–63; Pascoe, *Relations of Rescue*; Estelle B. Freedman, "Separatism as Strategy: Female Institution Building and American Feminism, 1870–1930," *Feminist Studies* 5 (Fall 1979): 512–29.

64. Historians critical of religious-based private welfare include Nathan Huggins, *Protestants Against Poverty: Boston's Charities, 1870–1900* (Westport, CT: Greenwood Press, 1971), and Paul Boyer, *Urban Masses and Moral Order in America, 1820–1920* (Cambridge: Harvard University Press, 1978). I

have made the same point about the vitality of the religious impulse in "Fallen Women, Federated Charities, and Maternity Homes, 1913–1973," *Social Service Review* 62 (March 1988): 61–82.

65. U.S. Government Printing Office, *Children Under Institutional Care, 1923* (Washington, D.C.: U.S. GPO, 1927), 14; Donnell M. Pappenfort et al., eds., *A Census of Children's Residential Institutions in the United States, Puerto Rico, and the Virgin Islands*, vol. 1 (Chicago: Aldine, 1970), table 34.

66. Memo to the author from Monica Haglund, activities coordinator, Booth Memorial Residence.

67. Pappenfort, *Census*, table 1.

68. F. Ellen Netting, "Secular and Religious Funding of Church-related Agencies," *Social Service Review* 56 (December 1982): 586–604. See also Edward H. McKinley, *Marching to Glory: The History of the Salvation Army in the United States, 1880–1980* (New York: Harper and Row, 1980), 212–14.

69. Esgar, "Women Involved in the Real World," 70.

CHAPTER 3

1. Roy Lubove, *The Professional Altruist: The Emergence of Social Work as a Career* (Cambridge: Harvard University Press, 1965), 1–54.

2. Amos G. Warner et al., *American Charities and Social Work* (New York: Thomas Y. Crowell, 1930), 41–56.

3. Lubove, *Professional Altruist*, 18–21.

4. Robert Morris, ed., *Encyclopedia of Social Work*, vol. 1 (New York: National Association of Social Workers, 1971), 258.

5. Morris, *Encyclopedia of Social Work*, 962; Clarke A. Chambers, "Women in the Creation of the Profession of Social Work," *Social Service Review* 60 (March 1986): 1–33.

6. Clara Kaiser, "Organized Social Work in Cleveland: Its History and Setting," Ph.D. dissertation, Ohio State University, 1936, 150.

7. Robyn L. Muncy, "Creating a Female Dominion in American Reform, 1890–1930," Ph.D. dissertation, Northwestern University, 1987. See also Molly Ladd Taylor, *Raising a Baby the Government Way, Mothers' Letters to the Children's Bureau, 1915–1932* (New Brunswick: Rutgers University Press, 1986).

8. Charles N. Crittenton, *The Brother of Girls: The Life Story of Charles N. Crittenton as Told by Himself* (Chicago: World's Events Co., 1910); Otto Wilson, *Fifty Years Work with Girls, 1833–1933* (Alexandria, Va.: National Florence Crittenton Mission, 1933), 30–35.

9. Wilson, *Fifty Years*, 38–39; Martha Morrison Dore, "Organizational Response to Environmental Change: A Case History Study of the National Florence Crittenton Mission," Ph.D. dissertation, University of Chicago, 1986,

37–39; Peter Romanofsky, ed., *Social Service Organizations* (Westport, CT: Greenwood Press, 1978), 306.

10. Wilson, *Fifty Years*, 132.

11. Wilson, *Fifty Years*, 35; Crittenton, *Brother of Girls*, 198.

12. Edward T. James, ed., *Notable American Women*, vol. 1 (Cambridge: Harvard University Press, 1971), 98–99; Emma O. Lundberg, *Unto the Least of These: Social Services for Children* (New York: D. Appleton-Century Co., 1947), 212–16.

13. Romanofsky, *Social Service Organizations*, 306–8; National Florence Crittenton Mission, Annual Report, 1918–19, 97; National Florence Crittenton Mission Papers, folder 7, Social Welfare History Archives, University of Minnesota, Minneapolis.

14. Kate Waller Barrett, *Some Practical Suggestions on the Conduct of a Rescue Home* (New York: Arno Press, 1974), 26, 110. This wonderful answer is quoted in Dore, "Organizational Response," 53. Barrett's book was originally published in 1903 by the National Florence Crittenton Association, Washington, D.C.

15. Barrett, *Practical Suggestions*, 7–8.

16. Like many women of her generation, Barrett believed that the ability to bear children was proof of women's superiority over men and that women functioned best and most usefully in their maternal role. This belief provided a powerful ideological rationale for contemporary Progressive reformers' demands for protective legislation for women and received triumphant endorsement in the 1908 *Muller v. Oregon* Supreme Court decision. The woman suffrage movement also made political capital out of motherhood, arguing that the vote would protect mothers and that mothers would make better voters. Motherhood was equally popular on the political left. Anarchist Emma Goldman named her newspaper "Mother Earth," and the labor agitator Mary Jones named herself "Mother Jones." See Mary P. Ryan, *Womanhood in America from Colonial Times to the Present* (New York: Franklin Watts, 1979), 136–50.

17. Quoted in Wilson, *Fifty Years*, 47, 172.

18. According to Katherine Aiken, "The Florence Crittenton combination of evangelism, practicality, and concern with morality and the family placed the NFCM in the mainstream of progressivism." This seems to me to underestimate Barrett's nineteenth-century roots. See Aiken, "The National Florence Crittenton Mission, 1883–1925: A Case Study in Progressive Reform," Ph.D. dissertation, Washington State University, 1980, 56, 79.

19. *Constitution and By-Laws, and Annual Report of the Florence Crittenton Home, 1913* (Cleveland, 1913), Western Reserve Historical Society (hereafter WRHS).

20. The Cleveland Home looked like the Crittenton homes in Terre Haute and Topeka, but unlike the imposing Crittenton Home and Hospital in Boston and Detroit; Wilson, *Fifty Years*, opposite 62, 254, opposite 462.

21. Wilson, *Fifty Years*, 253–57; Florence Crittenton Home Brochure, 1916–17, 8–9, WRHS.

22. *Constitution and By-Laws*, WRHS.

23. "The Physician in the Crittenton Home," *Florence Crittenton Magazine* 9 (February 1907), 1010, WRHS.

24. Wilson, *Fifty Years*, 255; Board of Managers, Florence Crittenton Services, Dec. 22, 1916, MS 3910, container 1, folder 3, WRHS. (The collection is titled after the agency's current name and hereafter will be referred to as FCS.)

25. Barrett, *Practical Suggestions*, 61.

26. Lubove, *Professional Altruist*, 183–219.

27. Thomas F. Campbell, *SASS: Fifty Years of Social Work Education* (Cleveland: Western Reserve University Press, 1967), 1–18.

28. Romanofsky, *Social Service Organizations*, 516–17.

29. Federation for Community Planning, Conference on Illegitimacy, Report of Sub-Committee on [State] Standards for Maternity Homes, MS 3788, container 30, folder 739, WRHS. (Hereafter this collection will be FCP MS 3788.)

30. Conference on Illegitimacy, May 1921, FCP MS 3788, container 30, folder 39, WRHS.

31. Michael B. Katz has called this "urban survival strategy," the chief service offered by the COS but also by nineteenth-century rescue workers like the Retreat missionary and Charles Crittenton himself; Katz, *In the Shadow of the Poorhouse: A Social History of Welfare in America* (New York: Basic Books, 1986), 65.

32. Regina G. Kunzel, "The Professionalization of Benevolence: Evangelicals and Social Workers in the Florence Crittenton Homes, 1915–1945," *Journal of Social History* 22 (Fall 1988): 26. Kunzel focuses on the implications of gender-based language, which is fascinating but misleading because she assumes that the rhetoric represents the reality of agency practices.

33. Conference on Illegitimacy, May 18, 1914, FCP MS 3788, container 21, folder 516, WRHS.

34. The policy also created problems, as in this case also reported to the conference: "Girl, now seventeen years old, has a baby a year old. The two have been in the Crittenton home over eleven months. The father of the baby is the husband of the girl's sister, with whom the girl was staying when the baby was born. The girl's mother is a drunk and has been in the Newbury insane asylum. . . . The girl wishes to leave the home and go to work. . . . She cannot leave the baby in the Crittenton Home . . . for she alone can handle the baby, which has a most nerve-wracking scream." Conference on Illegitimacy, April 6, 1914, FCP MS 3788, container 30, folder 739, and Oct. 6, 1913, container 21, folder 516, WRHS.

35. U.S. Department of Labor, Children's Bureau, *Illegitimacy as a Child-Welfare Problem*, part 3 (Washington, D.C.: U.S. Government Printing Office, 1924), 5.

36. U.S. Department of Labor, Children's Bureau, *Illegitimacy*, 8–9.

37. In addition to the 1924 publication cited above, the bureau published two other bulletins on illegitimacy in the 1920s: Emma O. Lundberg and Katherine F. Lenroot, *Illegitimacy as a Child-Welfare Problem, Part 1* (Washington, D.C.: U.S. Government Printing Office, 1920), and *Part 2* (Washington, D.C.: U.S. Government Printing Office, 1921). This reasoning suggests that the women were working class or immigrant, for baby formula was available and artificial feeding was becoming more and more popular with middle-class women and their doctors. Many doctors believed that although "civilized women" might not be able to nurse an infant successfully, "primitive women" could. Breast-feeding was also a tenet of the "maternal education" movement conducted by settlements and other social service agencies to teach poor women how to raise their children. See Rima D. Apple, *Mothers and Medicine: A Social History of Infant Feeding, 1890–1950* (Madison: University of Wisconsin Press, 1987), 73, and Richard A. Meckel, *Save the Babies: American Public Health Reform and the Prevention of Infant Mortality, 1850–1929* (Baltimore: Johns Hopkins University Press, 1990), 124–30.

38. Lundberg and Lenroot, *Illegitimacy, Part 1*, 28–29, 44–45.

39. Conference on Illegitimacy, June 14, 1926, FCP MS 3788, container 30, folder 739, WRHS. See also Eva Smill, "The Unmarried Mothers," *Family* 9 (November 1928): 241; Louise Drury, "Milestones in the Approach to Illegitimacy," parts 1 and 2, *Family* 6 (March 1925): 79–81, and (June 1925): 97–98.

40. *Florence Crittenton Bulletin* (May 1939): 38–41.

41. Letter, no author, to U.S. Children's Bureau, 1944, in Women's Social Service History folder, Salvation Army Archives, New York City.

42. Maud Morlock, "Wanted: A Square Deal for the Baby Born Out-of-Wedlock," reprinted from *The Child* 10 (1946): 167–69, in Robert H. Bremner, ed., *Children and Youth in America: A Documentary History*, vol. 3 (Cambridge: Harvard University Press, 1974), 819.

43. Kunzel, "The Professionalization of Benevolence," 34.

44. Viviana A. Zelizer, *Pricing the Priceless Child: The Changing Social Value of Childhood* (New York: Basic Books, 1985), 190, 199.

45. U.S. Department of Labor, Children's Bureau, *Essentials of Adoption Law and Procedures* (Washington, D.C.: U.S. Government Printing Office, 1944), 1–2; Children's Council, Study of Independent Placements, 1942–43, FCP MS 3788, container 31, folder 774, WRHS.

46. Dorothy Hutchinson, "How Can We Revise Agency Policies and Practices to Better Meet the Needs of Unmarried Mothers and Babies," *Florence Crittenton Bulletin* 24 (September 1949): 4, reprinted by U.S. Children's Bureau (Washington, D.C.: U.S. Government Printing Office, 1950).

47. Ethel Verry, *Meeting the Challenge of Today's Needs in Working with Unmarried Mothers*, reprinted by U.S. Children's Bureau (Washington, D.C.: U.S. Government Printing Office, 1945), 6–7.

48. Kunzel, "The Professionalization of Benevolence," 27.

49. Romanofsky, *Social Service Organizations*, 308–9; Dore, "Organizational Response," 139.

50. Dore, "Organizational Response," 99–100, 109–10.

51. Dore, "Organizational Response," 110–14; Resolution Adopted . . . 1943, *Florence Crittenton Bulletin* (July 1943), 19, National Florence Crittenton Mission Archives, Social Welfare History Archives, University of Minnesota, Minneapolis.

52. Alice Hunt Center Board minutes, Nov. 26, 1947, and April 27, 1949, Children's Services, MS 4020, container 5, folder 68, WRHS.

53. Children's Council, Study of Independent Placements, 1942–43, FCP MS 3788, container 31, folder 774, WRHS.

54. *Cleveland Press*, May 1, 1950, 15.

55. Dore, "Organizational Response," 147–48; Board of Trustees minutes, Florence Crittenton Home, Oct. 9, 1952, FCS MS 3910, container 2, folder 4, WRHS. Both the Federation and the *Cleveland Press* subsequently reported a decrease in gray market adoptions from the Crittenton Home. There were no comparable public scandals about the placement policies of other maternity homes, but Federation records reveal that St. Ann's and Mary B. Talbert, as well as Crittenton, were lax about reporting to the Ohio Department of Public Health and Welfare infants discharged to agencies or to persons other than their parents, as required by state law. *Cleveland Press*, March 20, 1951, 14; "Welfare Talks," 1953, FCP MS 3788, container 22, folder 540; correspondence, April 20, 1953, FCP MS 3788, container 22, folder 537, WRHS.

56. Report to the Steering Committee of the [Welfare Federation] Children's Council, March 16, 1953, Cleveland Foundation, MS 3627, container 4, folder 17, WRHS.

57. Board of Trustees minutes, Florence Crittenton Home, July 24 and Sept. 25, 1961, FCS MS 3910, container 1, folder 7, and April 23, 1962, container 1, folder 8, WRHS.

58. Board of Trustees minutes, Florence Crittenton Home, Aug. 8, 1956, FCS MS 3910, container 2, folder 4; Casework Council, Feb. 24, 1953, FCP MS 3788, container 49, folder 1178; correspondence, March 16, 1953, Cleveland Foundation, MS 3627, container 4, folder 17, WRHS.

59. Budget requests, Children's Council, 1955–63, FCP MS 3788, microfilm reel 33, WRHS.

60. Memo from FCH to Welfare Federation, July 6, 1956, FCP MS 3788, container 13, folder 303, WRHS.

61. "Program Contents Used in the Past," Cleveland Foundation, MS 3627, container 4, folder 17, WRHS.

62. Dore, "Organizational Response," 163.

63. Board of Trustees minutes, Florence Crittenton Home, Sept. 23, 1968, FCS MS 3910, container 1, folder 9, WRHS.

64. Board of Trustees minutes, Florence Crittenton Home, Jan. 22, 1968, and monthly meetings, 1967–79, FCS MS 3910, container 1, folders 9, 10, WRHS.

65. Dore, "Organizational Response," 164; Florence Crittenton Association of America, *Unwed Mothers* (Chicago: FCAA, 1967), 5–9.

66. Herman D. Stein, ed., *The Crisis in Welfare in Cleveland: Report of the Mayor's Commission* (Cleveland: Western Reserve University Press, 1969), 89.

67. Board of Trustees minutes, Florence Crittenton Home, Dec. 18, 1967, FCS MS 3910, container 1, folder 9, WRHS.

68. Correspondence, July 23, 1956, and Sept. 22, 1960, FCP MS 3788, container 13, folder 303; Residential Care . . . Committee, Feb. 26, 1970, FCP MS 3788, container 23, folder 561, WRHS.

69. Memorandum to Federation, 1970, FCS MS 3910, container 1, folder 10, WRHS.

70. Dore, "Organizational Response," 166.

71. See Peggy Pascoe, *Relations of Rescue: The Search for Female Moral Authority in the American West, 1874–1939* (New York: Oxford University Press, 1990), 191; Annette K. Baxter and Barbara Welter, *Inwood House: One Hundred and Fifty Years of Service to Women* (New York: Inwood House, 1980), 31.

72. Donnell M. Pappenfort et al., eds., *A Census of Children's Residential Institutions in the United States, Puerto Rico, and the Virgin Islands*, vol. 6 (Chicago: Aldine, 1970), table 134; Marian J. Morton, "Fallen Women, Federated Charities, and Maternity Homes, 1913–1973," *Social Service Review* 62 (March 1988): 61–82.

73. Dore, "Organizational Response," 155.

CHAPTER 4

1. David Rosner, *A Once Charitable Enterprise: Hospitals and Health Care in Brooklyn and New York, 1885–1915* (Cambridge: Cambridge University Press, 1982).

2. Morris J. Vogel, "The Transformation of the American Hospital, 1850–1920," in Susan Reverby and David Rosner, eds., *Health Care in America: Essays in Social History* (Philadelphia: Temple University Press, 1979), 105.

3. Paul Starr, *The Social Transformation of American Medicine* (New York: Basic Books, 1982), 146.

4. Starr, *Social Transformation*, 155–59.

5. See Pamela S. Eakins, ed., *The American Way of Birth* (Philadelphia: Temple University Press, 1986); Judith Walzer Leavitt, *Brought to Bed: Child-*

bearing in America, 1750–1850 (New York: Oxford University Press, 1986); Richard W. Wertz and Dorothy C. Wertz, *Lying-In: A History of Childbirth in America* (New York: Free Press, 1977).

6. Virginia Anne Metaxas Quiroga, "Poor Mothers and Babies: A Social History of Childbirth and Child Care Institutions in Nineteenth-Century New York City," Ph.D. dissertation, State University of New York, Stony Brook, 1984, 47–53.

7. By-Laws of Maternity Home of Cleveland, 1891, 1, University Hospitals Archives, Cleveland.

8. Quoted in Harold Speert, *The Sloane Hospital Chronicle* (Philadelphia: F. A. Davis, 1963), 81; Wertz and Wertz, *Lying-In*, 109–33.

9. John O'Grady, *Catholic Charities in the United States* (Washington, D.C.: National Conference of Catholic Charities, 1930), 71.

10. Mary Ewens, OP, "The Leadership of Nuns in Immigrant Catholicism," in Rosemary Radford Ruether and Rosemary Skinner Keller, eds., *Women and Religion in America, Volume 1: The Nineteenth Century* (San Francisco: Harper and Row, 1981), 101–3.

11. O'Grady, *Catholic Charities*, 343–68, 378, 395–96. For valuable statistical information, see Ursula Stepsis, CSA, and Dolores Liptak, RSM, eds., *Pioneer Healers: The History of Women Religious in American Health Care* (New York: Crossroads, 1989), 248–88.

12. Ewens, "The Leadership of Nuns," 102.

13. O'Grady, *Catholic Charities*, 200–201; Charles E. Rosenberg, *The Care of Strangers: The Rise of America's Hospital System* (New York: Basic Books, 1987), 111.

14. James J. Kenneally, *The History of the American Catholic Women* (New York: Crossroads, 1990), 43.

15. Joseph G. Mannard, "Maternity of the Spirit: Nuns and Domesticity in Antebellum America," *U.S. Catholic Historian* (Summer/Fall 1986): 316–22.

16. Donald P. Gavin, *In All Things Charity: History of the Sisters of Charity of St. Augustine, Cleveland, Ohio, 1851–1954* (Milwaukee: Catholic Life Publications, 1955), 59–60.

17. Mannard, "Maternity of the Spirit," 323.

18. Sr. Stanislaus Clifford, typescript history of St. Ann's, 1, Archives of the Sisters of Charity of St. Augustine, Mount Augustine, Richfield, Ohio (hereafter Richfield Archives); Michael J. Hynes, *History of the Diocese of Cleveland: Origin and Growth (1847–1952)* (Cleveland: Diocese of Cleveland, 1953), 168.

19. Quoted in Jay P. Dolan, *The Immigrant Church: New York's Irish and German Catholics, 1815–1865* (Baltimore: Johns Hopkins University Press, 1975), 132.

20. O'Grady, *Catholic Charities*, 171–73.

21. James C. Mohr, "Abortion in America," in Linda J. Kerber and Jane

DeHart Mathews, eds., *Women's America: Refocusing the Past* (New York: Oxford University Press, 1987), 190–201, excerpted from *Abortion in America: The Origins and Evolution of National Policy, 1800–1900* (New York: Oxford University Press, 1978).

22. Histories of the birth control movement include Linda Gordon, *Woman's Body, Woman's Right: A Social History of Birth Control in America* (New York: Grossman, 1976); David M. Kennedy, *Birth Control in America: The Career of Margaret Sanger* (New Haven: Yale University Press, 1970); James Reed, *From Private Vice to Public Virtue: The Birth Control Movement and American Society Since 1830* (New York: Basic Books, 1977).

23. O'Grady, *Catholic Charities*, 132, 139.

24. George F. Houck, *A History of Catholicity in Northern Ohio and in the Diocese of Cleveland* (Cleveland: Short & Forman, 1903), 739–40.

25. "Woman's Work," typescript copy of *Catholic Universe*, March 25, 1893, St. Ann's folder, Richfield Archives.

26. Correspondence, Sept. 30, 1926, St. Ann's Physicians and Staff, folder, and By Laws Governing the Visiting Staff of St. Ann's Infant Asylum and Maternity Hospital, Horstman, folder 11, Cleveland Catholic Diocesan Archives (hereafter CCDA).

27. St. Ann's Report, probably 1900, and Report . . . 1906, St. Ann's folder, CCDA.

28. Correspondence, Aug. 20, 1907, Horstman, folder 11, CCDA.

29. *Cleveland Medical Journal* (March 1910): 1–4.

30. Wertz and Wertz, *Lying-In*, 150–54; Leavitt, *Brought to Bed*, 116–41.

31. Cleveland Hospital Council, *Cleveland Hospital and Health Survey* (Cleveland: CHC, 1920), 276; City of Cleveland, Department of Public Health and Welfare, *Annual Report, 1925*, 19, and *Annual Report, 1930*, 36–37 (Cleveland, 1925, 1930).

32. City of Cleveland, Department of Public Health and Welfare, *Annual Report, 1930* (Cleveland, 1930), 36; Statistics folder and St. Ann's Board of Trustees minutes, Dec. 31, 1932, Richfield Archives.

33. O'Grady, *Catholic Charities*, 141.

34. Donald P. Gavin, *The National Conference of Catholic Charities, 1910–1960* (Milwaukee: Catholic Life Publications, 1962); Peter Romanofsky, ed., *Social Service Organizations* (Westport, CT: Greenwood Press, 1978), 476–80.

35. *Proceedings, First National Conference of Catholic Charities* (Washington, D.C.: NCCC, 1910), 303.

36. "Discussion," *Proceedings, Seventeenth National Conference of Catholic Charities* (Washington, D.C.: NCCC, 1931), 120.

37. "Official Visitation of St. Ann's Infant Asylum and Maternity Hospital, Oct. 26, 1910," 5, St. Ann's folder, CCDA.

38. Sister Annette, "Care of the Unmarried Mother in the Maternity Home," *Proceedings, Twenty-Fifth National Conference of Catholic Charities* (Washington, D.C.: NCCC, 1939), 147.

39. Ohio Department of Public Welfare, Report on St. Ann's, 1935, 35–39, Federation of Catholic Community Services/Catholic Charities Corporation (hereafter FCCS/CCC), box 23, CCDA, Federation for Community Planning, Conference on Illegitimacy, May 25, 1914, and Nov. 1923, MS 3788, container 21, folder 516, and container 30, folder 739, Western Reserve Historical Society (hereafter WRHS). (Hereafter this collection will be FCP MS 3788.) Bolt Report, Nov. 30, 1936, 15, FCP MS 3788, container 33, folder 829, WRHS. See also Marian J. Morton, "Seduced and Abandoned in an American City: Cleveland and Its Fallen Women, 1869–1936," *Journal of Urban History* 11 (August 1985): 443–69. See Percy G. Kammerer, *The Unmarried Mother: A Study of Five Hundred Cases* (Boston: Little, Brown, 1918), for similar data on this period.

40. This debate can be followed in Committee on Collections, March 4, 1942, and Committee on Maternity Homes, March 13, 1941, FCP MS 3788, container 33, folder 813; Committee on Maternity Homes, April 11, 1944, FCP MS 3788, container 33, folder 813, WRHS; Statistics, St. Ann's Hospital folder, Richfield Archives.

41. "Notes for a Talk," DePaul Infant Home folder, CCDA.

42. "A Study and Analysis of Booth Memorial Hospital and Mary B. Talbert Hospital for the Salvation Army," 1953, 111–14, Salvation Army Archives and Research Center, New York City. National figures for the Salvation Army and the Florence Crittenton Association also indicate the changed demographics of unwed mothers receiving institutional care: "Statistics for Calendar Year 1960 for National Report on Services to Unmarried Parents," 4, Salvation Army Archives, indicates that the great majority of the 7,943 women served were students or white-collar workers. See also, for example, Florence Crittenton Association of America, *Unwed Mothers* (Chicago: FCAA, 1967), 5–9.

43. Periodic Review, 1966–67, DePaul Maternity and Infant Home folder, CCDA.

44. Colleen McDannell, "Catholic Domesticity, 1860–1960," in Karen Kennelly, CSJ, ed. *American Catholic Women: A Historical Exploration* (New York: Macmillan, 1989), 75.

45. Committee on Unwed Mothers, Jan. 10, 1962, FCP MS 3788, container 22, folder 546, WRHS.

46. Conference on Illegitimacy, "The Unwed Mother and Her Child," FCP MS 3788, container 30, folder 738, WRHS; Herman Newman, "The Unmarried Mother of Borderline Mentality," *Proceedings of the National Conference on Social Work, 1915* (Chicago: NCSW, 1915), 118–20; Jean Wiedensall, "The Mentality of the Unmarried Mother," *Proceedings of the National Conference on Social Work, 1917* (Chicago: NCSW, 1917), 293.

47. Conference on Illegitimacy, April 16, 1928, FCP MS 3788, container 30, folder 740, WRHS.

48. Conference on Illegitimacy, April 16, 1928. See also Martha H. Field, "Social Casework Practice during the 'Psychiatric Deluge,'" *Social Service Review* 54 (December 1980): 482–89.

49. Robert Morris, ed., *Encyclopedia of Social Work*, vol. 1 (New York: National Association of Social Workers, 1971), 1237–45.

50. Martha Morrison Dore, "Organizational Response to Environmental Change: A Case History Study of the National Florence Crittenton Mission," Ph.D. dissertation, University of Chicago, 1986, 149–51.

51. Report to Case Work Council, Feb. 24, 1953, FCP MS 3788, container 49, folder 1178; Report of the Budget Committee to the Children's Council, June 20, 1955, FCP MS 3788, microfilm reel 33; Report of the Steering Committee to the [Welfare Federation] Children's Council, Cleveland Foundation, March 16, 1953, MS 3627, container 4, folder 17, WRHS.

52. Sr. M. deMontfort, "Unwed Mothers—Hide or Help," *Catholic Charities Review* 47 (April 1963): 7–9. Other examples of the psychiatric approach include Madge K. Gustin, "Goals in Casework with Unmarried Mothers," *Catholic Charities Review* 50 (February 1966): 22–23; Sr. Ann Gartner, "Psychiatric Consultation in a Maternity Hospital-Home," *Catholic Charities Review* 47 (February 1963): 8–11; George H. Zentz, "The Use of Therapeutic Groups with Unwed Mothers," *Catholic Charities Review* 54 (June 1970): 9–16.

53. Sr. Joseph Marie, "Individualized Services to Unmarried Mothers," *Proceedings of the National Conference of Catholic Charities* (Washington, D.C.: National Conference of Catholic Charities, 1965), 13, 15. See also Prudence M. Rains, "Moral Reinstatement: The Characteristics of Maternity Homes," *American Behavioral Scientist* 14 (1970–71): 219–35; DePaul Printed Materials, 1949–77, folder, FCCS/CCC, box 14, CCDA.

54. "Diary of the Annals of the Sisters of Charity of St. Augustine," DePaul Maternity and Infant Home folder, Richfield Archives.

55. Periodic Review, 1966–67, 7, DePaul Infant Home Reports folder, CCDA; Donnell M. Pappenfort et al., eds., *A Census of Children's Residential Institutions in the United States, Puerto Rico, and the Virgin Islands*, vol. 6 (Chicago: Aldine, 1970), tables 50, 54.

56. DePaul Maternity Homes Reports, 1969–72, 14, FCCS/CCC, box 4, CCDA.

57. Maternity Homes Consortium for Mental Health, 34, FCCS/CCC, box 4, CCDA.

58. "De Scoop," probably 1972, DePaul Printed Materials, 1949–77, folder, FCCS/CCC, box 14, CCDA.

59. Maternity Home Admissions, 1961–76, DePaul Statistics, 1959–72, folder, FCCS/CCC, box 14, CCDA.

60. Intake meeting, March 2, 1970, DePaul Reports, 1952–72, folder, FCCS/CCC, and correspondence, Dec. 18, 1972, Miscellaneous 1952 folder, FCCS/CCC, box 14, CCDA.

61. Maternity Home Admissions, 1961–76, DePaul Statistics, 1959–72, folder, FCCS/CCC, box 14, CCDA.

62. John D'Emilio and Estelle B. Freedman, *Intimate Matters: A History of Sexuality in America* (New York: Harper and Row, 1988), 330–36.

64. "The Problem of Out-of-Wedlock Pregnancy," April 1971, 3, FCP MS 3788, container 21, folder 515, WRHS.

64. D'Emilio and Freedman, *Intimate Matters*, 252.

65. See Wertz and Wertz, *Lying-In*; Eakins, *American Way of Birth*; Leavitt, *Brought to Bed*.

66. Typescript, Excerpts . . . 1933, St. Ann's folder, Richfield Archives.

CHAPTER 5

1. Kathleen C. Berkeley, "'Colored Ladies Also Contributed': Black Women's Activities from Benevolence to Social Welfare, 1866–1896," in Walter J. Fraser et al., eds., *The Web of Southern Social Relations: Women, Family, and Education* (Athens: University of Georgia Press, 1985), 188–91; David J. Rothman, in David J. Rothman and Stanton Wheeler, *Poverty and Policy in American History* (Philadelphia: Academic Press, 1983), 101.

2. Andrew Billingsley and Jeanne M. Giovannoni, *Children of the Storm: Black Children and American Child Welfare* (New York: Harcourt Brace Jovanovich, 1972), 51; Rachel B. Marks, "Institutions for Dependent and Delinquent Children: Histories, Nineteenth-Century Statistics, and Recurrent Goals," in Donnell M. Pappenfort et al., eds., *Child-Caring: Social Policy and the Institution* (Chicago: Aldine, 1973), 38–39.

3. Marks, "Institutions for Dependent and Delinquent Children," 39–41; Billingsley and Giovannoni, *Children*, 72. On differential treatment of blacks by the COS, see Alvin B. Kogut, "The Negro and the Charity Organization Society in the Progressive Era," *Social Service Review* 44 (March 1970): 11–21.

4. W. E. B. DuBois, *Some Efforts of American Negroes for Their Own Social Betterment* (Atlanta: Atlanta University, 1898), 28.

5. Examples include the Sisters of Friendship and the Daughters of Bethlehem of Petersburg, Virginia, the Ladies' Relief and Missionary Corps of Fort Smith, Arkansas, and the Colored Woman's League of Washington, D.C.; Du Bois, *Some Efforts*, 18, 30.

6. Dorothy Salem, *To Better Our World: Black Women in Organized Reform, 1890–1920* (Brooklyn: Carlson, 1990), 3; Linda Gordon, "Black and White Visions of Welfare: Women's Welfare Activism, 1890–1945," *Journal of American History* 78 (September 1991), 561–69.

7. Quoted in Berkeley, "'Colored Ladies,'" 185.

8. Philip Jackson, "Black Charity in Progressive Era Chicago," *Social Service Review* 52 (September 1978): 403.

9. Quoted in Salem, *To Better Our World*, 26.

10. W. E. B. DuBois, *Efforts for Social Betterment among Negro Americans* (Atlanta: Atlanta University, 1909), 102–3; Salem, *To Better Our World*, 45–46, 91–92; DuBois, *Some Efforts*, 30, 51.

11. Edward H. McKinley, *Marching to Glory: The History of the Salvation Army in the United States, 1880–1980* (New York: Harper and Row, 1980), 52.

12. Quoted in McKinley, *Marching to Glory*, 52.

13. David D. Van Tassel and John J. Grabowski, eds., *The Encyclopedia of Cleveland History* (Bloomington: Indiana University Press, 1987), 866.

14. McKinley, *Marching to Glory*, 11.

15. McKinley, *Marching to Glory*, 4, 44.

16. Quoted in *Cleveland Plain Dealer*, Oct. 30, 1983, 7; McKinley, *Marching to Glory*, 21.

17. McKinley, *Marching to Glory*, xi; William Booth, quoted in McKinley, *Marching to Glory*, 33; Peter Romanofsky, ed., *Social Service Organizations* (Westport, CT: Greenwood Press, 1978), 652.

18. McKinley, *Marching to Glory*, 58–60, 105.

19. McKinley, *Marching to Glory*, 195.

20. Flora Larsson, *My Best Men are Women* (London: Hodder and Stoughton, 1974), 13–14, 64–65; Catherine Booth, "Female Ministry; or Woman's Right to Preach the Gospel," in John D. Waldron, ed., *Women in the Salvation Army* (Canada: The Salvation Army, 1983), 3–4.

21. Norman H. Murdoch, "Female Ministry in the Thought and Work of Catherine Booth," *Church History* (September 1984): 349.

22. Quoted in Rosemary Radford Ruether and Rosemary Skinner Keller, eds., *Women and Religion in America, Volume 3: 1900–1968* (San Francisco: Harper and Row, 1986), 257–58.

23. Larsson, *My Best Men*, 170–71; Waldron, *Women in the Salvation Army*, 143–44; Murdoch, "Female Ministry," 359–60.

24. Quoted in Herbert A. Wisbey, Jr., *Soldiers Without Swords: The History of the Salvation Army in the United States* (New York: Macmillan, 1955), 100.

25. "The Development of the Women's Social Work in One Year," *War Service Herald and Social News* (May 1920): 4.

26. "Women Uplift Fallen Sisters," newspaper clipping, in author's possession; Salvation Army Rescue Home, Cleveland, *Annual Report, 1893* (Cleveland, 1893), 6, Western Reserve Historical Society (hereafter WRHS).

27. Salvation Army Rescue Home, *Annual Report, 1893*, 6–8, WRHS.

28. Salvation Army Rescue Home, *Diamonds in the Rough: Annual Report, Salvation Army Rescue Work in Cleveland, 1905* (Cleveland, 1905), 4, 6.

29. "Development of the Women's Social Work," *War Service Herald*: 4–5.

30. Edward H. McKinley, *Somebody's Brother: A History of the Salvation Army Men's Social Service Department, 1891–1985* (Lewiston: Edwin Mellen, 1986), 184.

31. Raymond Mohl, *The New City: Urban America in an Industrial Age, 1860–1920* (Arlington Heights, IL: Harlan Davidson, 1985), 20.

32. U.S. Government Printing Office, *Children Under Institutional Care, 1923* (Washington, D.C.: U.S. GPO, 1927), 107–8.

33. Charles W. Chesnutt, "The Negro in Cleveland," *Clevelander* (November 1930): 4.

34. Russell H. Davis, *Black Americans in Cleveland From George Peake to Carl B. Stokes, 1796–1969* (Washington, D.C.: Associated Publishers, 1972), 194–95; Kenneth Kusmer, *A Ghetto Takes Shape: Black Cleveland, 1870–1930* (Urbana: University of Illinois Press, 1980), 250–69.

35. Van Tassel and Grabowski, *Encyclopedia of Cleveland History*, 535, 768–69.

36. Emma O. Lundberg and Katherine F. Lenroot, *Illegitimacy as a Child-Welfare Problem, Part 1* (Washington, D.C.: U.S. Government Printing Office, 1920), 24–26.

37. Federation for Community Planning, Conference on Illegitimacy, May 25, 1914, MS 3788, container 21, folder 516, WRHS (hereafter this collection will be FCP MS 3788).

38. Conference on Illegitimacy minutes, Jan. 9, 1922, and "Illegitimate birth situation 1923," FCP MS 3788, container 30, folder 739, WRHS.

39. Conference on Illegitimacy, June 21, 1924, FCP MS 3788, container 30, folder 739, WRHS.

40. Emma O. Lundberg and Katharine F. Lenroot, *Illegitimacy as a Child Welfare Problem, Part 2* (Washington, D.C.: U.S. Government Printing Office, 1921), 22.

41. Elsie Johnson McDougald, "The Double Tasks: The Struggle of Negro Women for Sex and Race Emancipation," *Survey Graphic* 6 (March 1925): 691, quoted in Gerda Lerner, ed., *Black Women in White America: A Documentary History* (New York: Vintage, 1972), 170.

42. Conference on Illegitimacy, Dec. 14, 1925, FCP MS 3788, container 30, folder 739, WRHS; Van Tassel and Grabowski, *Encyclopedia of Cleveland History*, 119.

43. Conference on Illegitimacy, June 21, 1924, FCP MS 3788, container 30, folder 739, WRHS.

44. Typescript, Council of Colored Women Meet at Mary B. Talbert Hos-

pital, probably mid-1950s, scrapbook, Booth Memorial Hospital, and also at Cleveland Metropolitan General Hospital Archives (hereafter CMGH).

45. Conference on Illegitimacy, Dec. 14, 1925, FCP MS 3788, container 30, folder 739, WRHS.

46. A 1926 Children's Bureau study of maternity homes in Minnesota and Pennsylvania indicated that few admitted black women; U.S. Department of Labor, Children's Bureau, *A Study of Maternity Homes in Minnesota and Pennsylvania* (Washington, D.C.: U.S. Government Printing Office, 1926), 20, 55. The 1930 White House Conference on Child Health and Protection remarked upon the lack of facilities for black women: "Institutions and agencies available for the care of unmarried mothers and their children are rarest among the Negro group." The conference findings are quoted in Billingsley and Giovannoni, *Children of the Storm*, 83.

47. Bolt Report, Nov. 30, 1936, 6, FCP MS 3788, container 33, folder 829, WRHS.

48. Bolt Report, 16.

49. Committee on Unmarried Mothers, Oct. 1, 1936, FCP MS 3788, container 33, folder 829, WRHS.

50. Bolt Report, 6, 8.

51. Committee on Unmarried Mothers, Oct. 1, 1936.

52. Bolt Report, 2, 4.

53. Van Tassel and Grabowski, *Encyclopedia of Cleveland History*, 102.

54. Billingsley and Giovannoni, *Children of the Storm*, 126–27.

55. Billingsley and Giovannoni do not discuss the Federation debate, which can be followed in FCP MS 3788. In 1945 the Federation Subcommittee on Children's Institutions found the segregation of children's institutions "unacceptable"; May 29, 1945, container 48, folder 1153. The modification of the Cleveland Chapter of the AASW Statement of Principles Concerning Racial, Religious, or National Minority Groups is in the minutes of the Race Relations Committee of the Group Work Council, April 6, 1950. The agencies' limitations are listed in the Report of the Joint Committee of the Case Work and Children's Councils, June 28, 1949, container 48, folder 1153, WRHS.

56. Billingsley and Giovannoni, *Children of the Storm*, 126–27.

57. Maud Morlock, "Services to Unmarried Mothers as Kate Waller Barrett Might Have Wanted Them Today," *Florence Crittenton Bulletin*, August 1944, 17, National Florence Crittenton Mission Archives, Social Welfare History Archives, University of Minnesota, Minneapolis.

58. "A Study of the Needs of Unmarried Mothers," 1948, 12, table 1, FCP MS 3788, container 33, folder 830, WRHS.

59. "A Study of the Needs of Unmarried Mothers," 14.

60. Billingsley and Giovannoni, *Children of the Storm*, 125–30.

61. "Tabulations of Social Data For All Cases Closed by the Four Maternity Homes . . . 1952," FCP MS 3788, container 48, folder 1154, WRHS; "A Study of the Needs of Unmarried Mothers," 7, 13.

62. Summary of Service Data for the Four Maternity Homes in Cuyahoga County in the 4th Quarter of 1952, tables 2, 4, FCP MS 3788, container 48, folder 1154, WRHS.

63. Maternity Home Costs and Earned Income, 1951, FCP MS 3788, container 13, folder 303, WRHS.

64. Mary B. Talbert Home, Annual Report, 1952, Salvation Army Archives and Research Center, New York City.

65. "A Study and Analysis of Booth Memorial Hospital and Mary B. Talbert Hospital for the Salvation Army," 1952, Introduction, 4–7; V, 1–13; III, 4, Salvation Army Archives.

66. "Study and Analysis," II, 3–14; Introduction, 7.

67. Typescript, "The Mary B. Talbert Hospital: Its Origin and Present Service," 2, probably 1950, Booth Memorial Hospital and also at CMGH; Lt. Col. Eveline C. Skinner, "Merger of Catherine Booth Hospital and Evangeline Booth Hospital," 1983; Brief, "The Catherine Booth Home and Hospital," Aug. 15, 1943; Summary of Minutes of Catherine Booth Hospital, 1940–61, in Closed Hospitals folder, Salvation Army Archives.

68. Statistics compiled by the Cleveland Urban League for 1962 show that 81 percent of the city's illegitimate births were to black women; Cleveland Urban League, "The Negro in Cleveland, 1950–1963" (Cleveland: CUL, 1964), 50.

69. Report on the Traditional Role of the Salvation Army Maternity Home and Hospital, Feb. 13–14, 1956; Directory of Salvation Army Maternity Hospitals and Homes in the U.S.A., January 1959, Salvation Army Archives.

70. Prudence M. Rains, *Becoming an Unwed Mother: A Sociological Account* (Chicago: Aldine-Allerton, 1971), 40; P. Frederick Delliquadri, *Services Keyed to Future Families* (Washington, D.C.: Florence Crittenton Association of America, 1968), 5.

71. Gisela Konopka, *A Changing Culture Asks for Changing Services* (Chicago: Florence Crittenton Association of America, 1966), 5–9; Morris A. Wessel, "A Physician Looks at Services for Unmarried Parents," *Social Casework* 49 (1968): 12.

72. Konopka, *Changing Culture*, 7–8; Vera Shlakman, "Unmarried Parenthood: An Approach to Social Policy," *Social Casework* 47 (1966): 497–98.

73. Wessel, "Physician," 11–12; Patricia G. Morisey, *Improving Service Delivery to the Unwed Mother and Her Family* (Washington, D.C.: Florence Crittenton Association of America, 1968), 3–19.

74. Shlakman, "Unmarried Parenthood," 498; Morisey, *Improving Service*, 11–19.

75. John B. Turner, ed., *Encyclopedia of Social Work* (New York: National Association of Social Workers, 1977), 1626; Federation for Community Planning, *An Overview of Teenage Pregnancy: A Local and Ohio Perspective* (Cleveland: FCP, 1987), 6.

76. Report of Unmarried Parents Planning Committee, 2, FCP MS 3788, container 49, folder 1171, WRHS.

77. Samuel Miller, "Institutions for Unmarried Pregnant Girls," in Pappenfort et al., eds., *Child-Caring*, 237.

78. Maj. Mary E. Verner, "Administrative Concepts in Comprehensive Services for Unmarried Parents," in National Council on Illegitimacy, *Unmarried Parenthood: Clues to Agency and Community Action* (New York: NCI, 1967), 43, 46.

79. Verner, "Administrative Concepts," 47.

80. Brig. Dorothy Purser and Joan L. Lindsey, "Clinic Serves Unwed Parents," *Hospitals* 48 (Feb. 16, 1974): 58–61.

81. Child Welfare League of America, *Standards for Services for Unmarried Parents* (New York: CWLA, 1960, 1971, 1976). See also Michael Sedlak, "Youth Policy and Young Women, 1870–1972" *Social Service Review* 56 (September 1982): 457–59; Ursula M. Gallagher, "Comprehensive Services for the Unmarried Parent," in National Council on Illegitimacy, *Illegitimacy: Today's Realities* (New York: NCI, 1971), 37–43.

82. Delliquadri, "Services," 2–7; Ellen Winston, *Unmarried Parents and Federal Programs of Assistance* (Washington, D.C.: Florence Crittenton Association of America, 1966), 1–7.

83. Report of the Unmarried Parents Planning Committee, 1971, table 3, FCP MS 3788, container 49, folder 1171, WRHS.

84. Report of the Unmarried Parents Planning Committee, 1971, 13, 20.

85. McKinley, *Marching to Glory*, 208.

86. Memo to the author from Monica Haglund, activities coordinator, Booth Memorial Residence; Review, Women's and Children's Social Service Department, April 25, 1977, Salvation Army Archives.

87. "The Undiscussed Tragedy," *Cleveland Edition* (Dec. 6–12, 1990): 7.

88. Steven J. Diner, "Chicago Social Workers and Blacks in the Progressive Era," *Social Service Review* 44 (December 1970): 393–410; Kogut, "The Negro and the Charity Organization Society in the Progressive Era"; Howard N. Rabinowitz, "From Exclusion to Segregation: Health and Welfare Services for Southern Blacks, 1865–1890," *Social Service Review* 48 (September 1974): 327–54; Billingsley and Giovannoni, *Children of the Storm*; Frances Fox Piven and Richard A. Cloward, *Regulating the Poor: The Functions of Public Welfare* (New York: Pantheon, 1971).

CHAPTER 6

1. Harry F. Dowling, *City Hospitals: The Undercare of the Underprivileged* (Cambridge: Harvard University Press, 1982).

2. David M. Katzman, *Seven Days a Week: Women and Domestic Service in Industrializing America* (Urbana: University of Illinois Press, 1981), 287; William Ganson Rose, *Cleveland: The Making of a City* (Cleveland: World Publishing, 1950), 608.

3. Records of the Consumers' League of Ohio, Annual Report, 1912, 30, MS 3546, reel 2, folder 1, Western Reserve Historical Society (hereafter WRHS). See also Lois Scharf, "A Woman's View of Cleveland's Labor Force: Two Case Studies," in Thomas F. Campbell and Edward M. Miggins, eds., *The Birth of Modern Cleveland, 1865–1930* (Cleveland: WRHS, 1988), 172–94.

4. Susan Tiffin, *In Whose Best Interest? Child Welfare Reform in the Progressive Era* (Westport, CT: Greenwood Press, 1982), 121–26.

5. Emma O. Lundberg, *Public Aid to Mothers with Dependent Children: Extent and Fundamental Principles* (Washington, D.C.: U.S. Government Printing Office, 1928), 1–2.

6. Lundberg, *Public Aid to Mothers*, 6; Agnes K. Hanna, "Changing Care of Children Born Out-of-Wedlock," in Robert H. Bremner, ed., *Children and Youth in America: A Documentary History, Vol. 3: 1933–1973* (Cambridge: Harvard University Press, 1974), 815.

7. Sherman C. Kingsley et al., *Cleveland Relief Agencies* (Cleveland: Cleveland Foundation, 1914), 11, 41.

8. Mimi Abramowitz, *Regulating the Lives of Women: Social Welfare Policy from Colonial Times to the Present* (Boston: South End Press, 1988), 193–203.

9. Tiffin, *In Whose Best Interest?* 133; Cleveland Hospital Council, *Cleveland Hospital and Health Survey* (Cleveland: CHC, 1920), 575.

10. Kingsley et al., *Cleveland Relief Agencies*, 11, 30, 67.

11. Cleveland Associated Charities, Annual Report, 1921, 7, Family Services Papers, MS 3290, container 15, folder 1, WRHS.

12. Annual reports of the AC are in Family Services Papers, MS 3290, containers 13, 14, and 15, WRHS. Linda Gordon, *Heroes of Their Own Lives: The Politics and History of Family Violence. Boston, 1880–1960* (New York: Viking Press, 1988), 82–115, points out that "single mothers" received discriminatory treatment by child-protection agencies during this period. AC records, however, indicate that most women who received relief were "single"—not only never-married or unwed but "divorced," "deserted," and so forth.

13. Dowling, *City Hospitals*, 27.

14. James E. Pelikan and Rebecca Pelikan, eds., *The History of City Hos-*

pital and the Discovery and Interpretation of a Hospital's Past (Cleveland: Cuyahoga County Hospital Archives, 1981), 146.

15. Pelikan and Pelikan, *History of City Hospital,* 154.

16. City of Cleveland, *Annual Report, 1910* (Cleveland, 1910), 21.

17. Cleveland Hospital Council, *Hospital and Health Survey,* 930–31, 991.

18. Quoted in Pelikan and Pelikan, *History of City Hospital,* 185.

19. Dowling, *City Hospitals,* 137–38, 149.

20. Cleveland Hospital Council, *Hospital and Health Survey,* 838.

21. Cleveland Hospital Council, *Hospital and Health Survey,* 953, 956.

22. David D. Van Tassel and John J. Grabowski, eds., *The Encyclopedia of Cleveland History* (Bloomington: Indiana University Press, 1987), 521.

23. City Hospital, Annual Report, 1914, 1205, MetroHealth Medical Center Archives, Cleveland (hereafter MHMC).

24. Cleveland Centennial Commission, *The History of the Charities of Cleveland, 1796–1896* (Cleveland: Centennial Commission, 1896), 52; By-Laws of the Maternity Home of Cleveland, 1891, 15, University Hospital Archives, Cleveland.

25. In 1919, 74 percent of reported births in Cleveland took place at home. Thirty-four percent of those births were delivered by midwives, but a growing number of home births were attended by Maternity Hospital physicians: 1,156 in 1919 and 1,868 in 1922. See Cleveland Hospital Council, *Hospital and Health Survey,* 275–77; Burdett Wylie, "Obstetrics and Gynecology and the Cleveland Hospital Obstetric Society," in Kent Brown, ed., *Medicine in Cleveland and Cuyahoga County, 1810–1976* (Cleveland: Cleveland Academy of Medicine, 1977), 244.

26. Federation for Community Planning, Conference on Illegitimacy, May 1921 and March 9, 1925, MS 3788, container 30, folder 738, WRHS. (Hereafter this collection will be FCP MS 3788.)

27. Annual Report of the University Hospitals of Cleveland, 1928, 234, University Hospitals Archives; City of Cleveland, Department of Public Health and Welfare, *Annual Report, 1928* (Cleveland, 1928), table 1.

28. Florence T. Waite, *A Warm Friend for the Spirit: A History of the Family Service Association of Cleveland and Its Forebears, 1830–1952* (Cleveland: Family Service Association, 1960), 222–24; Van Tassel and Grabowski, eds., *Encyclopedia of Cleveland History,* xlv, 1037.

29. Waite, *Warm Friend,* 252.

30. Howard Whipple Green, *Nine Years of Relief: Greater Cleveland, 1928–1937* (Cleveland: Cleveland Health Council, 1937), 2; Lucia Johnson Bing, *Social Work in Greater Cleveland* (Cleveland: Welfare Federation of Cleveland, 1938), 23.

31. See Hanna, "Changing Care," 815–16.

32. Letter from Henry L. Zucker to Maud Morlock, March 30, 1939, FCP MS 3788, container 30, folder 742, WRHS.

33. Pelikan and Pelikan, *History of City Hospital*, 221–33.

34. City of Cleveland, Department of Public Health and Welfare, *Annual Report, 1930* (Cleveland, 1930), 36; Bolt Report, Nov. 30, 1936, tables 4, 8, FCP MS 3788, container 33, folder 829, WRHS.

35. Bolt Report, Nov. 30, 1936, tables 4, 8, FCP MS 3788, container 33, folder 829, WRHS.

36. Bolt Report, tables 4, 8.

37. Bolt Report, 4, 9, 11, 12, 16, 19, 23; Committee on Unwed Mothers, May 4, 1936, FCP MS 3788, container 33, folder 829, WRHS.

38. City Hospital, Annual Report, 1945, 8, MHMC.

39. City of Cleveland, *Vital Statistics, 1980* (Cleveland, 1980), table 15, and *Vital Statistics, 1945* (Cleveland, 1945).

40. City of Cleveland, Department of Public Health and Welfare, *Annual Report, 1930* (Cleveland, 1930), 3. In 1957, City Hospital received praise from the president of the Cleveland National Association for the Advancement of Colored People as the only hospital in the city "where integration as we understand the process has occurred." Quote in Dowling, *City Hospitals*, 156.

41. "A Study of the Needs of Unmarried Mothers," 1948, 11, 13, FCP MS 3788, container 33, folder 830, WRHS.

42. Social Service Department, Annual Report, 1948, typescript, MHMC.

43. Division of City Hospital, Annual Report, 1952, 3, CMGH; City of Cleveland, *Vital Statistics, 1950* (Cleveland, 1950), shows that 526 of 758 home births were to black women; "A Study and Analysis of Booth Memorial Hospital and Mary B. Talbert Hospital for the Salvation Army," 1952, 4, 111, Salvation Army Archives, New York City. A 1952 Urban League study also concluded that in most cities black unwed mothers had their babies at the public hospital where there were few social services, especially adoption: "The 'maternity home' for Black women was, in effect— . . . in most communities today—the obstetric ward of the county hospital, which was not supplied with adoption-oriented casework service"; Andrew Billingsley and Jeanne M. Giovannoni, *Children of the Storm: Black Children and American Child Welfare* (New York: Harcourt Brace Jovanovich, 1972), 145.

44. Report on Services to the Unmarried Mother, March 30, 1960, FCP MS 3788, container 22, folder 546, WRHS. A letter from the social worker at Cleveland Metropolitan General Hospital to the Federation Committee on Unmarried Mothers, July 7, 1958, MR 33, MS 3788, simply refers to all the births to unmarried women as "illegitimate." I have decided to be more cautious.

45. Michael B. Katz, *In the Shadow of the Poorhouse: A Social History of Welfare in America* (New York: Basic Books, 1986), 257, 266–67.

46. Herman D. Stein, ed., *The Crisis in Welfare in Cleveland: Report of*

the Mayor's Commission (Cleveland: Case Western Reserve University Press, 1969), 97.

47. Stein, *The Crisis in Welfare*, 97.

48. Tom Joe and Cheryl Rogers, *By the Few for the Few: The Reagan Welfare Legacy* (Lexington, MA: Lexington Books, 1985), 21; Michael B. Katz, *The Undeserving Poor: From the War on Poverty to the War on Welfare* (New York: Pantheon, 1989), 68–69. Frances Fox Piven and Richard A. Cloward, *The Mean Season: The Attack on the Welfare State* (New York: Pantheon, 1987), 48, contend that hostility to AFDC stems from hostility to blacks. Marital status also seems key, as suggested in this chapter and earlier.

49. Cleveland Metropolitan General Hospital, Annual Report, 1962, 6, MHMC.

50. Quoted in Stein, *Crisis in Welfare*, 65; National Association of Social Workers, *The Delivery of Health Services to the Poor in Cleveland: Report of the Task Force* (Cleveland: NASW, 1969), 7.

51. City of Cleveland, Department of Public Health and Welfare, *Vital Statistics, 1963* (Cleveland, 1963).

52. Terri Combs-Orme, "Infant Mortality and Social Work: Legacy of Success," *Social Service Review* 62 (March 1988): 83–102.

53. Report of the Unmarried Parents Planning Committee, 1971, 16, FCP MS 3788, container 49, folder 1171, WRHS.

54. Report of the Unmarried Parents Planning Committee, 1971, table 3, FCP MS 3788, container 49, folder 1171, WRHS; City of Cleveland, *Vital Statistics, 1980* (Cleveland, 1980), table 15.

55. Maternity and Infant Health Care, Annual Report, 1988, Maternity and Infant Care Project Office, MHMC.

56. The study actually was critical of both, especially of the institutions' care of unwed mothers, but found the public facility most deficient. The study's author, Nancy Stoller Shaw, concluded that City Hospital (not its real name) "represents an extreme form of the dehumanized routinized style of clinic. The basic attitude of the staff is that the patients are not paying for care and that the staff therefore has the right to treat people in any way they see fit, short of physical damage (which sometimes occurs anyway)." The black and Hispanic women were "perceived by the nursing staff as less moral, less deserving of good care, less intelligent." These negative attitudes affected the treatment of women and their children: infant care was "horrifying," Shaw maintained. Nurses "focus[ed] on stereotypes of family life, sexual behavior, and the presumed immorality associated with extra-marital pregnancy. These notions add[ed] to the nurses' beliefs that women, especially black women who are patients at the hospital, deserve the [bad] treatment they get at City," Shaw concluded. She also discovered that patients at the private facility were pressured to go onto AFDC so that medical costs would be borne by Medicaid and the hospital would be compensated.

Nancy Stoller Shaw, *Forced Labor: Maternity Care in the United States* (New York: Pergamon, 1974), 9, 54, 110–11, 114.

57. Cleveland Metropolitan General Hospital, Annual Report, 1972, 29, MHMC.

58. Van Tassel and Grabowski, *Encyclopedia of Cleveland History*, 318.

59. Van Tassel and Grabowski, *Encyclopedia of Cleveland History*, 1037; *Cleveland Plain Dealer*, June 4, 1985, 1C.

60. Katz, *In the Shadow*, 274.

61. Katz, *Undeserving Poor*, 216 and *In the Shadow*, 287.

62. Earl Landau, "Child Welfare in Cuyahoga County," November 1986, 59, typescript in author's possession.

63. Cleveland Metropolitan General Hospital, Annual Report, 1980, 26, MHMC.

64. Cleveland Metropolitan General Hospital, Annual Report, 1982, 11–12, MHMC.

65. Maternity and Infant Care Project, Annual Report, 1983 and 1988, Maternity and Infant Care Project Office, MetroHealth Medical Center.

66. Memo to the author from Vic Hersch, computer laboratory, Metro-Health Medical Center, Feb. 18, 1988.

67. *Cleveland Plain Dealer*, Feb. 21, B1, 1988; Paul Starr, *The Social Transformation of American Medicine* (New York: Basic Books, 1982), 435.

68. Dowling, *City Hospitals*, 187.

CHAPTER 7

1. Charles Murray, *Losing Ground: American Social Policy, 1950–1980* (New York: Basic Books, 1984), 156–64. See also his "White Welfare Families, 'White Trash,'" *National Review* (March 28, 1986): 30–34.

◆ Bibliography ◆

Abbott, Edith. *Public Assistance: American Principles and Policies.* Chicago: University of Chicago Press, 1940.

Abbott, Grace. *The Child and the State: Select Documents.* 2 vols. Chicago: University of Chicago Press, 1938.

Abramowitz, Mimi. "The Family Ethic: The Female Pauper and Public Aid, Pre-1900." *Social Service Review* 59 (March 1985): 121–35.

———. *Regulating the Lives of Women: Social Welfare Policy from Colonial Times to the Present.* Boston: South End Press, 1988.

Adams, Hanna. *Social Services for Unmarried Mothers and Their Children Provided Through Public and Voluntary Child Welfare Agencies.* Washington, D.C.: U.S. Children's Bureau, 1962.

Ahlstrom, Sydney, E. *A Religious History of the American People.* New York: Doubleday, 1975.

Aiken, Katherine G. "The National Florence Crittenton Mission, 1883–1925: A Case Study in Progressive Reform." Ph.D. dissertation, Washington State University, 1980.

Amidon, Beulah. "Front Line Officer." *Survey Graphic* (October 1948).

Anderson, Odin W. *The Uneasy Equilibrium: Private and Public Financing of Health Services in the United States, 1875–1965.* New Haven: College and University Press, 1968.

Annette, Sr. "Care of the Unmarried Mother in the Maternity Home." In *Proceedings, Twenty-Fifth National Conference of Catholic Charities.* Washington, D.C.: NCCC, 1939, 143–47.

Apple, Rima D. *Mothers and Medicine: A Social History of Infant Feeding, 1890–1950.* Madison: University of Wisconsin Press, 1987.

———. "Picturing the Hospital: Photographs in the History of an Institution." In *The American General Hospital: Communities and Social Contexts,* edited by Diana Elizabeth Long and Janet Golden. Ithaca: Cornell University Press, 1989, 67–81.

Ashby, LeRoy. *Saving the Waifs: Reformers and Dependent Children, 1890–1917.* Philadelphia: Temple University Press, 1984.

Austin, David M. "The Flexner Myth and the History of Social Work." *Social Service Review* 57 (September 1983): 359–77.

Axxin, June, and Herman Levin, eds. *Social Welfare: A History of the American Response to Need.* New York: Harper and Row, 1975.

Bagan, Denise. "Case Work with the Unmarried Mothers." In *Proceedings, Twenty-third National Conference of Catholic Charities.* Washington, D.C.: NCCC, 1937, 107–19.

Barrett, Kate Waller. *Some Practical Suggestions on the Conduct of a Rescue Home.* New York: Arno Press, 1974. (Reprint of 1903 edition, National Florence Crittenton Mission, Washington, D.C.)

Bass, Herbert J., ed. *The State of American History.* Chicago: Quadrangle, 1970.

Baxter, Annette K., and Barbara Welter. *Inwood House: One Hundred and Fifty Years of Service to Women.* New York: Inwood House, 1980.

Berg, Barbara. *The Remembered Gate: Origins of American Feminism: The Woman and the City, 1800–1860.* New York: Oxford University Press, 1978.

Berkeley, Kathleen C. "'Colored Ladies Also Contributed': Black Women's Activities from Benevolence to Social Welfare, 1866–1896." In *The Web of Southern Social Relations: Women, Family, and Education,* edited by Walter J. Fraser, Jr., Frank Saunders, Jr., and John L. Wakelyn. Athens: University of Georgia Press, 1985, 181–203.

Bernard, Jessie. *Marriage and Family Among Negroes.* Englewood Cliffs, NJ: Prentice-Hall, 1966.

Billingsley, Andrew, and Jeanne M. Giovannoni. *Children of the Storm: Black Children and American Child Welfare.* New York: Harcourt Brace Jovanovich, 1972.

Billington, Ray Allen. *The Protestant Crusade.* New York: Macmillan, 1938.

Bing, Lucia Johnson. *Social Work in Greater Cleveland.* Cleveland: Welfare Federation of Cleveland, 1938.

Blauvelt, Martha Tomhave. "Women and Revivalism." In *Women and Religion in America, Volume 1: The Nineteenth Century,* edited by Rosemary Radford Ruether and Rosemary Skinner Keller. San Francisco: Harper and Row, 1981, 1–9.

Bledstein, Burton J. *The Culture of Professionalism: The Middle Class and the Development of Higher Education in America.* New York: W.W. Norton, 1976.

Block, Fred, Richard A. Cloward, Barbara Ehrenreich, and Frances Fox Piven. *The Mean Season: The Attack on the Welfare State.* New York: Pantheon, 1987.

Booth, Catherine. "Female Ministry; or Woman's Right to Preach the Gospel." In *Women in the Salvation Army,* edited by John D. Waldron. Canada: Salvation Army, 1983, 3–4.

Booth-Tucker, Frederick. *The Salvation Army in America: Selected Reports, 1899–1903.* New York: Arno Press, 1972.

Bordin, Ruth. *Woman and Temperance: The Quest for Power and Liberty, 1873–1900.* Philadelphia: Temple University Press, 1981.

Boyer, Paul. *Urban Masses and Moral Order in America, 1820–1920.* Cambridge: Harvard University Press, 1978.

Bremner, Robert H. *From the Depths: The Discovery of Poverty in the United States.* New York: New York University Press, 1964.

———. "The State of Social Welfare History." In *The State of American History,* edited by Herbert J. Bass. Chicago: Quadrangle, 1970, 89–98.

————, ed. *Children and Youth in America: A Documentary History.* 6 vols. Cambridge: Harvard University Press, 1970–74.

Brenzel, Barbara M. *Daughters of the State: A Social Portrait of the First Reform School for Girls in North America, 1865–1905.* Cambridge: MIT Press, 1983.

Brown, Kent, ed. *Medicine in Cleveland and Cuyahoga County, 1810–1976.* Cleveland: Cleveland Academy of Medicine, 1977.

Brumberg, Joan Jacobs. "'Ruined Girls': Changing Community Responses to Illegitimacy in Upstate New York, 1890–1920." *Journal of Social History* (Winter 1984): 247–72.

Burns, Jeffrey M. "Catholic Laywomen in the Culture of American Catholicism in the 1950s." *U.S. Catholic Historian* (Summer/Fall 1986): 385–400.

Burrows, James G. *Organized Medicine in the Progressive Era: The Move Toward Monopoly.* Baltimore: Johns Hopkins University Press, 1977.

Campbell, Thomas F. *SASS: Fifty Years of Social Work Education.* Cleveland: Western Reserve University Press, 1967.

————, and Edward M. Miggins, eds. *The Birth of Modern Cleveland, 1865–1930.* Cleveland: Western Reserve Historical Society, 1988.

Chambers, Clarke A. "Toward a Redefinition of Welfare History." *Journal of American History* 73 (September 1986): 407–33.

————. "Women in the Creation of the Profession of Social Work." *Social Service Review* 60 (March 1986): 1–33.

Chapman, Edmund H. *Cleveland: Village to Metropolis: A Case Study of Urban Development in Nineteenth Century America.* Cleveland: Western Reserve Historical Society, 1950.

Chaskel, Ruth. "Changing Patterns of Services for Unmarried Parents." *Social Casework* 49 (1968): 3–10.

Chestnutt, Charles W. "The Negro in Cleveland." *Clevelander* (November 1930).

Child Welfare League of America. *Child Welfare League of America Standards for Services for Unmarried Parents.* New York: CWLA, 1960, 1971, 1976.

City of Cleveland, Annual reports, 1856–1912. Cleveland: City of Cleveland.

City of Cleveland, Department of Public Health and Welfare. Annual reports, 1925, 1928, 1930, 1963. Cleveland: City of Cleveland.

————. Vital Statistics, 1945–1980. Cleveland: City of Cleveland.

City of Cleveland, Division of Charities and Correction. Annual reports, 1913–1930. Cleveland: City of Cleveland.

Clark, Mary Vida. "The Almshouse." In *Proceedings of the National Conference on Charities and Corrections, 1900.* Chicago: NCCC, 1900, 146–58.

Clement, Priscilla Ferguson. *Welfare and the Poor in the Nineteenth-Century City, Philadelphia, 1800–1854.* London: Associated University Presses, 1985.

Cleveland Centennial Commission. *A Centennial History of Cleveland's Charities, 1796–1896.* Cleveland: CCC, 1896.

Cleveland Federation for Charity and Philanthropy. *The Social Year Book.* Cleveland: CFCP, 1913.

Cleveland Hospital Council. *Cleveland Hospital and Health Survey.* Cleveland: CHC, 1920.

Cleveland Medical Gazette 2 (1887).

Cleveland Urban League. "The Negro in Cleveland, 1950–1963." Cleveland: CUL, 1964.

Combs-Orme, Terri. "Infant Mortality and Social Work: Legacy of Success." *Social Service Review* 62 (March 1988): 83–102.

Connelly, Mark Thomas. *The Response to Prostitution in the Progressive Era.* Chapel Hill: University of North Carolina Press, 1980.

Cooley, Harris R. "The Organization and Development of Our City Infirmary." In *Proceedings of the National Conference on Charities and Corrections, 1912.* Chicago: NCCC, 1912, 437–39.

Coulton, Claudia J., Julian Chow, and Shanta Pandey. "An Analysis of Poverty and Related Conditions in Cleveland Area Neighborhoods." Cleveland: Case Western Reserve University, Center for Urban Poverty and Social Change, Mandel School of Applied Social Sciences, January 1990.

Crittenton, Charles N. *The Brother of Girls: The Life Story of Charles N. Crittenton as Told by Himself.* Chicago: World's Events Co., 1910.

Davis, Russell H. *Black Americans in Cleveland From George Peake to Carl B. Stokes, 1796–1969.* Washington, D.C.: Associated Publishers, 1972.

Day, Phyllis J. "Sex Role Stereotypes and Public Assistance." *Social Service Review* 53 (March 1979): 106–15.

Dehey, Elinor Tong. *Religious Orders of Women in the United States.* Hammond, IN: W. B. Conkey, 1930.

Delliquadri, P. Frederick. *Services Keyed to Future Families.* Washington, D.C.: Florence Crittenton Association of America, 1968.

D'Emilio, John, and Estelle B. Freedman. *Intimate Matters: A History of Sexuality in America.* New York: Harper and Row, 1988.

deMontfort, Sr. M. "Unwed Mothers—Hide or Help." *Catholic Charities Review* 47 (April 1963): 7–9.

DePaul, Sr. Mary. "A Discussion." In *Proceedings, Seventeenth National Conference of Catholic Charities.* Washington, D.C.: NCCC, 1931, 120–25.

"The Development of the Women's Social Work in One Year." *War Service Herald and Social News,* May 1920.

Diner, Steven J. "Chicago Social Workers and Blacks in the Progressive Era." *Social Service Review* 44 (December 1970): 393–410.

Dolan, Jay P. *The Immigrant Church: New York's Irish and German Catholics, 1815–1865.* Baltimore: Johns Hopkins University Press, 1975.

D'Olier, Kathleen. "Foster Care for the Unmarried Mother." *Catholic Charities Review* 23 (1939): 138–41.

Dore, Martha Morrison. "Organizational Response to Environmental Change: A Case History Study of the National Florence Crittenton Mission." Ph.D. dissertation, University of Chicago, 1986.

Dowling, Harry F. *City Hospitals: The Undercare of the Underprivileged.* Cambridge: Harvard University Press, 1982.

Downs, Susan Whitelaw, and Michael W. Sherraden. "The Orphan Asylum in the Nineteenth Century." *Social Service Review* 57 (June 1983): 272–90.

Drachman, Virginia G. *Hospital With a Heart: Women Doctors and the Paradox of Separatism at the New England Hospital, 1862–1969.* Ithaca: Cornell University Press, 1984.

Drury, Louise. "Milestones in the Approach to Illegitimacy, I." *Family* 6 (March 1925): 79–81.

———. "Milestones in the Approach to Illegitimacy, II." *Family* 6 (June 1925): 97–98.

DuBois, W. E. B. *Efforts for Social Betterment Among Negro Americans.* Atlanta: Atlanta University, 1909.

———. *The Philadelphia Negro: A Social Study.* New York: Benjamin Blom, 1899.

———. *Some Efforts of American Negroes for Their Own Social Betterment.* Atlanta: Atlanta University, 1898.

Eakins, Pamela S., ed. *The American Way of Birth.* Philadelphia: Temple University Press, 1986.

Earnest Worker (1873–1875).

Edelman, Marian Wright. *Families in Peril: An Agenda for Social Change.* Cambridge: Harvard University Press, 1987.

Ehrenreich, John H. *The Altruistic Imagination: A History of Social Work and Social Policy in the United States.* Ithaca: Cornell University Press, 1985.

Epstein, Barbara L. *The Politics of Domesticity: Women, Evangelism, and Temperance in the Nineteenth Century.* Middletown, CT: Wesleyan University Press, 1981.

Esgar, Mildred. "Women Involved in the Real World: A History of the Young Women's Christian Association of Cleveland, Ohio, 1868–1968." Unpublished typescript, 1968. Western Reserve Historical Society.

Ewens, Mary, OP. "The Leadership of Nuns in Immigrant Catholicism." In *Women and Religion in America, Volume 1: The Nineteenth Century,* edited by Rosemary Radford Ruether and Rosemary Skinner Keller. San Francisco: Harper and Row, 1981, 101–7.

———. *The Role of the Nun in Nineteenth-Century America.* New York: Arno Press, 1978.

Federation for Community Planning. *An Overview of Teenage Pregnancy: A Local and Ohio Perspective.* Cleveland: FCP, 1987.

Field, Martha H. "Social Casework Practice during the 'Psychiatric Deluge.'" *Social Service Review* 54 (December 1980): 482–89.

Florence Crittenton Association of America. *Services to and Characteristics of Unwed Mothers.* Chicago: FCAA, 1965.

———. *Unwed Mothers.* Chicago: FCAA, 1967.

Folks, Homer. *The Care of Destitute, Neglected, and Deliquent Children.* New York: Macmillan, 1902.

Fraser, Walter J., Jr., Frank Saunders, Jr., and John L. Wakelyn, eds. *The Web of Southern Social Relations: Women, Family, and Education*. Athens: University of Georgia Press, 1985.

Frazier, E. Franklin. *The Negro Family in the United States*. New York: Dryden Press, 1951.

Freedman, Estelle B. "Separatism as Strategy: Female Institution Building and American Feminism, 1870–1930." *Feminist Studies* 5 (Fall 1979): 512–29.

———. *Their Sister's Keepers: Women's Prison Reform in America, 1830–1930*. Ann Arbor: University of Michigan Press, 1981.

Frey, Sylvia, and Marian J. Morton, eds. *New World, New Roles: A Documentary History of Women in Pre-Industrial America*. Westport, CT: Greenwood Press, 1986.

Gallagher, Ursula M. "Comprehensive Services for the Unmarried Parent." In National Council on Illegitimacy, *Illegitimacy: Today's Realities*. New York: NCI, 1971, 37–43.

Gartner, Sr. Ann. "Psychiatric Consultation in a Maternity Hospital-Home." *Catholic Charities Review* 47 (February 1963): 8–11.

Gavin, Donald P. *In All Things Charity: History of the Sisters of Charity of St. Augustine, Cleveland, Ohio, 1851–1954*. Milwaukee: Catholic Life Publications, 1955.

———. *The National Conference of Catholic Charities, 1910–1960*. Milwaukee: Catholic Life Publications, 1962.

Ginzberg, Lori D. *Women and the Work of Benevolence: Morality, Politics, and Class in the Nineteenth-Century United States*. New Haven: Yale University Press, 1990.

Gordon, Linda. "Black and White Visions of Welfare: Women's Welfare Activism, 1890–1945." *Journal of American History* 78 (September 1991): 559–90.

———. *Heroes of Their Own Lives: The Politics and History of Family Violence. Boston, 1880–1960*. New York: Viking Press, 1988.

———. *Woman's Body, Woman's Right: A Social History of Birth Control in America*. New York: Grossman, 1976.

———, ed. *Women, the State, and Welfare*. Madison: University of Wisconsin Press, 1990.

Green, Howard Whipple. *Hospitals and Their Use in Northeast Ohio*. Cleveland: Cleveland Health Council, 1961.

———. *Infant Mortality and Economic Status, Cleveland Five-City Area*. Cleveland: Cleveland Health Council, 1939.

———. *Nine Years of Relief: Greater Cleveland, 1928–1937*. Cleveland: Cleveland Health Council, 1937.

———. *Population Characteristics of Population Tracts, Cleveland, Ohio*. Cleveland: Plain Dealer Publishing, 1931.

Griffith, Katherine. "A Discussion." In *Proceedings, Seventeenth National Conference of Catholic Charities, 1931*, Washington, D.C.: NCCC, 1931, 109–14.

Grob, Gerald. *Mental Institutions in America: Social Policy to 1875.* New York: Free Press, 1973.

Grossberg, Michael. *Governing the Hearth: Law and the Family in Nineteenth-Century America.* Chapel Hill: University of North Carolina Press, 1985.

Gustin, Madge K. "Goals in Casework with Unmarried Mothers." *Catholic Charities Review* 50 (February 1966): 22–23.

Haller, John S., Jr. *American Medicine in Transition, 1840–1910.* Urbana: University of Illinois Press, 1981.

Hanna, Agnes K. "Changing Care of Children Born Out-of-Wedlock." In *Children and Youth in America: A Documentary History, Vol. 3: 1933–1973,* edited by Robert H. Bremner. Cambridge: Harvard University Press, 1974, 812–28.

Helen, Sr. Mary. "A Pioneer Maternity Hospital and Infant Home Reports." In *Proceedings, Thirty-Sixth National Conference of Catholic Charities, 1951.* Washington, D.C.: NCCC, 1951, 94–98.

Henderson, Charles A. "Poor Laws of the United States." In *Proceedings of the National Conference on Charities and Corrections, 1897.* Chicago: NCCC, 1897, 256–63.

Hewitt, Nancy. *Women's Activism and Social Change: Rochester, New York, 1822–1872.* Ithaca: Cornell University Press, 1984.

Hodges, Margaret B. *Social Work Year Book.* New York: Russell Sage Foundation, 1949.

Hopkins, Charles H. *A History of the YMCA in North America.* New York: Association Press, 1951.

———. *The Rise of the Social Gospel in American Protestantism, 1865–1915.* New Haven: Yale University Press, 1940.

Hopkirk, Howard W. *Institutions Serving Children.* New York: Russell Sage Foundation, 1944.

Houck, George F. *A History of Catholicity in Northern Ohio and in the Diocese of Cleveland.* Cleveland: Short & Forman, 1903.

Howard, Marion. *Multi-Service Programs for Pregnant School Girls.* Washington, D.C.: U.S. Department of Health, Education, and Welfare, 1968.

Huggins, Nathan I. *Protestants Against Poverty: Boston's Charities, 1870–1900.* Westport, CT: Greenwood Press, 1971.

Hutchinson, Dorothy. "How Can We Revise Agency Policies and Practices to Better Meet the Needs of Unmarried Mothers and Babies." Washington, D.C.: U.S. Government Printing Office, 1950.

Hynes, Michael J. *History of the Diocese of Cleveland: Origin and Growth (1847–1952).* Cleveland: Diocese of Cleveland, 1953.

Ingham, Mary. *Women of Cleveland and Their Work: Philanthropic, Education, Literary, Medical and Artistic.* Cleveland: W. A. Ingham, 1893.

International Messenger (March 1901).

Irving, Frederick C. *Safe Deliverance.* Boston: Houghton Mifflin, 1942.

Jackson, Philip. "Black Charity in Progressive Era Chicago." *Social Service Review* 52 (September 1978): 400–17.

James, Edward T., ed. *Notable American Women*. Vol. 1. Cambridge: Harvard University Press, 1971.

James, Janet Wilson, ed. *Women in American Religion*. Philadelphia: University of Pennsylvania Press, 1980.

Joe, Tom, and Cheryl Rogers. *By the Few for the Few: The Reagan Welfare Legacy*. Lexington, MS: Lexington Books, 1985.

Johnson, Tom L. *My Story*. Seattle: University of Washington Press, 1910.

Kaiser, Clara. "Organized Social Work in Cleveland: Its History and Setting." Ph.D. dissertation, Ohio State University, 1936.

Kammerer, Percy G. *The Unmarried Mother: A Study of Five Hundred Cases*. Boston: Little, Brown, 1918.

Katz, Michael B. *In the Shadow of the Poorhouse: A Social History of Welfare in America*. New York: Basic Books, 1986.

———. *Poverty and Policy in American History*. New York: Academic Press, 1983.

———. *The Undeserving Poor: From the War on Poverty to the War on Welfare*. New York: Pantheon, 1989.

Katzman, David M. *Seven Days a Week: Women and Domestic Service in Industrializing America*. Urbana: University of Illinois Press, 1981.

Keller, Rosemary Skinner. "Lay Women in the Protestant Tradition." In *Women and Religion in America. Volume 1: The Nineteenth Century*, edited by Rosemary Radford Ruether and Rosemary Skinner Keller. San Francisco: Harper and Row, 1981, 242–53.

Kenneally, James J. *The History of the American Catholic Women*. New York: Crossroads, 1990.

———. "Reflections on Historical Catholic Women." *U.S. Catholic Historian* (Summer/Fall 1986): 411–18.

Kennedy, Aileen E. *The Ohio Poor Law and Its Administration*. Chicago: University of Chicago Press, 1934.

Kennedy, David M. *Birth Control in America: The Career of Margaret Sanger*. New Haven: Yale University Press, 1970.

Kennelly, Karen, C.S.J., ed. *American Catholic Women: A Historical Exploration*. New York: Macmillan, 1989.

Kerber, Linda J., and Jane DeHart Mathews, eds. *Women's America: Refocusing the Past*. New York: Oxford University Press, 1987.

Kessler-Harris, Alice. *Out to Work: A History of Wage-Earning Women in the United States*. Oxford: Oxford University Press, 1982.

Kett, Joseph F. *The Formation of the American Medical Profession: The Role of Institutions, 1780–1860*. New Haven: Yale University Press, 1968.

Kingsley, Sherman C., Amelia Sears, and Allen T. Burns. *Cleveland Relief Agencies*. Cleveland: Cleveland Foundation, 1914.

Kogut, Alvin B. "The Negro and the Charity Organization Society in the Progressive Era." *Social Service Review* 44 (March 1970): 11–21.

Konopka, Gisela. *A Changing Culture Asks for Changing Services*. Chicago: Florence Crittenton Association of America, 1966.

Kozol, Jonathan. *Rachel and Her Children: Homeless Families in America*. New York: Ballantine, 1988.

Kunzel, Regina G. "The Professionalization of Benevolence: Evangelicals and Social Workers in the Florence Crittenton Homes, 1915–1945," *Journal of Social History* 22 (Fall 1988): 21–44.

Kurtz, Russell H., ed. *Social Work Year Book*. New York: Russell Sage Foundation, 1945.

Kusmer, Kenneth. *A Ghetto Takes Shape: Black Cleveland, 1870–1930*. Urbana: University of Illinois Press, 1980.

Labaree, Mary S. "Unmarried Parenthood Under the Social Security Act." In *Proceedings of the National Conference on Social Work, 1939*. Chicago: NCSW, 446–57.

Larsson, Flora. *My Best Men are Women*. London: Hodder and Stoughton, 1974.

Laslett, Peter, Karla Oosterveen, and Richard Michael Smith, eds. *Bastardy and Its Comparative History*. Cambridge: Harvard University Press, 1980.

Leavitt, Judith Walzer. *Brought to Bed: Childbearing in America. 1750–1850*. New York: Oxford University Press, 1986.

Leiby, James. *A History of Social Welfare and Social Work in the United States*. New York: Columbia University Press, 1978.

Lerner, Gerda, ed. *Black Women in White America: A Documentary History*. New York: Vintage, 1972.

Long, Diana Elizabeth, and Janet Golden, eds. *The American General Hospital: Communities and Social Contexts*. Ithaca: Cornell University Press, 1989.

Lubove, Roy. *The Professional Altruist: The Emergence of Social Work as a Career*. Cambridge: Harvard University Press, 1965.

Luckin, Bill. "Towards a Social History of Institutionalization." *Social History* 8.1 (January 1983): 87–96.

Lundberg, Emma O. *Child Dependency in the United States*. New York: Child Welfare League of America.

———. *Children of Illegitimate Birth and Measures for their Protection*. Washington, D.C.: U.S. Government Printing Office, 1926.

———. *Public Aid to Mothers with Dependent Children: Extent and Fundamental Principles*. Washington, D.C.: U.S. Government Printing Office, 1928.

———. *Unto the Least of These: Social Services for Children*. New York: D. Appleton-Century Co., 1947.

———, and Katharine F. Lenroot. *Illegitimacy as a Child-Welfare Problem, Part 1*. Washington, D.C.: U.S. Government Printing Office, 1920.

———. *Illegitimacy as a Child-Welfare Problem, Part 2*. Washington, D.C.: U.S. Government Printing Office, 1921.

Lurie, Harry L., ed. *Encyclopedia of Social Work*. New York: National Association of Social Workers, 1965.

Lynaugh, Joan E. "From Respectable Domesticity to Medical Efficiency: The Changing Kansas City Hospital, 1875–1920." In *The American General*

Hospital: Communities and Social Contexts, edited by Diana Elizabeth Long and Janet Golden. Ithaca: Cornell University Press, 1989, 21–39.

Mannard, Joseph G. "Maternity of the Spirit: Nuns and Domesticity in Antebellum America." *U.S. Catholic Historian* (Summer/Fall 1986): 305–24.

Magnuson, Norris. *Salvation in the Slums*. Metuchen, NJ: Scarecrow Press, 1977.

Marie, C.S.A., Sr. Joseph. "Individualized Services to Unmarried Mothers." In *Proceedings, Fifty-first National Conference of Catholic Charities, 1965.* Washington, D.C.: NCCC, 1965, 13–16.

Marks, Rachel B. "Institutions for Dependent and Delinquent Children: Histories, Nineteenth-Century Statistics, and Recurrent Goals." In *Child-Caring: Social Policy and the Institution*, edited by Donnell M. Pappenfort, Dee Morgan Kilpatrick, and Robert W. Roberts. Chicago: Aldine, 1973, 32–58.

Marsden, George M. *Religion and American Culture*. San Diego: Harcourt Brace Jovanovich, 1990.

Mattingly, Mabel H. *The Unmarried Mother and Her Child: A Fact-Finding Study of Fifty-three Cases of Unmarried Mothers Who Kept Their Children.* Cleveland: Western Reserve University, School of Applied Social Sciences, 1928.

May, Henry. *Protestant Churches in Industrial America*. New York: Harper Torchbook, 1967.

McAdoo, Hariette Pipes, ed. *Black Families*. Beverly Hills: Sage Publications, 1981.

McCarthy, Kathleen D. *Noblesse Oblige: Charity and Cultural Philanthropy in Chicago, 1849–1929.* Chicago: University of Chicago Press, 1982.

———, ed. *Lady Bountiful Revisited: Women, Philanthropy and Power.* New Brunswick: Rutgers University Press, 1990.

McCollum, Marguerite. "Foster Home Care of the Unmarried Mother." *Family* 16 (January 1936): 276–79.

McDannell, Colleen. "Catholic Domesticity, 1860–1960." In *American Catholic Women: A Historical Exploration*, edited by Karen Kennelly, C.S.J. New York: Macmillan, 1989, 48–80.

———. *The Christian Home in Victorian America, 1840–1900.* Bloomington: Indiana University Press, 1986.

McDougald, Elsie Johnson. "The Double Tasks: The Struggle of Negro Women for Sex and Race Emancipation." *Survey Graphic* 6 (March 1925): 688–91.

McKinley, Edward H. *Marching to Glory: The History of the Salvation Army in the United States, 1880–1980.* New York: Harper and Row, 1980.

———. *Somebody's Brother: A History of the Salvation Army Men's Social Service Department, 1891–1985.* Lewiston: Edwin Mellen, 1986.

Meagher, Timothy J. "Sweet Good Mothers and Young Women Out in the World: The Roles of Irish American Women in Late Nineteenth and Early Twentieth Century Worcester, Massachusetts." *U.S. Catholic Historian* (Summer/Fall 1986): 325–43.

Meckel, Richard A. *Save the Babies: American Public Health Reform and the Prevention of Infant Mortality, 1850–1929.* Baltimore: Johns Hopkins University Press, 1990.

Meier, August. *Negro Thought in America, 1880–1915: Racial Ideologies in the Age of Booker T. Washington.* Ann Arbor: University of Michigan Press, 1963.

Michella, Sr. Anna. "Social Policy of Institutions Caring for Unmarried Mothers." In *Proceedings, Ninth National Conference of Catholic Charities, 1923.* Washington, D.C.: NCCC, 283–88.

Miller, Carol Poh, and Robert Wheeler. *Cleveland: A Concise History, 1796– 1990.* Bloomington: Indiana University Press, 1990.

Miller, Dorothy C. *Women and Social Welfare: A Feminist Analysis.* New York: Praeger, 1990.

Miller, Samuel. "Institutions for Unmarried Pregnant Girls." In *Child-Caring: Social Policy and the Institution,* edited by Donnell M. Pappenfort, Dee Morgan Kilpatrick, and Robert W. Roberts. Chicago: Aldine, 1973.

Miller, Zane L. *The Urbanization of Modern America: A Brief History.* New York: Harcourt Brace Jovanovich, 1973.

Mohl, Raymond. *The New City: Urban America in an Industrial Age, 1860– 1920.* Arlington Heights, IL: Harlan Davidson, 1985.

———. *Poverty in New York, 1783–1825.* New York: Oxford University Press, 1971.

Mohr, James E. *Abortion in America: The Origins and Evolution of National Policy, 1800–1900.* New York: Oxford University Press, 1978.

Morisey, Patricia G. *Improving Service Delivery to the Unwed Mother and Her Family.* Washington, D.C.: Florence Crittenton Association of America, 1968.

Morlock, Maud. "Services to Unmarried Mothers as Kate Waller Barrett Might Have Wanted Them Today." *Florence Crittenton Bulletin* (August 1944): 16–20.

———. "Wanted: A Square Deal for the Baby Born Out-of-Wedlock." In *Children and Youth in America: A Documentary History,* Vol. 3, edited by Robert Bremner. Cambridge: Harvard University Press, 1974, 818–22.

Morris, Robert, ed. *Encyclopedia of Social Work.* Vol. 1. New York: National Association of Social Workers, 1971.

Morton, Marian J. "Fallen Women, Federated Charities, and Maternity Homes, 1913–1973." *Social Service Review* 62 (March 1988): 61–82.

———. "'Go and Sin No More': Maternity Homes in Cleveland, 1869–1936." *Ohio History* 93 (Fall 1984): 117–46.

———. "Homes for Poverty's Children: Cleveland's Orphanages, 1851–1933." *Ohio History* 98 (Winter-Spring 1989): 5–22.

———. "Seduced and Abandoned in an American City: Cleveland and Its Fallen Women, 1869–1936." *Journal of Urban History* 11 (August 1985): 443–69.

———. "Temperance, Benevolence, and the City: The Cleveland Non-Partisan Woman's Christian Temperance Union." *Ohio History* 91 (Annual 1982): 58–73.

Muncy, Robyn L. "Creating a Female Dominion in American Reform, 1890– 1930." Ph.D. dissertation, Northwestern University, 1987.

Murdoch, Norman H. "Female Ministry in the Thought and Work of Catherine Booth," *Church History* (September 1984): 348–62.

Murray, Charles. *Losing Ground: American Social Policy, 1950–1980.* New York: Basic Books, 1984.

Murray, Charles. "White Welfare Families, 'White Trash.'" *National Review* (March 28, 1986): 30–34.

National Association of Social Workers. *The Delivery of Health Services to the Poor in Cleveland: Report of the Task Force.* Cleveland: NASW, 1969.

National Conference of Social Work. *Proceedings of the National Conference of Social Work Index, 1874–1933.* Chicago: University of Chicago Press, 1935.

National Council on Illegitimacy. *Unmarried Parenthood: Clues to Agency and Community Action.* New York: NCI, 1967.

National Florence Crittenton Mission. *Fourteen Years Work with Street Girls.* Washington, D.C.: NFCM, 1897.

Netting, F. Ellen. "Secular and Religious Funding of Church-related Agencies." *Social Service Review* 56 (December 1982): 586–604.

Newman, Herman. "The Unmarried Mother of Borderline Mentality." In *Proceedings of the National Conference on Social Work, 1915.* Chicago: NCSW, 1915.

Northrop, Flora L. *The Record of a Century, 1834–1934.* New York: American Female Guardian Society, 1934.

O'Grady, John. *Catholic Charities in the United States.* Washington, D.C.: National Conference of Catholic Charities, 1930.

O'Neill, William L., ed. *Insights and Parallels: Problems and Issues of American Social History.* Minneapolis: Burgess, 1973.

Pappenfort, Donnell M. *Journey to Labor: A Study of Births in Hospitals and Technology.* Chicago: University of Chicago Press, 1964.

———, Dee Morgan Kilpatrick, and Alma M. Kuby, eds. *A Census of Children's Residential Institutions in the United States, Puerto Rico, and the Virgin Islands.* Vols. 1, 6. Chicago: Aldine, 1970.

———, Dee Morgan Kilpatrick, and Robert W. Roberts, eds. *Child-Caring: Social Policy and the Institution.* Chicago: Aldine, 1973.

Parmenter, Laura S. "The Case of an Unmarried Mother Who Has Cared for Her Child, and Failed." In *Proceedings of the National Conference on Social Work, 1917.* Chicago: National Conference on Social Work, 1917, 285.

Pascoe, Peggy. *Relations of Rescue: The Search for Female Moral Authority in the American West, 1874–1939.* New York: Oxford University Press, 1990.

Peck, Emelyn Foster. *Adoption Laws in the United States.* Washington, D.C.: U.S. Government Printing Office, 1925.

Pelikan, James E., and Rebecca Pelikan, eds. *The History of City Hospital and the Discovery and Interpretation of a Hospital's Past.* Cleveland: Cuyahoga County Hospital Archives, 1981.

Pickett, Robert S. *House of Refuge: Origins of Juvenile Reform in New York State.* Syracuse: Syracuse University Press, 1969.

Pittsburgh and Allegheny Women's Christian Association. *Annual Report, 1874.* Pittsburgh: Pittsburgh and Allegheny Women's Christian Association, 1874.

Pivar, David. *The Purity Crusade: Sexual Morality and Social Control.* Westport, CT: Greenwood Press, 1973.

Piven, Frances Fox, and Richard A. Cloward. *Regulating the Poor: The Functions of Public Welfare.* New York: Pantheon, 1971.

Proceedings of the National Conference of Catholic Charities. Washington, D.C.: National Conference of Catholic Charities, 1910–1965.

Purser, Brig. Dorothy, and Joan L. Lindsey. "Clinic Serves Unwed Parents." *Hospitals* 48 (Feb. 16, 1974): 58–61.

Quiroga, Virginia Anne Metaxas. "Poor Mothers and Babies: A Social History of Childbirth and Child Care Institutions in Nineteenth-Century New York City." Ph.D. dissertation, State University of New York, Stony Brook, 1984.

Rabinowitz, Howard N. "From Exclusion to Segregation: Health and Welfare Services for Southern Blacks, 1865–1890." *Social Service Review* 48 (September 1974): 327–54.

Rains, Prudence M. *Becoming an Unwed Mother: A Sociological Account.* Chicago: Aldine-Allerton, 1971.

———. "Moral Reinstatement: The Characteristics of Maternity Homes." *American Behavioral Scientist* 14 (1970–71): 219–35.

Reagan, Leslie. "'About to Meet Her Maker': Women, Doctors, Dying Declarations, and the State's Investigation of Abortion, Chicago, 1867–1940." *Journal of American History* 77 (March 1991): 1240–64.

Reed, James. *From Private Vice to Public Virtue: The Birth Control Movement and American Society Since 1830.* New York: Basic Books, 1977.

Reverby, Susan, and David Rosner, eds. *Health Care in America: Essays in Social History.* Philadelphia: Temple University Press, 1979.

Ringenbach, Paul T. *Tramps and Reformers, 1873–1916: The Discovery of Unemployment in New York.* Westport, CT: Greenwood Press, 1973.

Romanofsky, Peter, ed. *Social Service Organizations.* Westport, CT: Greenwood Press, 1978.

Rose, William Ganson. *Cleveland: The Making of a City.* Cleveland: World Publishing, 1950.

Rosen, Ruth. *The Lost Sisterhood: Prostitution in America, 1900–1918.* Baltimore: Johns Hopkins University Press, 1982.

Rosenberg, Charles C. *The Care of Strangers: The Rise of America's Hospital System.* New York: Basic Books, 1987.

———. "Inward Vision and Outward Glance: The Shaping of the American Hospital, 1880–1914." In *Social History and Social Policy,* edited by David J. Rothman and Stanton Wheeler. New York: Academic Press, 1981.

Rosner, David. "Business at the Bedside: Health Care in Brooklyn, 1890–1915." In *Health Care in America: Essays in Social History,* edited by Susan Reverby and David Rosner. Philadelphia: Temple University Press, 1979.

———. *A Once Charitable Enterprise: Hospitals and Health Care in Brooklyn and New York, 1885–1915.* Cambridge: Cambridge University Press, 1982.

Rothman, David J. *Conscience and Convenience: The Asylum and Its Alternatives in Progressive America*. Boston: Little, Brown, 1980.

———. *The Discovery of the Asylum: Social Order and Disorder in the New Republic*. Boston: Little, Brown, 1971.

Rothman, David J., and Stanton Wheeler. *Poverty and Policy in American History*. Philadelphia: Academic Press, 1983.

———. *Social History and Social Policy*. New York: Academic Press, 1981.

Rothman, Sheila. *Woman's Proper Place: A History of Changing Ideals and Practices, 1870 to the Present*. New York: Basic Books, 1978.

Ruether, Rosemary Radford, and Rosemary Skinner Keller, eds., *Women and Religion in America. Volume 1: The Nineteenth Century*. San Francisco: Harper and Row, 1981.

———, eds. *Women and Religion in America. Volume 3: 1900–1968*. San Francisco: Harper and Row, 1986.

Ruggles, Steven. "Fallen Women: The Inmates of the Magdalen Asylum of Philadelphia, 1836–1908." *Journal of Social History* 16 (Summer 1983): 107–35.

Ryan, Mary P. *Womanhood in America from Colonial Times to the Present*. New York: Franklin Watts, 1979.

Sadlier's Catholic Directory. New York: D. and J. Sadlier, 1871.

Salem, Dorothy. *To Better Our World: Black Women in Organized Reform, 1890–1920*. Brooklyn: Carlson, 1990.

Salvation Army. *War Service Herald and Social News*. May 1920.

Salvation Army Rescue Home. *Annual Report, 1893*. Cleveland: Salvation Army, 1893.

———. *Links of Love: Annual Report, Salvation Army Rescue Work in Cleveland, 1904*. Cleveland: Salvation Army, 1904.

———. *Diamonds in the Rough: Annual Report, Salvation Army Rescue Work in Cleveland, 1905*. Cleveland: Salvation Army, 1905.

Sandall, Robert. *The History of the Salvation Army, Vols. 1–3, 1883–1953*. London: T. Nelson, 1947–1973.

Scharf, Lois. "A Woman's View of Cleveland's Labor Force: Two Case Studies." In *The Birth of Modern Cleveland, 1865–1930*, edited by Thomas F. Campbell and Edward M. Miggins. Cleveland: Western Reserve Historical Society, 1988, 172–94.

Schlossman, Steven L. *Love and the American Delinquent: The Theory and Practice of "Progressive" Juvenile Justice, 1825–1930*. Chicago: University of Chicago Press, 1977.

Sedlak, Michael W. "Youth Policy and Young Women, 1870–1972." *Social Service Review* 56 (September 1982): 448–64.

Shapiro, Deborah. "Attitudes, Values, and Unmarried Motherhood." In National Council on Illegitimacy, *Unmarried Parenthood: Clues to Agency and Community Action*. New York: NCI, 1967.

Shaw, Nancy Stoller. *Forced Labor: Maternity Care in the United States*. New York: Pergamon, 1974.

Shlakman, Vera. "Unmarried Parenthood: An Approach to Social Policy." *Social Casework* 47 (1966): 494–500.

Sidel, Ruth. *Women and Children Last: The Plight of Poor Women in Affluent America.* New York: Penguin, 1986.

Sims, Mary S. *The Natural History of a Social Institution: The YWCA.* New York: Woman's Press, 1936.

Smill, Eva. "The Unmarried Mothers." *Family* 9 (November 1928): 240–42.

Smith, Billy G., and Cynthia Shelton, eds. "The Daily Occurrence Docket of the Philadelphia Almshouse, 1800." *Pennsylvania History* 52.2 (April 1985): 86–116.

———. "Selected Entries, 1800–1804." *Pennsylvania History* 52.3 (July 1985): 183–205.

Smith, Daniel Scott, "The Long Cycle in American Illegitimacy and Prenuptial Bastardy." In *Bastardy and Its Comparative History,* edited by Peter Laslett, Karla Oosterveen, and Richard Michael Smith. Cambridge: Harvard University Press, 1980.

Smith, Timothy L. *Revivalism and Social Reform: American Protestantism on the Eve of the Civil War.* New York: Harper Torchbooks, 1957.

Smith-Rosenberg, Carroll. *Religion and the Rise of the American City: The New York City Mission Movement, 1812–1870.* Ithaca: Cornell University Press, 1971.

Snyder, John. "An Analysis of Relationships: Unwed Mothers and Putative Fathers." *Catholic Charities Review* 55 (September 1971): 2–12.

Speert, Harold. *The Sloane Hospital Chronicle.* Philadelphia: F. A. Davis, 1963.

Starr, Paul. *The Social Transformation of American Medicine.* New York: Basic Books, 1982.

Stein, Herman D., ed. *The Crisis in Welfare in Cleveland: Report of the Mayor's Commission.* Cleveland: Case Western Reserve University Press, 1969.

Steiner, Gilbert Y. *Social Insecurity: The Politics of Welfare.* Chicago: Rand McNally, 1966.

———. *The State of Welfare.* Washington, D.C.: Brookings Institute, 1971.

Stepis, Ursula, CSA, and Dolores Liptak, RSM., eds. *Pioneer Healers: The History of Women Religious in American Health Care.* New York: Crossroads, 1989.

Stevens, Rosemary. *American Medicine and the Public Interest.* New Haven: Yale University Press, 1971.

Taylor, Molly Ladd. *Raising a Baby the Government Way. Mothers' Letters to the Children's Bureau, 1915–1932.* New Brunswick: Rutgers University Press, 1986.

Tiffin, Susan. *In Whose Best Interest? Child Welfare Reform in the Progressive Era.* Westport, CT: Greenwood Press, 1982.

Tinney, Mary C. "Illegitimacy." In *Proceedings, Sixth National Conference of Catholic Charities, 1920.* Washington, D.C.: NCCC, 99–104.

Trattner, Walter I. *From Poor Law to Welfare State: A History of Social Welfare in America.* New York: Free Press, 1984.

Trolander, Judith Ann. *Settlement Houses and the Great Depression.* Detroit: Wayne State University Press, 1975.

Turner, John B., ed. *Encyclopedia of Social Work.* New York: National Association of Social Workers, 1977.

Tyor, Peter L., and Jamil S. Zainaldin. "Asylum and Society: An Approach to Institutional Change." *Journal of Social History* 13 (Fall 1979): 23–48.

"The Undiscussed Tragedy." *Cleveland Edition* (December 6–12, 1990): 7.

U.S. Department of Health, Education, and Welfare. *Trends in Illegitimacy in the United States, 1940–1965.* Washington, D.C.: U.S. Government Printing Office, 1968.

U.S. Department of Labor, Children's Bureau. *A Study of Maternity Homes in Minnesota and Pennsylvania.* Washington, D.C.: U.S. Government Printing Office, 1926.

———. *Essentials of Adoption Law and Procedures.* Washington, D.C.: U.S. Government Printing Office, 1944.

———. *Illegitimacy as a Child-Welfare Problem, Part 3.* Washington, D.C.: U.S. Government Printing Office, 1924.

———. *Standards of Legal Protection for Children Born Out of Wedlock.* Washington, D.C.: U.S. Government Printing Office, 1921.

U.S. Government Printing Office. *Children Under Institutional Care, 1923.* Washington, D.C.: U.S. GPO, 1927.

Van Tassel, David D., and John J. Grabowski, eds. *Cleveland: A Tradition of Reform.* Kent: Kent State University Press, 1986.

———. *The Encyclopedia of Cleveland History.* Bloomington: Indiana University Press, 1987.

Verner, Maj. Mary E. "Administrative Concepts in Comprehensive Services for Unmarried Parents." In National Council on Illegitimacy, *Unmarried Parenthood: Clues to Agency and Community Action.* New York: NCI, 1967, 43–51.

Verry, Ethel. *Meeting the Challenge of Today's Needs in Working with Unmarried Mothers.* Washington, D.C.: U.S. Government Printing Office, 1945.

Vinovskis, Maris A. *An "Epidemic" of Adolescent Pregnancy.* New York: Oxford University Press, 1988.

Vogel, Morris J. "The Transformation of the American Hospital, 1850–1920." In *Health Care in America: Essays in Social History*, edited by Susan Reverby and David Rosner. Philadelphia: Temple University Press, 1979.

Waite, Florence T. *A Warm Friend for the Spirit: A History of the Family Service Association of Cleveland and Its Forebears.* Cleveland: Family Service Association, 1960.

Waite, Frederick C. *Western Reserve University Centennial History of the School of Medicine.* Cleveland: Western Reserve University Press, 1946.

Waldron, John D., ed. *Women in the Salvation Army.* Canada: Salvation Army, 1983.

Ware, Susan. *Holding Their Own: American Women in the 1930s.* Boston: Twayne, 1982.

Warner, Amos G., Stuart A. Queen, and Ernest B. Harper. *American Charities and Social Work*. New York: Thomas Y. Crowell, 1930.

Weaver, Mary Jo. "Feminist Perspectives and American Catholic History." *U.S. Catholic Historian* (Summer/Fall 1986): 401–18.

———. *New Catholic Women: A Contemporary Challenge to Traditional Religious Authority*. San Francisco: Harper and Row, 1985.

Welter, Barbara. "The Feminization of American Religion." In *Insights and Parallels: Problems and Issues of American Social History*, edited by William L. O'Neill. Minneapolis: Burgess, 1973.

Welter, Barbara. "She Hath Done What She Could: Protestant Women's Missionary Careers in Nineteenth Century America." In *Women in American Religion*, edited by Janet Wilson James. Philadelphia: University of Pennsylvania Press, 1980, 111–26.

Wertz, Richard W., and Dorothy C. Wertz. *Lying-In: A History of Childbirth in America*. New York: Free Press, 1977.

Wessel, Morris A. "A Physician Looks at Services for Unmarried Parents." *Social Casework* 49 (1968): 11–14.

West, Guida. *The National Welfare Rights Movement: The Social Protest of Poor Women*. New York: Praeger, 1981.

Wiebe, Robert. *The Search for Order, 1877–1920*. New York: Hill and Wang, 1963.

Wiedensall, Jean. "The Mentality of the Unmarried Mother." In *Proceedings of the National Conference on Social Work, 1915*. Chicago: NCSW, 287–93.

Wilson, Elizabeth. *Fifty Years of Association Work among Young Women, 1866–1916*. New York: Young Women's Christian Association, 1916.

Wilson, Otto. *Fifty Years Work with Girls, 1833–1933*. Alexandria, VA: National Florence Crittenton Mission, 1933.

Winston, Ellen. *Unmarried Parents and Federal Programs of Assistance*. Washington, D.C.: Florence Crittenton Association of America, 1966.

Wisbey, Herbert A., Jr. *Soldiers Without Swords: The History of the Salvation Army in the United States*. New York: Macmillan, 1955.

Woloch, Nancy. *Women and the American Experience*. New York: Alfred A. Knopf, 1984.

Works Progress Administration of Ohio. *Annals of Cleveland, 1818–1935*. Vols. 48, 52. Cleveland: WPA, 1937.

Wright, A. O. "Employment in Poorhouses." In *Proceedings, National Conference on Charities and Corrections, 1889*. Chicago: NCCC, 197–200.

Wylie, Burdett. "Obstetrics and Gynecology and the Cleveland Hospital Obstetric Society." In *Medicine in Cleveland and Cuyahoga County, 1810–1976*, edited by Kent Brown. Cleveland: Cleveland Academy of Medicine, 1977.

Young, Leontine. *Out of Wedlock: A Study of the Problems of the Unmarried Mother and Her Children*. New York: McGraw Hill, 1954.

Zelizer, Viviana A. *Pricing the Priceless Child: The Changing Social Value of Children*. New York: Basic Books, 1985.

Zentz, George H. "The Use of Therapeutic Groups with Unwed Mothers." *Catholic Charities Review* 54 (June 1970): 9–16.

Zitner, Rosalind, and Shelby H. Miller. *Our Youngest Parents: A Study of the Use of Support Services by Adolescent Mothers.* New York: Child Welfare League of America, 1980.

MANUSCRIPT COLLECTIONS AT THE WESTERN RESERVE HISTORICAL SOCIETY ARCHIVES, CLEVELAND

Children's Services, MS 4020.
Cleveland Foundation, MS 3627.
Cleveland Workhouse and House of Refuge and Correction, MS 3681.
Florence Crittenton Services, MS 3910.
Federation for Community Planning, MS 3788.
Young Women's Christian Association, Cleveland, MS 3516.

OTHER ARCHIVES CONSULTED

Cleveland Catholic Diocesan Archives
MetroHealth Medical Center Archives, Cleveland
Rockefeller Family Archives, Tarrytown, New York
Salvation Army Archives and Research Center, New York City
Sisters of Charity of St. Augustine Archives, Richfield, Ohio
Social Welfare History Archives, University of Minnesota, Minneapolis
University Hospital Archives, Cleveland

◆ Index ◆

Cleveland Conference on Illegitimacy, 11, 61–64, 82, 96–99, 111. *See also* Cleveland Federation for Charity and Philanthropy/Welfare Federation/Federation for Community Planning
Cleveland Council of Colored Women, 19–20, 97, 98
Cleveland Federation for Charity and Philanthropy/Welfare Federation/Federation for Community Planning, 7, 8, 18, 20, 48–50, 54, 70, 80–81, 85, 113; cuts subsidies to maternity homes, 68–69, 101, 104; endorses family planning, 86; and Florence Crittenton Home, 66–71; and professionalization of social work, 61–64; and racial integration, 99, 100
Cleveland Foundation, 53, 67
Cleveland Hospital Survey, 109, 111
Cleveland Humane Society, 15, 61, 62, 63
Cleveland Infirmary, 3, 7–8, 9, 17, 21–36, 74, 77, 89; founding of, 24–26; medical care in, 27; men and women in, 28–36; regimen, 26–27; removal of unwed mothers, 31–36; unwed mothers in, 27–34. *See also* Cleveland City Hospital
Cleveland MetroHealth Services, 7–8, 120–21. *See also* Cleveland City Hospital; Cleveland Metropolitan General Hospital
Cleveland Metropolitan General Hospital, 7–8, 105; black women at, 116, 117–19, 120; unwed mothers at, 116, 117–19, 120. *See also* Cleveland City Hospital; Cleveland MetroHealth Services
Cleveland Protestant Orphan Asylum, 46, 48. *See also* Beech Brook
Cleveland Welfare Federation, 7, 8, 9, 14, 15. *See also* Cleveland Federation for Charity and Philanthropy/Welfare Federation/Federation for Community Planning
Comprehensive services for unwed mothers, 103
Consumers League of Ohio, 107
Convent of the Good Shepherd, 43, 44, 47
Cooley, Rev. Harris R., 24
Crittenton, Charles, 13, 54, 56–57, 91

Cuyahoga County Department of Human Services, 119

Daughters of Charity, 75
D'Emilio, John, 86
DePaul Family Services, 7, 85, 122
DePaul Infant and Maternity Home, 7, 8, 12, 51, 52, 53, 81, 83–85, 104, 118; admissions, 84–85. *See also* DePaul Family Services; St. Ann's Infant and Maternity Asylum
Dependent children, 39, 47–48, 56; black, 89; in Cleveland, 31–35; public support of, 99–100
Depression, the, 48, 112–13
Doctors, and childbirth, 73–74, 78–79
Dowling, Harry F., 107

Eels, Mrs. Daniel P., 42
Evangeline Booth Home (Cincinnati), 94–95, 101, 105
"Fallen women," 40–41
Federated charity organizations, 54
Feeblemindedness, 82
Fitch, Sarah, 42
Florence Crittenton Association of America, 66, 69. *See also* Florence Crittenton Services; National Florence Crittenton Mission
Florence Crittenton Home (Atlanta), 90
Florence Crittenton Home (Cleveland), 7, 8, 9, 12, 14, 15, 18, 36, 50, 54–71, 80, 81, 83, 84, 96, 104, 114, 118, 120, 122; adoptions at, 66–67; clientele, 69; costs, 67, 68–69; founding of, 59; volunteers at, 60–61, 66
Florence Crittenton Services, 7, 8, 50–53, 69. *See also* Florence Crittenton Home (Cleveland); National Florence Crittenton Mission
Freedman, Estelle B., 52, 86

Gender, and social policy, 2, 70, 125–26
Gilmour, Bp. Richard, 76, 77

Hanna, Mark, 92
Herrick, Myron T., 92
Home for Aged Colored People (Eliza Bryant Home), 90, 95
Hospitals, Catholic, 75; childbirth in,